signs & seasons

signs & seasons

An Astrology Cookbook

AMY ZERNER AND MONTE FARBER WITH CHEF JOHN OKAS

ILLUSTRATIONS BY AMY ZERNER AND PHOTOGRAPHY BY MONTE FARBER

HARPER**ELIXIR**

An Imprint of HarperCollinsPublishers

SIGNS AND SEASONS. Copyright © 2017 by Monte Farber and Amy Zerner. All rights reserved. Printed in the United States of America. No part of this book may be used or reproduced in any manner whatsoever without written permission except in the case of brief quotations embodied in critical articles and reviews. For information, address HarperCollins Publishers, 195 Broadway, New York, NY 10007.

HarperCollins books may be purchased for educational, business, or sales promotional use. For information, please email the Special Markets Department at SPsales@harpercollins.com.

FIRST EDITION

Library of Congress Cataloging-in-Publication Data has been applied for.

ISBN 978–0–06–246134–6

17 18 19 20 21   LSC   10 9 8 7 6 5 4 3 2 1

CONTENTS

Introduction   1

How Each Sign Eats, Cooks,
and Entertains   12

SPRING 36

SUMMER 86

FALL 132

WINTER 186

Holiday Celebrations
and Feasts   243

Acknowledgments   252

Universal Conversion Chart   253

Index   254

About the Authors   263

LONG BEFORE
ANY NATIONS OR
EVEN HUNTER-
GATHERER TRIBES
EVOLVED, OUR
BODIES WERE
IMPRINTED WITH
THE MANTRA
"WHAT'S TO EAT?"

INTRODUCTION

Are you looking to find epicurean as well as spiritual satisfaction? Do you want to make meals not only a time of communion with family and friends but also an opportunity to deepen your understanding of your appetite and how it connects you to the cycle of the seasons and thus to nature and the very universe itself? If you'd like to know more about how cosmic influences work in the realm of food and how each of the signs prefers to eat and cook, then this book is for you. *Signs and Seasons* is all about an astrological approach to cooking and eating, one which emphasizes both sensual nourishment and psychic satisfaction.

Long before any nations or even hunter-gatherer tribes evolved, our bodies were imprinted with the mantra "What's to eat?" On the physical level, our appetites are at the root of our being. Our need for food is the most basic thing about us. Within every human being there is an emptiness, an implacable vacuum that becomes increasingly insistent after mere hours of not eating.

And as humans, our sensual, social, and spiritual needs coexist with our biological needs. Besides being a necessity, food is undeniably the most consistent and reliable pleasure we have. Food has a social function.

It's a means for contact between people. Certainly, one of the best things about a good meal is sharing the experience with others. And eating food is a sacrament. As a living instance of the mystery of matter becoming energy, a meal is communion with the spirit.

As the cosmic wheels turn, the energies particular to each astrological Zodiac sign are at play in some way or at some time in all our lives. The basic premise of astrology is that the position of the sun at the moment of your birth makes you part of a Zodiac sign like Aries, Taurus, etc. Astrologers believe each sign is inclined to perceive the world and act upon it in very specific ways, overlaid with their individual predilections, genetic imperatives, and experiences. Astrology, as we see it, is a kind of psychological language. The signs add their unique flavor to the planets (the word *planet* is derived from the Greek word for "wanderer") as they move through the narrow band of space we call the Zodiac. The sun in one's chart represents the ego; the moon, emotional intelligence; Mercury, the logical mind; Venus, that to which one is attracted; Mars, the energy available to one's ego to fulfill its goals; Jupiter, how one grows when things are going well; Saturn, how one grows when things require discipline, limits,

1

and focus; and the outer planets Uranus, Neptune, and Pluto represent generational influences that both unite and separate.

This human-centered approach to astrology informs every page of *Signs and Seasons*. It can help us better understand ourselves as individuals, help us balance our appetites, reduce conflict and stress about food, and increase pleasure, happiness, gratitude, love for others, and awe for the mystery of creation.

Astrology has been around for thousands of years, and its popularity proves, if not its accuracy and efficacy as a predictor of human traits and even events, then at least that there must be something to this intriguing theory. Observing the order of the heavens, the corresponding seasonal order on earth, and the regularity of the biological processes of plants and animals that depend on this order, is it not logical to assume that a similar comprehensible arrangement exists within the seeming chaos of our psyches, that our inner lives, our tastes and desires, are part of a naturally regulated process? And if our personality (essentially what we like and dislike) and our behavior are tied to the astrological position of the sun, then our tastes and appetites are also somewhat predetermined by these heavenly influences.

The spirit is nourished through the senses. To truly enjoy ourselves, we must be satisfied in our thoughts, emotions, senses, and imaginings. And to gain such satisfaction, we must give everything, our bodies, our minds, our hearts, and our souls, to the pursuit. For the self-aware, if it's good to you, it's good for you. When the stomach is full, the mind is content; when the heart is warm and joyful, the soul can take flight.

Each Zodiac sign experiences these various needs in different measure and with different levels of intensity and urgency. We study the Zodiac to learn harmony and balance. Harmony and balance also happen to be basic principles of fine cooking and sound eating. By thinking "more of this and less of that" rather than "this is forbidden and that is compulsory," we can revive our attitudes toward eating and cooking and toward life. As each phase of the Zodiac represents different pulls, different approaches to fulfillment are necessary.

You will soon come to understand the real reason astrology has survived as a part of daily life for over five thousand years—and why it has so much to teach us about life in the kitchen and at the table. *Astrology is inextricably tied to the cycle of the seasons, to nature at its most basic level.* The origins of Western astrology are firmly rooted in the agrarian cycle of the Northern Hemisphere where it developed. Studying the movements of the heavens empowered our ancestors to track and predict the seasons, critical to their ability to grow food. In fact, it was a matter of life or death.

So our distant ancestors watched the starry night sky closely. Not only was it incomparably beautiful, it provided a fixed backdrop against which the movement of the moon, planets, and sun could be measured. Our ancestors called this belt of sky, through which the moon, planets, and sun move as they appear to circle the Earth, the Zodiac (from the Greek *kyklos zodiakos,* meaning "circle of life"). They divided the Zodiac into twelve sections, based on their observations of the monthly waning and waxing of the moon: every twenty-nine days or so the moon swelled full, and as it did so, it moved to the next section of the Zodiac (they also noticed that some of the stars moved, too, and they called these special stars "planets"). Our ancestors identified the fixed group of stars in each section of the Zodiac as a unit called a "constellation" (which means, appropriately, "a group of stars"). Each constellation was assigned a meaningful name and symbol, a "sign" that captured the natural events taking place on Earth during the time of the year when the sun was moving through that

particular constellation. And so, through this association of signs and seasons, did astrology develop.

For our ancestors, the first day the sun entered Aries, the first sign of the Zodiac, marked (and still marks) the day when the whole Earth was particularly glad to be alive: it was the first day of spring and another winter had been endured. Rams, the symbol for Aries, as well as other creatures, began their energetic mating battles, butting their heads against each other fiercely. Everyone got busy frantically preparing for the hunting and growing season ahead. Metal tools were sharpened; arrows and knives, as well as plows and scythes, were readied for action in the fresh new season.

OUR ANCESTORS
KNEW THAT
A BALANCED,
LOVING
RELATIONSHIP WAS
A TRULY VALUABLE
COMMODITY
ON THOSE
COOLING
NIGHTS.

When the sun entered Taurus, symbolized by the bull, people started harnessing their oxen. Slowly, methodically, they plowed the earth into beautiful and practical rows, and planted the seeds they had prudently saved from last year. How well they had planned and saved their resources from the past year determined the production of that year. They prayed for fertility as the warmer weather allowed them to enjoy the sensuous sights, sounds, and smells of a reawakening earth.

When Gemini, the sign ruled by Mercury—the planet of communication—and symbolized by a pair of twins, finally arrived, the necessity to concentrate solely on the compelling duties of planting had somewhat subsided. People were now able to catch up on the many other areas of their lives that had been put aside. Not only other areas of farm life, but also quick, short trips to visit with friends, neighbors, and relatives became possible. The joy of seeing familiar faces after a long winter overrode any petty disagreements of the past. It was a time for exchanging family news and local gossip as well as discussing techniques for farming, hunting, cooking, and living in general.

The ancient astrologers chose a crab or sometimes a turtle—both creatures that carry their homes with them in the form of a shell—to symbolize Cancer, the sign that concerns itself with the home and its most important figure, the mother. At that time of the year the home, and consequently the mother, became the center of attention. There were home repairs and improvements to be made, usually at Mother's direction. The early harvests were prepared for both eating and storage in the real center of every home, the kitchen. And there was that most precious gift, the mothering needed to nurture and protect the lives and feelings of a family living through the summer, a time when warm days and warm nights facilitated an exponential increase in human interactions of all kinds, especially among young people experimenting with adulthood. It takes not only unconditional love, but also the ability to be in touch with feelings and intuitions to make a house a home.

During the sun's passage through Leo, the heat of the days was so intense that our ancestors were inclined to act like the Lion, Leo's symbol, and just play, eat, and catnap the day away in royal splendor. The threshing scythe that is the glyph used to represent Leo in an astrological chart is a reminder that despite our ancestors' desire to loll about, it was also a time to prepare for the work of the coming harvest. It took the noble heart, commanding presence, and organizational skill of a king—and the lion is the king of the jungle—plus a bit of roaring, to motivate the population to stop having fun in the sun and ready themselves for the harvest.

By the time of Virgo, symbolized by a woman holding shafts of wheat, even the most fun-loving person couldn't deny that the crops were ready for harvest. The work to be done was analyzed in detail, fueled by worry about the time remaining to get all jobs done perfectly. Close attention was paid to the logical and most efficient techniques necessary to produce maximum results. Both weeding by hand and natural insect repellents were necessary to ensure the health of the mature plants and thereby the people and their livestock.

The scales of Libra, the only sign of the Zodiac that is neither human nor animal, reminds us that the time of Libra was when the harvest was weighed and then measured against other years' and other farmers' yields. Public declarations of contractual partnerships were made and fulfilled as goods were exchanged for their fair market value. But the perfect balance of the Libran scales was also a reminder that the first six warming full moons of the lunar year had passed and that the challenges of the next six cooling full moons were at hand. Our ancestors knew that a balanced, loving relationship was a truly valuable commodity on those cooling nights.

As the sun enters Scorpio, its heat begins to wane and the days grow shorter. Leaves fall from the trees; flowers and crops die. In the time of our ancestors, the least prized of the livestock were killed and the meat preserved for the coming winter. All this death must have reminded our ancestors of their own mortality. But they knew that the leaves and the perennial crops and flowers would return in the spring, and the annual crops and flowers would live on through their seeds. The animals that were killed would live on in their offspring and through the people who ate their flesh to survive. The reality of a kind of life after death in their everyday world suggested the promise of a life after death for themselves.

The arrow of Sagittarius represents Chiron, the bow-wielding Centaur, half-man and half-horse, and first doctor of herbal medicine, sage, and tutor of Achilles. The legend of Chiron may have started out with stories of a wise and skillful hunter, perhaps the leader of the first tribe to hunt from the back of a horse. As hunting parties from different places crossed paths, the generous and open-minded among them would exchange information about best practices, herd movements, and even invitations to freshly caught dinner. Sagittarius's association with philosophy, the love of learning, and sharing life's truths with the world beyond one's homeland is descended from the time when hunters sat around a fire under the night sky discussing the faraway lands and the different religions, philosophies, and customs they had seen in their long journeys, made possible by travel on horseback.

The day the sun enters Capricorn marks the time of the Winter Solstice: the shortest, bleakest day of the year. But the next day, the sun begins its northward climb, and with each succeeding midday sky it moves toward spring and the season of rebirth. Our ancestors knew that they could get through the privations of winter only by being disciplined and conservative in the truest sense of the word. If the hunt and the harvest had been successful and conserved correctly, then the limitations imposed by winter could be patiently endured. Capricorn's association with authority, time, and timing harken back to an era that required stern guardians to allot the proper rations to their stir-crazy neighbors, with everyone counting the days until spring and life returned to the earth.

By the time the sun entered the sign of Aquarius, our ancestors were beginning to feel confined. Those who weren't snowed in would only bother to visit their closest friends or neighbors with whom they had agreed to band together to survive the winter. With their friends they could escape the monotony of the winter days by telling stories and dreaming about a literally brighter future. In a setting like this, one fueled by camaraderie and a desire to stave off boredom, we can imagine our ancestors may have felt particularly free to share their wildest hopes and wishes for the future, making this a season for inspired visions and ideas about how to create a better world to come.

Pisces is the last sign of the Zodiac. Its symbol is two fish swimming in opposite directions, reminding us that this is a moment in time that marks a cusp, the point where one year is coming to a close as another is beginning. Winter, though

not over, is coming to an end, and spring, though on the horizon, has not yet arrived. One year is dying as another is being born. For our ancestors, the ideals of Aquarius were tempered by the sad realities of Pisces. At winter's end, supplies were at their lowest and food shortages were not uncommon. The strong and the compassionate were required to do without so that the children, the elderly, and the less fortunate could survive. Sometimes people even gave their lives so that others would live. It was an emotional time.

The return of the sun to the portion of the Zodiac occupied by the constellation Aries marked the return of spring. And so the cycle began again, as it will until the end of time.

Five thousand years of observation have further taught astrologers that the twelve Zodiac signs can be understood even more precisely by applying to each sign several classifications: a ruling planet, a "quality," and an element.

A sign's ruling planet is the planet that, due to its mythological traits and its effect on an astrological chart, most closely aligns with the traits of a particular sign. In modern Western astrology, the sun represents the ego and rules the self-assured sign of Leo. Mars, which represents the energy available to one's ego to go out in the world and get what it wants, rules assertive Aries—this is the best example of an affinity between a planet and a sign, as "Mars" is the Roman name for the Greek "Aries." Venus, which represents one's ability to attract, create, and appreciate beauty, rules Taurus and Libra. Mercury, which represents one's logical mind and its ability to communicate and assimilate information, rules Gemini and Virgo. The moon, the protective "mother" that always faces the Earth, rules the sign of Cancer, the sign associated with the home, the past, and one's nurturing caregiver. Jupiter, the biggest planet, represents how one grows when things go well and rules Sagittarius, the sign that gifts the rest of us with honest opinions. Saturn represents how one grows when time, discipline, and structure limit one's experience and rules Capricorn, the sign that acquires authority through diligence and patience. Uranus, the only planet that inclines its north pole at the sun and spins like a wheel as it orbits, rules Aquarius, the sign symbolizing eccentricity, disruptive thinking, and genius. Neptune, named after the god of the sea and symbol of the often overwhelming effect of emotions, positive or negative, rules the sign of Pisces, the sign symbolizing the part of ourselves willing to sacrifice for the good of others. Finally, Pluto (forever a planet to astrologers no matter what astronomers call it), which symbolizes our ability to render powerful judgment as displayed by its namesake, the god who decided who went to heaven and who did not, rules the sign of Scorpio, the sign that concerns itself with power in all its forms and exchanges.

Ancient astrologers further enhanced the precise meaning of the signs by assigning to each the quality of either cardinal, fixed, or mutable. They associated four signs with each quality. The four *cardinal* signs are those whose first day corresponds with the first day of each season: Aries (spring), Cancer (summer), Libra (fall), and Capricorn (winter). The cardinal quality is associated with initiating projects or being enterprising. Each of the cardinal signs begins at a time when one season has ended and another is starting, a time when there are specific goals that must be accomplished if the rest of the season is to be successfully navigated and utilized for the good of all. For this reason, these four cardinal signs are said to have the quality of being goal-oriented, though how they decide what suits them varies widely and can change course as they see fit.

The four *fixed* signs follow the cardinal, goal-oriented signs and are inclined to "fix" the actions put in place by the cardinal signs. The fixed signs are Taurus, Leo, Scorpio, and Aquarius. Fixed signs are characterized by dependability, determination, and stability. Though people born with the fixed signs prominent also have goals, once they decide on how to proceed, they are resistant to changing course. For this reason, in astrology, the fixed signs are known as the stubborn signs. They apply their basic mind-set to the accomplishing of their goals and to their approach to all aspects of their life.

The four *mutable* signs follow the fixed, stubborn signs and precede the cardinal, goal-oriented sign that begins the next season. They must therefore be flexible and able to bridge one season to the succeeding season. The mutable signs are Gemini, the last sign of spring; Virgo, the last sign of summer; Sagittarius, the last sign of fall; and Pisces, the last sign of winter. Mutable signs are characterized by a concern with adapting and blending. The mutable signs also have goals, but they accomplish them by being flexible and adjusting their course when they find information that appeals to them at the moment.

The signs of the Zodiac are further classified as being from four groups of elements: fire, air, water, and earth. The three *fire* signs are Aries, Leo, and Sagittarius. Fire signs concern themselves with the realm of action, and they burn with desire and the faith that they will succeed. Fire symbolizes energy, action, and creativity. The three *air* signs are Gemini, Libra, and Aquarius.

THE SIGNS OF THE ZODIAC ARE FURTHER CLASSIFIED AS BEING FROM FOUR GROUPS OF ELEMENTS: FIRE, AIR, WATER, AND EARTH.

Air signs concern themselves with the realm of ideas. Air symbolizes ideas, intellect, and communication. The three *water* signs are Cancer, Scorpio, and Pisces. Water signs concern themselves with the realm of emotions. Water symbolizes emotion, intuition, and empathy. The three *earth* signs are Taurus, Virgo, and Capricorn. Earth signs concern themselves with the realm of the material world and practical matters. Earth symbolizes substance, practicality, and grounding.

The qualities (cardinal, fixed, and mutable) and the elements (fire, air, water, and earth) combine differently in each of the twelve signs of the Zodiac. The seasons, signs, planets, qualities, and elements are like intermeshing gears that power the year here on planet Earth.

At its core, astrology is simply an expression of life as an annual cyclical process. The Zodiac is a rotating symbol of the seasonal expansion and contraction of the periods of darkness and light—on earth as it is in the heavens. The cycle of the year— its various states of vegetation and animal behavior—offers us what we need to know to be in harmony with the Zodiac. What is more Aries than mint, lamb, and asparagus? More Pisces than fish and chips? Seasonal ingredients make spring and summer

meals lighter, fall and winter meals more substantial.

As the planets, physical entities with predictable movements, are named from the Greco-Roman gods, the recipes in this book are Mediterranean, drawn primarily from Italy and Greece, with support from Southern France and Spain, and the Middle East, the fertile crescent where Western culture was born. We offer these robust, all-natural recipes, as well as our astrological insights as guidance as you determine the way you really want to eat and prepare nourishment for your soul.

HOW TO USE THIS BOOK

There is a rhythm in Nature. The Earth turns and the sun seems to move across the sky. Astrology is grounded in the idea that whatever comes into being at a certain moment in this cycle partakes of the spirit of that phase of it. The recipes in this book were written from the perspective that when the sun is in a certain sign, all individuals, regardless of their dates of birth, share in the characteristics and energy matrix of that stage and season of the cycle.

For example, to some extent, we are all Aries-impulsive in early spring, Cancer-moony in June, Scorpio-spooky at Halloween, Piscesotherworldly at winter's end. Every year we all take a trip around the sun. As we go around and around, to be in tune with the Universe, when the sun is in Aries, we tap our inner Aries; when the sun is in Taurus, we tap our inner Taurus; and so forth.

Rather than try to cater to individual appetites, the sign designations of the recipes in this book refer primarily to the recipes themselves. The seasonality of the ingredients and the method of their preparation reflect certain aspects of the mind-set of that sign.

Appetites come from Nature. Depending on the level of awareness, within each sign we find a wide spectrum of thoughts and feelings about eating and tastes that are specific to the individual. The Lion is the King of Beasts, but not all Leos are carnivorous. Abstemiousness is a Virgo trait, but not all Virgos eat with moderation. Feasting is Jupiter's second most favorite pastime, but all Sagittarians do not necessarily overeat.

So, you're a Virgo and you're having a Scorpio over for dinner (or the reverse). Or perhaps you're entertaining mixed company of a Virgo and a Scorpio. How do you design a beautiful and sustaining meal that will make all parties happy?

The first step is to read the "How Each Sign Eats, Cooks, and Entertains" section. The second step we suggest is to choose from some of the recipes appropriate for each sun sign—dishes from the season of each sign that are particularly suited to each sign—to make sure there is food on your menu that each person would like. The third step would be to balance your menu to have a starter, main course, sides, and a variety of offerings that blend and balance beautifully, choosing how many dishes you feel are needed for the size and formality of the event and looking for those that serve the needs of both: simple but luxurious dishes, bold but familiar in flavor, that are not fussy to eat but will still make for an engaging dining experience are the ticket. It makes for interesting conversations as well!

Food allergies and sensitivities can affect anyone. Astrology aside, if you entertain, proper etiquette dictates that there be something on the table for everyone to enjoy. Asking your dinner guests beforehand about what they do and do not eat is the most reliable way to do this. Then you might want to ask about their sun sign and let intuition and creativity (and a few of the suggestions here) be your guide.

Our friends come from all around the Zodiac. Similarly, a varied diet, all things in their proper time and place, is the Golden Rule. Dining under the stars, there's a dish for every purpose under heaven.

HOW EACH SIGN EATS, COOKS, AND ENTERTAINS

ARIES

MARCH 21 to APRIL 19

Ruling planet: Mars

Quality: cardinal

Element: fire

Aries foods: asparagus, radishes, red peppers, deviled eggs, lamb, black olives, grapefruit

Herbs: ginger, cayenne

Personal qualities: honest, brave, headstrong

Key words: initiation • challenge • adventure • exploration • daring • courage • honesty • competition • innocence • action • aggression • spontaneity • discovery • creativity

HOW THEY EAT

Aries sun sign people are here to show us the pure life force and selfless focus necessary to achieve one's goals. Aries are cardinal fire. They know how to initiate action, how to push and work toward furthering their goals. They cannot wait to do what they have in mind to do. Aries is the first sign, and its natives usually like to be served first. They do not have time for long meals because they are constantly busy. They are usually completely focused on the task they've set for themselves, but don't get between Aries and their food when they finally realize they are hungry. The only thing an Aries fears is being afraid. Because hunger can simulate the sensation of fear—a sense of weakness and diminution of power—Aries may confuse the two, leading them to panic if they don't eat quickly. In general, Aries love food that can be made and eaten quickly without fussing. They can often have a meal ready before the rest of the family, who walked in the door with them, have put their things away and sat down at the table. Aries also have a habit of eating too quickly. Aries-born are, in their own individual way, warriors, and when their tempers flare they should not eat at all.

Their tempers cool quickly, but even so they should stick to lighter fare following any confrontations.

Hot and spicy food figures prominently among their dietary preoccupations; Aries either love spiciness, hate it, or can't eat it. They favor fiery and bold tastes. Aries natives should stay away from sweets and carbonated drinks. Small bites suit them. They love starters and appetizers as well as breakfasts. Piquant flavors and red foods attract them.

HOW THEY COOK

Aries have no patience with seven-course meals or any meal that takes a long time to prepare, unless it is for those they care about. They must get an entire meal prepared as quickly as possible, so they tend to use shortcuts like packages of chopped onions or ready-to-cook fresh vegetables. Stir-frying is a perfect way for an Aries to whip up a dish.

Preparation is an Aries special talent. Their refrigerators are filled with ingredients arranged together and ready to cook. This is their secret to preparing an intricate dinner in the amount of time it takes another sun sign to put on an apron. The famous Aries

impatience will make an appearance if they have to rush at the last minute.

Aries chefs must be careful not to burn themselves or what they're cooking, and should avoid impetuous, sudden, overly rapid movements, especially at the end of their cooking effort when rushing to put the food on the table.

HOW THEY ENTERTAIN

Aries can throw a party together fast. Fiery Arians enjoy bold color and light, so cheerful and bright flowers and fabrics will attract them. This energy means it's easy for them to enter almost any social setting as a host or as a guest. Aries people love little bites before they eat a real meal, as they are always starving when they arrive or just before an event. A selection of zesty finger foods with brash, exciting flavors such as those from around the Mediterranean—bright notes of lemon, herbs, garlic, and olive oil—will please. Once they have something to eat, the Aries' enthusiasm for life can be contagious as they share tips and original ideas on how to do more, be more, see more. They could also start arguing about social injustices, or cause a stir by being too direct with other guests.

TAURUS

APRIL 20 *to* MAY 20

Ruling planet: Venus

Quality: fixed

Element: earth

Taurus foods: carrots, lima beans, peas, cheddar, cod, new potatoes, avocados, bananas

Herbs: cardamom, cloves

Personal qualities: loyal, pragmatic, good-humored, reliable, musical

Key words: slow • steady • values • money • caution • control • security • tenacity • texture • beauty • habits • supplies • kindness • calmness • romance • sensuality

HOW THEY EAT

Taurus sun sign people are here to show us that slow but steady wins the race. Taurus are fixed earth. They know how to sustain an effort in matters that concern talent, security, values, and finances. They do not like quick changes. Taureans are the most sensual of all the Zodiac signs. The majority of true gastronomes are Taureans. They like to eat slowly, savoring every morsel. They dislike food fads, trends, or diets of any kind. They like big helpings and creamy dishes like quiche, chocolate mousse, and prime rib. Their inability to resist high-calorie foods can eventually lead to weight issues. To bring balance to their diet, they need to adapt their ingredients, using substitutes for sugar, salt, and butter, and add delicious but lower-fat meals to their dietary regimen, as they tend to overindulge.

A Taurus wants to feel relaxed and comfortable throughout the meal. They hate interruptions while eating, preferring to focus on their enjoyment of the food at hand. For some this could even mean little to no conversation during meals except that which centers on the food at hand. Their love of comfort extends to all aspects of the dining experience. Plates, tablecloths, napkins, and all utensils must convey a sense of luxury, even for casual meals and picnics. Sitting comfortably is crucial, so if your chairs or picnic blanket is not sufficiently cushioned you may find your Taurus guest is not as pleased as you think they might be, given their obvious enjoyment of the meal.

HOW THEY COOK

The Taurean goal for living the good life often translates into their love for the entire process of cooking. They prepare carefully and cook at their leisure, so no involved recipe, expensive or hard-to-come-by ingredient, or seven-course meal is too much for them to attempt. They take pleasure in studying recipes before they enter the kitchen.

You can learn many new recipes from people born under this sign, but when you make one for them they will show an uncanny ability to tell if you did not stick to it as they gave it to you. Taurus natives love to show the world how strong they are and do so by enduring what no other sign can. They will do whatever it takes to create a gastronomic event that will be legendary among those who attended. Their patience is also legendary, and there are no shortcuts for them. They will follow the recipes, no matter how intricate and time consuming.

Taurus is all about the appreciation of living well: what can be touched and savored and often what can be possessed. So, expect to see the finest kitchen equipment they can afford. Their spice collection contains everything they've ever seen mentioned in their impressive collection of cookbooks, even if they haven't prepared that recipe yet (they have it on their list to cook when the time is right).

HOW THEY ENTERTAIN

Venus's children are better-than-average cooks and better-than-average decorators, too. Emphasis for a Taurus is on the aesthetic aspects of the meal: beautiful presentation, table setting, flowers, and music. Taurus people love crafts, centerpieces, and arrangements that are handmade. They will splurge on fresh flowers. Taurus prefers a rather traditional and friendly environment when it comes to sustenance. Though they have a fondness for the good life, luxury foods, and the pleasure of eating, they also possess a large share of common sense. They delight in preparing a cozy, home-cooked dinner and feeding people they like even more than going out to a fancy gala. The rustic classics will always work for a Taurus host. Their favorite moment is just after dinner when everyone is gabbing and enjoying dessert.

GEMINI

MAY 21 *to* JUNE 20

Ruling planet: Mercury

Quality: mutable

Element: air

Gemini foods: citrus, mangos, lettuce, ramps, cucumbers, snap peas, feta, celery

Herbs: oregano, dill

Personal qualities: witty, changeable, versatile, talkative, well-read

Key words: duality • social skills • communication • mischief • cleverness • logic • restlessness • gossip • versatility • curiosity • precocity • duality • quick wit

HOW THEY EAT

Gemini sun sign people are here to show us the wisdom of seeing all sides in every issue. Geminis are mutable air. They know how to adjust and improvise their style of communication to deal with fluctuations. Geminis can adapt themselves to their environment. It's fitting that the Twins are the symbol for Gemini, because there often seems to be at least two different people inside every one of them: their tastes can change from meal to meal or even mid-meal. Their need for mental stimulation keeps them constantly on the go, and snacks and finger foods keep them energized. If you assembled their day's food supply in front of them, they might be quite surprised at the quantity and the diversity.

When they actually sit down to eat, Geminis need a variety of foods to choose from in any given meal, as well as at least two beverages available to them at all times. They love to learn while they nibble, so be prepared for questions of all kinds about every aspect of what you have prepared. And you'll learn a lot if a Gemini is cooking for you. For Geminis, a lively and interesting conversation during the meal is just as important as the food. Guests must be sufficiently quick-witted and amusing to keep Geminis from experiencing what they dread the most, boredom. A bored Gemini may fall relatively silent and only pick at even the most delicious and well-prepared dishes.

Earthy foods can help keep Geminis grounded, but they will avoid heavy dishes that require them to sit and digest after a meal; they would rather move on to the next part of the evening's festivities.

HOW THEY COOK

There are few things as interesting to watch as a Gemini at work in the kitchen. Fortunately, the Gemini love of communication means that they often set up their kitchen and dining areas with as few obstructions between them as possible, so that the chef and guests can see each other and converse easily. Geminis are the masters of multitasking and actually need to do other things while cooking. When cooking alone, they talk on the phone, watch TV, and walk around. They are nervous types, so they might drop utensils and forget they have a pot on the stove when they get distracted.

They love to read cookbooks, even when they are nowhere near a kitchen. Their culinary creativity is legendary, often the result of having to compensate for important ingredients or recipe details omitted.

HOW THEY ENTERTAIN

Geminis love parties and opportunities to socialize. The challenge for Geminis is to balance their on-the-go, hand-to-mouth impulses with their need for contact and communication with loved ones. Hands-on foods and mini-meals give Geminis the option of sitting down, being present, and paying attention to their food as well as those around them . . . or not. They are energetic whirling dervishes who can eat, talk, tell jokes, and flirt all at the same time.

Their environment usually has a lot of places to sit along with displays of their many collections, which are conversation pieces. Many Geminis are happiest playing games after dinner—how about charades or Trivial Pursuit? If you know authors or journalists, you will impress a Gemini. Sometimes they are so busy meeting and greeting that they forget about the food! They always have a fresh take on different subjects that make for lively talk, but as guests they may have to leave early so that they don't miss another event somewhere else, as they may have double-booked, due to indecision.

CANCER

JUNE 21 *to* JULY 22

Ruling planet: moon

Quality: cardinal

Element: water

Cancer foods: arugula, coconuts, figs, crab, pine nuts, duck, zucchini, eggs, lettuces

Herbs: chamomile, bay leaf

Personal qualities: caring, tenacious, sensitive, nurturing, practical

Key words: clairvoyant • protective • heredity • emotions • moods • feelings • intuitions • reflect • respond • adapt • habits • cycles • motherhood • unconditional love • our past

HOW THEY EAT

Cancer sun sign people are here to show us that we must all take care of one another. Cancers are cardinal water. They know how to give and nurture as well as how to understand emotional processes. Cancer is the Zodiac sign that "rules" our stomach and also the nurturing that caregivers display by putting food on the table. Because they are natural caregivers, subject to the tremendous emotional swings that can occur when you are responsible for another's well-being, Cancer natives are prone to transfer their emotional state to their digestive system. Therefore Cancer natives are very sensitive and have sensitive stomachs. They generally like good-size portions and family-style settings and are attracted to comfort foods such as macaroni and cheese, apple pie, rice pudding or any meal that reminds them of good times past. If you want to understand a Cancer's eating habits, ask them about their childhood and their relationship with their mother. Unsurprisingly, a Cancer enjoys dining at home more than dining out. They love anything homemade and freshly baked and will patronize restaurants and shops that add love and pride to their dishes and use traditional cooking methods. Drinking plenty of pure water and eating foods high in water content are good for them. They have definite ideas about seafood.

It is important for a Cancer to eat at regular times in a calm atmosphere, with people who make them feel safe and secure. They should never eat when they are upset, because they have a tendency to mix their food with their emotional state and will "eat" their anger, sorrow, or other emotion. If you have a Cancer living with you, do not be surprised if during an argument about something else, they suddenly make a big emotional display about a particular dish they do not like but have eaten without complaint for your sake.

HOW THEY COOK

Cancerians enjoy cooking for the comfort and nurturing it offers those they love. Cooking, for a Cancer, is part of creating their ideal home. They love to make recipes that have been handed down to them from family members and will do so using inherited, cherished cooking equipment with which the recipes were originally made, if possible. They love having a kitchen large enough to accommodate a dining table so that their family and friends feel cozy and are never far from them while they prepare meals.

They are patient, thoughtful cooks and excellent bakers who can be counted on to improve every recipe by tailoring it for the tastes of those they care about. They do want to know how you would improve what they have made, but they are quite sensitive so be gentle with your constructive criticism. They will know it if you fib.

They especially enjoy children in the kitchen and will patiently show them how their meals are made if they seem interested. They can inspire both young and old with stories about how they came by their specialties and recipes.

HOW THEY ENTERTAIN

Cancers are attracted to other people who are as much into nurturing as they are. For them, the dining area is a protective, homey shell that often includes the gentle colors of the ocean. They love to have a dear friend come by, even if unexpected, so they can share some gossip over tea and cookies. Cancer chooses its acquaintances carefully. They are so warmhearted and sensitive when entertaining—they always make sure there will be enough for everyone.

Cancers love to fuss over guests and make them feel comfy with their tender care. If you are a good host or hostess and know how to make others feel at home, a Cancer will adore you. And get ready to meet the relatives! You can find their photos in the picture gallery displayed in a Cancer's home.

LEO

JULY 23 *to* AUGUST 22

Ruling planet: sun

Quality: fixed

Element: fire

Leo foods: corn, peaches, tomatoes, sunflower seeds, clams, spinach, mozzarella, mustard

Herbs: rosemary, saffron

Personal qualities: creative, dramatic, proud, organized, romantic

Key words: self-assertion • creativity • recognition • theatricality • hobbies • leadership • love • pleasure • fun • hospitality • openheartedness • appreciation • playfulness • entertainment

HOW THEY EAT

Leo sun sign people are here to show us that every minute we are alive is special and worthy of our full attention. Leos are fixed fire. They know how to persevere and be respected by becoming a steady and focused creative force. They like to be in leadership roles. Leos are flamboyant and like to make a performance out of everything they do. When they eat they like to let everyone know how delightful or distasteful the food is. Leos like to eat in a royal way. Like the male lion that is their symbol, they prefer to have their food brought to them. They are fond of expensive foods and drink and will always buy the best they can afford. They are the ones to ask if you want to know what the smart set is doing.

Leos like "dressed-up" dishes that are especially difficult to prepare, stuffed, or layered. They are more likely than not to be attracted to rich food and wine. A lifetime of this behavior can adversely affect the heart, the part of the body ruled by Leo. For this reason, wise Leos will add what their doctor considers to be heart-healthy foods to the royal menu plan. Their vanity will also help to keep their overindulgences in check. Whether they are eating a snack or a full-course meal, there is a good chance that it will contain some kind of animal protein, especially meat.

HOW THEY COOK

Every meal is a cooking show to a Leo. Even on the rare occasion when they are cooking for only themselves, they will execute every aspect of preparation as if the cameras were rolling. They prefer to interact with others, their audience, and are one of the few signs that can work with another chef in the kitchen—every king and queen needs their court. Their specialty is theater, so do not be surprised if you and the other guests get drafted into "performing" some task to make a Leo's party special. Their kitchen is their favorite stage and they are always the life of every party.

Leos need to be complimented and admired. They demand attention for each and every one of their culinary achievements. If for some reason they are not getting the compliments, admiration, or affection that they crave, Leos will roar a little and complain a lot. Fortunately, they are truly generous and have big hearts, so these party animals truly enjoy entertaining others. They love to see that their events brought smiles to the faces of their friends and family.

HOW THEY ENTERTAIN

Entertaining is an art form for Leos. They like to be surrounded by rich shades of yellow and gold. Leos love company—hosting a big barbecue with lots of grilled meat and fish, creative salads, and slaws. For Leos, meals are a venue for creativity and an opportunity to impress others. Leos are self-assured and want their gatherings to be opulent and done with grand style. They choose recipes and table settings that project the Leo elegance, pride, hospitality, generosity, noblesse oblige, and romance.

They like to show off their excellent taste and efforts in the kitchen and will make showy entrances with their creations. Leos need to be treated like royalty, so be sure to give them extra attention. Leos will not like being seated next to someone who is not willing to listen to their stories. They will tell you exactly what they mean. They are leaders, and trouble will start and you might hear a roar if you don't let them lead. But they can have the warmest, biggest hearts of all.

VIRGO

AUGUST 23 *to* **SEPTEMBER 22**

Ruling planet: Mercury

Quality: mutable

Element: earth

Virgo foods: wheat, chicken, little tomatoes, string beans, shrimp, raspberries, blueberries

Herbs: mint, fennel

Personal qualities: analytical, discreet, practical, intelligent, detail oriented

Key words: energy • thought • observation • study • discernment • division into component parts • criticism • reason • logic • connection • adaptation • health

HOW THEY EAT

Virgo sun sign people are here to show us that the whole is the sum of its parts. Virgos are mutable earth. They know how to

be of service and how to review, fix, edit, and adjust to circumstances. Virgos can be critical and analytical. Virgo is the sign that rules digestion, and as such, Virgos in particular need foods that contain fiber and enzymes that aid digestion. Because Virgos have very active, analytical minds, their health is directly tied to how much or how little they worry, and they need foods that calm them.

Even the most carefree Virgos should not consume too much food at once; small, nourishing, and frequent meals work best. Virgos are fidgety and like to eat on the go or standing. They are the most finicky eaters in the Zodiac though you might not think so because they always seem to be eating something. Virgos are usually thrifty except when it comes to buying their groceries. They like food that is simple yet special, like the best granola with a perfectly ripe banana, a picture-perfect grilled fish, or organic roast chicken.

HOW THEY COOK

Virgos are often meticulous perfectionists, which is why they make both excellent chefs and food critics. They usually have a well-stocked kitchen with simple, functional, well-made equipment and gadgets for every purpose. They work hard to keep everything neat and clean. When cooking with people who are messy or disorganized, Virgos may become irritable and unable to apply themselves to the tasks at hand in their customary efficient manner. Their fastidiousness can get in the way when a dish requires making a mess, however, which can cause their meal to suffer.

Developing their skills and confidence in themselves as hardworking people is more important to Virgos than the praise of the crowd. Though they are surprisingly independent, they will follow a recipe to the letter because they know that information is power. If they are not able to execute a recipe as it is written, they will take more time than any other sign weighing the pros and cons of substituting versus leaving out an ingredient or process. That said, they will berate themselves if their creations are not up to their exacting standards. When this happens they need a lot of tender support.

Virgos love details, and their attention to the little things that make a plain dish look fancy or a good dish taste great is what makes them such excellent cooks. Virgos have an abundance of nervous energy and usually prefer to keep moving from dish to dish while they cook. They are one of the signs that always know the best places to shop for gourmet ingredients and specialty items.

HOW THEY ENTERTAIN

Virgos have an extremely critical eye. Soft colors, warm woods, and floor lamps, a table, and chairs in clean lines and minimalist styles will appeal. They will polish the silver, lay out the napkins, and arrange the flowers up to the last minute, to make sure every detail is in place. They adore stylish storage containers. Enlist a Virgo friend to help you plan a party! They like to contribute to any undertaking without too much ego. They will immediately assess the dinner to see if you or they forgot anything.

Make sure you check for food allergies if you have a Virgo as a guest. They can be picky eaters. Note that the wear and tear of responsibility can often be exhausting to the Virgo perfectionist. They have excellent memories, so be careful you don't serve the same recipe you made the last time. Sometimes they will ask a lot of questions before they try something new. They will be eager to dissect the latest movies and current events.

LIBRA

SEPTEMBER 23 *to* OCTOBER 22

Ruling planet: Venus

Quality: cardinal

Element: air

Libra foods: apples, walnuts, scallops, fennel, capers, pomegranates, broccoli, oats

Herbs: vanilla, cinnamon

Personal qualities: artistic, refined, poised, intelligent, tactful

Key words: partnership • union • sophistication • good taste • yin and yang • balance • cooperation • fairness • quality control • aesthetics • harmony • romance • opinions • diplomacy

HOW THEY EAT

Libra sun sign people are here to help us understand judgment. Libras are cardinal air.

They can be diplomatic as well as aggressive in communications. The time of Libra is when the harvest is weighed and measured against other years and other farmers. Libras want everything to be fair and equal. They are very aware of portion size and presentation.

It is often difficult for Libras to decide what they want to eat, especially when they are by themselves. Having another person's choice to react to activates their decision-making ability. Many Libras overeat when they are not happy, as if in hope that by filling themselves with beautiful delicious food they can feel equally beautiful and desired.

Eating is an art to a Libra. They are the consummate epicures, and their approach to culinary perfection requires that what they eat has to be absolutely garden fresh and also look photo ready. They avoid unattractive foods. Their love of beauty means that packaging and presentation make a difference to them, whether they are ordering simple refreshments or continuing their search for the ultimate in fine dining.

Libras do not like extremes and prefer dishes that are neither too spicy nor too bland. Libras enjoy simple menus with an elegant, gourmet flare. They like a cornucopia of foods that not only taste good but also smell and look equally as good.

A delicate soup, poached fruit straight from the farm, a plate of their favorite cheeses, and fresh baked bread—any of these could be as satisfying to a Libra as dinner at the best restaurant in their area.

HOW THEY COOK

Libras expend a lot of mental energy attempting to decide what needs to be done before and after cooking commences to make their creations perfect. They need to balance their love of and immersion in idealized mental imagery of what is to come—a veritable feature film in their mind's eye of how the cooking and the event itself should proceed—with getting to work on the meal, or else they may find themselves drained of energy and enthusiasm before the prep work has begun.

Librans look for a harmonious blend in all things, whether it is the equipment and layout of their kitchen, the appearance of their table, the colors and flavors in their dishes, or the way they get along with their guests and other chefs. They sometimes may have a hard time deciding what to make, and having a partner involved is more of a necessity for them than an option.

The aesthetic appearance of the food and table is especially important to the Libra. They have excellent design skills and can make wonderful flower arrangements, decorations, and place settings. Guests at a Libra's table must make an extra effort to avoid disharmony in any form or find themselves never invited back. Though Libra is the sign of diplomacy, negotiating, and conflict resolution skills and they are willing to fight for peace, they detest having to do so.

HOW THEY ENTERTAIN

Libras make great hosts. They are the incarnation of cultivation, good taste, and diplomacy and are usually quite levelheaded and calm. They like a dining room with uniformity: matching chairs and balanced elements. Their talents ensure that all the table settings harmonize beautifully. They will usually have interesting art objects. You can always count on a Libra to create the right mood and to handle any social situation correctly, with polished manners. They will introduce their guests to one another, making connections. They will make sure you are so well cared for that you will feel very special. The Libra guest and host will always be classy and dressed to perfection. But at times indecision, vacillation, and a lack of sensible, consistent reference points will cause delays.

SCORPIO

OCTOBER 23 *to* NOVEMBER 21

Ruling planet: Pluto

Quality: fixed

Element: water

Scorpio foods: pumpkin, chocolate, oysters, artichokes, mushrooms, onions, beets, lobster

Herbs: cumin, garlic

Personal qualities: intense, obsessive, loyal, determined, passionate

Key words: investigation • conscience • secrets • magical • psychology • precision • mysteries • good detective • transformation • power • legacy • sex • regeneration

HOW THEY EAT

Scorpios are here to show us how to gain and use power. Scorpios are fixed water. They understand what motivates them and what makes others tick. They are emotionally reactive but seek to heal. They are the most passionate sign of the Zodiac, and their list of favorite foods will usually include some of those sensuous foods known to arouse passions, such as oysters, chocolate, avocados, cheese, asparagus, or spicy foods prepared with chilies. They get really into the luxurious, sexy, satisfying experience of eating, though they are secretive and would only do so while alone or with a desired romantic partner. Scorpios will do their best to eat alone or hidden in some way when they have to eat in public. When eating with others, Scorpios cannot pretend when food is not cooked according to their taste, though they will only say this out loud if they have a reason to put someone in their place.

Scorpios crave intensity, and the foods they are drawn to usually exhibit pure, strong flavors and aromas. Buttered lobster, linguine with clam sauce, or creamy fondue would all appeal to a Scorpio. Scorpios are the embodiment of Oscar Wilde's brilliant statement, "I can resist anything except temptation." They eat what they want when they want it. They would feel less than alive if they were not able to have their cake and eat it, too, though out of sight.

HOW THEY COOK

Their strong personality is very controlling in the kitchen, as elsewhere. Scorpios prefer to cook alone in kitchens whose design allows them to feel hidden and protected. Their equipment will be as close to commercial level as they can afford, large and powerful enough to make any dish. Their goal is to make their dishes the clear equal to any similar dishes made by the finest kitchens. Scorpios are the Zodiac's best detectives and will dedicate themselves to finding out how to re-create any dish they consider worthy. Most Scorpios have a treasured set of recipes they have inherited from beloved relatives and friends. Scorpios are secretive, so do not waste your time asking them for their recipes unless you have passed their test and can be trusted not to reveal them to others.

Scorpios need a powerful reason to share their cooking prowess with a group of people. When they want to weave their magic spell, they will approach the planning and execution of a meal as a way of seducing a potential lover, powerful friend, or business partner. In that case, they would enjoy planning a special eight-course meal of exotic dishes perfectly prepared that would be the stuff of legend. They are the only judge of what they make, however, so do not feel that you must overly compliment them.

HOW THEY ENTERTAIN

Scorpios tend to be brooding, emotionally intense, and deep. Change the music and you will change their mood! Candlelight and dramatic bouquets add a touch of transformational magic. They love antiques and treasures. You might catch them giving some probing, sexy, dark looks, or catch them sulking if they don't get their way or if something offends them.

Things of a mysterious nature fascinate a Scorpio. They are attracted to warm, lusty, dark, exciting atmospheres and food to keep the cold away, loved ones close, and enemies closer. Trick or treat? They are suspicious, so they need to make sure everything is planned for carefully. They love masquerade-themed parties. They enjoy anything to do with the occult or psychology, so these are good topics for conversation.

SAGITTARIUS

NOVEMBER 22 *to* DECEMBER 21

Ruling planet: Jupiter

Quality: mutable

Element: fire

Sagittarius foods: turkey, salmon, beans, squash, plums, persimmons, pecans, dates

Herbs: nutmeg, curry

Personal qualities: generous, cosmopolitan, humorous, optimistic, well-traveled, honest to a fault

Key words: freedom • theories • teaching • learning • world travel • philosophy • expansion • nature • increase • encouragement • prosperity • jovial • positive outlook • luck

HOW THEY EAT

Sagittarians are here to show us how to appreciate the best that other cultures and philosophies have to offer. Sagittarians are mutable fire. They know how to share their belief system while teaching, learning, and adjusting with optimism. They are dedicated to enjoying life's bounty. They are the sign most likely to be champions of the emerging Philosophy of Food movement, considering such issues as vegetarianism, agricultural ethics, food rights, biotechnology, and gustatory aesthetics, as well as the globalization of food, the role of technology, and the rights and responsibilities of consumers and producers.

Sagittarians know that we are what we eat. As lovers of nature, they need lots of pure water and fresh foods of every variety; overly processed foods do not agree with their health or their belief system, but otherwise they are not fussy or picky eaters—in fact, quite the opposite.

Their desire to know all that the world has to offer impels them to try almost every international cuisine they can. Eating is an important part of their lifelong learning program, and every meal is an opportunity to learn. You can expect them to be surprisingly blunt and honest about their likes and dislikes, even if their opinion was not solicited.

Their numerous other interests and outdoor activities can cause them to skip meals. The jovial Jupiter influence can sometimes lead a Sagittarian into compensating for meals missed by bingeing on rich food or alcoholic beverages when they finally sit down.

HOW THEY COOK

Sagittarians are eager for new experiences and so will study and employ the techniques of cuisine from all over the world. They can be the most adventurous cooks and will attempt the most difficult recipes with hard-to-find ingredients, using authentic cooking methods and utensils from around the globe.

Their love of nature inclines them to be outstanding farmers or outdoorsmen and women, so you may find yourself treated to the freshest meats, fish, or poultry you have ever tasted. You may even find them cooking over an outdoor fire. At the very least they will be experts at using an outdoor grill and smoker. They will not be shy about sharing information about any aspect of raising, culling, processing, and preparing any of their catch, so only ask if you are prepared to hear it.

Some Sagittarians emulate the mystic-philosopher Gurdjieff, who taught his students as he cooked them all dinner and then sat down to eat and discuss the lesson.

It is rare to attend a dinner cooked by a Sagittarius after which you do not come away saying, "I never knew that before. I really learned something tonight."

HOW THEY ENTERTAIN

Sagittarians are always fun and they are champions of other cultures, so expect an interesting mix of different dishes and native textiles when they host a party. Sagittarians love a potluck. There is a natural conflict between the Sagittarian intellect, which may crusade for food that is local and in season; the Sagittarian palate, which hungers for exotic flavors and foreign affairs; and the Sagittarian optimism, which indulges cravings. They are drawn to sustainable cuisine and green living, so the materials and decor they use will reflect that. Their bookcases are always crammed with interesting titles.

They probably just returned from a trip and are eager to share their adventures and to show the other party guests their photos. They love philosophical discussions and are very outspoken and exuberant. A bit of a fanatic and a puritan, Sagittarius may go overboard worrying about the good of humankind. A good long walk after dinner will suit Sagittarians well.

CAPRICORN

DECEMBER 22 *to* JANUARY 19

Ruling planet: Saturn

Quality: cardinal

Element: earth

Capricorn foods: leeks, cranberries, beef, cauliflower, fennel, bread, kale, quinoa

Herbs: tarragon, thyme

Personal qualities: ambitious, prudent, self-disciplined, thrifty, traditional

Key words: permanence • tradition • conservation • organization • responsibility • realism • definition and understanding of rules and limits • test of time • authority • concern

HOW THEY EAT

Capricorns are here to show us how applying oneself diligently and with persistence in the face of difficult circumstances can help one attain expertise and authority. Capricorns are cardinal earth. They know how to be disciplined in matters of resources and goal planning. They take action based on practical needs. Capricorns are traditional and like their meals served regularly and on time. They know what they like. They prefer to eat the things they have eaten since childhood. Many of them can eat the same thing every day for a particular meal, without becoming bored. Even if Capricorns become quite wealthy, they may cling to the foods they grew up with; it shows them how far they've come, yet how true they've stayed to their authentic self. This could be a steak dinner or a peanut butter and jelly sandwich. They are drawn to quality, however, though they may say they worry about the expense.

Capricorns can be surprisingly sensuous and will sometimes prefer the kind of creamy, buttery rich foods one might think more appropriate for a Taurus or its opposite sign, Scorpio. Like Scorpios, Capricorns have a secret side, and it is a rare Capricorn who does not have a treat they consider a guilty pleasure. Since they are disciplined and well-behaved so much of the time, they need to be "bad" in small and subtle ways to reward themselves.

When they eat with other people, Capricorns like to be respected for their choices and their knowledge about the food (and everything else). They would rather sit silently and be thought shy than speak up and risk being thought ignorant. Do not worry if you find yourself serving them a dish you have offered them before if they liked it the first time.

HOW THEY COOK

Capricorns take great pride in maintaining a beautiful and well-appointed kitchen that will impress guests. They appreciate tried-and-true recipes that call for ingredients they're familiar with and will follow them to the letter. They love tradition and re-creating meals that have an important meaning to their family or history.

A Capricorn's pantry is often the mirror image of their favorite specialty food shop, complete and alphabetized. Timing is very important to them so they may also have a collection of kitchen timers. It is a rare Capricorn who does not have a bottle of champagne, a jar of caviar, or a box of chocolates on hand, so they can celebrate an achievement any time.

Though they often present a stoic exterior, they do need recognition for their culinary triumphs and a generous helping of emotional support for any failures. Their goal is not only to become the best chef possible, but also a recognized culinary authority, at least among their friends and family. To this end they devour cookbooks, food lore, and cooking shows.

HOW THEY ENTERTAIN

Capricorns are patient and like to prepare hearty dinners. Their persistence coupled with their desire to adhere to tradition helps to make their gatherings as pleasant and special as possible. Though fairly conventional, Capricorns usually have very good taste, and they work hard to realize it in their homes. They like a sturdy table, a thick oriental rug, and a roaring fire for atmosphere. They might prefer to run the show than be the guest. Dinner gatherings are a way of celebrating family, coworkers, friends, and special occasions with foods that have traditional meaning. The conservation of resources always remains an issue with Capricorns, as they balance luxury with earthy common sense, "waste not, want not" principles, and self-discipline. Even though Capricorns are fundamentally serious and a bit spartan, they know how to loosen up and have fun when there is a party.

AQUARIUS

JANUARY 20 *to* FEBRUARY 18

Ruling planet: Uranus

Quality: fixed

Element: air

Aquarius foods: potatoes, Brussels sprouts, broccoli, chestnuts, sausage, wild rice, vinegar

Herbs: parsley, lemon balm

Personal qualities: unique, brilliant, inventive, articulate, progressive

Key words: humanitarian • inventive • detached • radical • altruistic • rebellious • scientific • eclectic • genius • eccentric • alternative • original • futuristic • history buff

HOW THEY EAT

Aquarians are here to show the world how to think outside the box. Aquarians are fixed air. They know how to be a friendly, innovative, methodical, futuristic, and stabilizing resource. They have original ideas. Aquarians love to eat with friends and prefer a no-fuss atmosphere where they are free to be themselves. When they eat alone at home, they do so as if they're camping out, no plates or utensils required. Aquarians thrive on being rebellious and different so they will be the vegan at the barbecue or the one who orders the token meat dish in the natural foods restaurant. They don't like schedules, so don't take it personally if they show up late or even early.

Aquarians study the past to improve the future and will experiment with both the most cutting-edge food craze or foods from the past that they sense are needed to benefit present and future generations. As students of history, they will appreciate any dish or table setting that harkens back to another time, though don't expect them to abide by the etiquette of that or any time—for Aquarians, rules are made to be broken. Hosts may find that when they present their Aquarian guest with their own nontraditional experimental menu offering, there is a good chance the Aquarian will rebel against this perceived restriction on their freedom and ask for a grilled cheese sandwich or other conventional dish.

Their concern for the good of all means that

they may eat in a way oriented more toward saving the planet than anything else. They are innovative and usually on the cutting edge of new thought regarding food as medicine. Freshness, sustainability, and humane farming are all important to them.

HOW THEY COOK

Aquarians do not like following instructions, and as a result, they are the sign most likely to invent new recipes and to experiment with different ways of making a dish. They are unpredictable and love to surprise their guests with the unusual and unexpected. The Aquarian specialty is walking into any kitchen, regardless of its strange conglomeration of ingredients (the stranger the better the challenge), and then whipping up a mini-masterpiece.

Their kitchens are an eclectic mixture of the latest technology and devices from the past; an Aquarian chef is just as likely to own a hand-cranked food mill as a sous vide machine. They value innovation, but also those tools that may have fallen out of vogue, which they can resurrect—a form of innovation in its own right.

Aquarians think like scientists, and every meal is an experiment in some way, even one they have made numerous times. They may add a new ingredient or eliminate a tried-and-true one. Aquarians can, however, go too far in their desire to make something different and end up by making something that is inedible. They will often hide the evidence of their failures in a most eccentric way, not by throwing out what they've made but by eating it themselves. This serves as a punitive lesson designed to overcome the Aquarian tendency to forget things and to make sure that they never do it that way again.

HOW THEY ENTERTAIN

Mixing, meeting, and mingling are an Aquarian's favorite things, and dining rooms can be one of the best places to spend some great time. As a host, they like to serve diverse fusion foods, which break through the barriers of race, religion, and national origin. They have many connections and are the cool, emotionally restrained, and cultivated sign of the Zodiac. They are good at analyzing other people's relationships, and usually their detached intellectual conversation is accomplished with a great sense of humor. They also love to talk about their enthusiasm for planning the future. With Aquarius you can always expect the unexpected. They may have a flowing fountain in their home.

PISCES

FEBRUARY 19 *to* MARCH 20

Ruling planet: Neptune

Quality: mutable

Element: water

Pisces foods: pears, flounder, spinach, honey, almonds, eggplant, sweet potatoes, melon

Herbs: seaweed, sage

Personal qualities: empathetic, artistic, compassionate, selfless, psychically attuned

Key words: sensitivity • spiritualism • receptivity • moodiness • caring • intuition • otherworldliness • inspiration • faith • idealism • fantasy • imagination

HOW THEY EAT

Pisces are here to show us that others are equally important and deserving of compassion as are we ourselves. Pisces are mutable water. They know how to shift, dissolve, merge, and change and be highly sensitive and empathetic to the emotional needs of others. While eating, a Pisces can often seem distracted; they may even give the impression that something's bothering them, but this is not usually the case. Typically, what is really happening is that they are experiencing their meal on a deep soul level, feeling the subtle energies of the various ingredients. They have emotional attachments to certain foods that remind them of important experiences in the past, so when eating they may be miles away, lost in vivid memories attached to similar foods and settings.

Pisceans love delicate, gentle food that is prepared simply and does not remind them of the harsher side of what is necessary to bring food to market and table. Many of them are vegetarians for moral reasons. They may have a sweet tooth, as they long for sweetness in all areas of life. Empathic, more so than any other sign, they need foods that restore balance and lift the spirits, like seafood, complex carbohydrates, nuts, fruits, and vegetables rich with blues-beating nutrients.

HOW THEY COOK

Pisceans like to lose themselves in the art of cooking. They can be inspired by acts as humble as peeling an onion or chopping vegetables, so much so that you may see them do a little dance when adding the veggies to a simmering pot. They love to mix, blend, and stir. The combining, dissolving, and blending of ingredients is akin to a religious experience for them. You are also likely to see them sample the cooking wine or sip some bubbly while they are at it.

Pisces chefs will pay attention to every look, gesture, and sound made by their guests in reaction to their gastronomic efforts. They are very sensitive and will take to heart any and all disapproval of their talents, though they may not show it for fear of causing equal pain in their guests. They are quite sentimental and you may find them store and use—usually out of sight of their guests—inherited and gifted cooking items and even chipped plates that other sun signs would have long thrown away.

HOW THEY ENTERTAIN

Pisces are sweet-natured dreamers with a romantic view of life. Love is the most important ingredient to a Pisces. Watery colors and whimsical elements make them happy. As hosts, they will float around the room, with an innate air of thoughtfulness for their guests, refreshing their drinks with love, healing, and deep insights. They never want anyone to feel left out. As guests, they have great sympathy and would rather eat something they do not like than cause their host to feel uncomfortable. To Pisceans, cooking and entertaining is an art that they cherish, and they delight in sharing meals that are full of charm and delicacy. Because they have highly attuned artistic impulses, they find a way to channel that talent into their cooking abilities. Their presentations of even the most familiar dishes can be masterful to the point where they become the new standard for everyone lucky enough to be invited to their home. Pisces dinner companions are intrigued by their intuitive and spiritual natures. They possess other-worldly perceptions and will gladly share with those they consider worthy.

SPRING

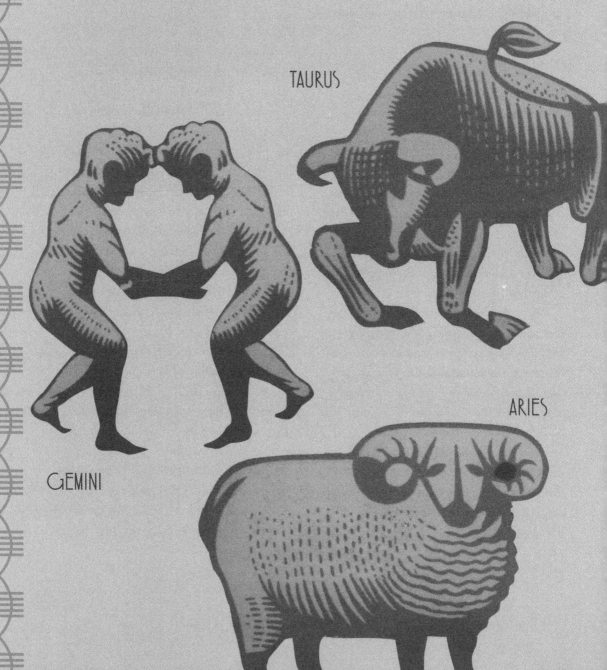

TAURUS

GEMINI

ARIES

STARTERS

Deviled Eggs and Diablo Slaw (A)

Watercress-Parsley Soup (T)

Endives with Parmesan, Olives, and Walnuts (G)

SALADS

Couscous and Cracked Wheat Tabbouleh (A)

Iceberg Wedge with Green Goddess Avocado Dressing (T)

Farro and Fiddleheads (G)

PASTA

Asparagus and Fresh Favas Fettucine (A)

Baby Arugula Pesto and Baby Peas Conchiglie (T)

Linguine and Ramps al Olio (G)

VEGETARIAN

Arancini and Ceci Arrabiata (A)

Spring Vegetable Quiche with New Potatoes, Arugula, and Cheddar (T)

Pan-Roasted Tomato and Kalamata Spanakopita (G)

SEAFOOD

Sriracha Salmon Cakes (A)

Roasted Black Cod and Sesame Spinach (T)

Sweet and Sour Snapper with Mango-Citrus Relish (G)

MEAT

Merguez Moussaka (A)

Classic Passover Brisket (T)

Tagine of Chicken with Potato, Preserved Lemon, and Apricot (G)

SIDES

Roasted Radishes (A)

Mashed Baby Limas (T)

Stir-Fried Snap Peas (G)

DESSERTS

Carrot Cupcakes (A)

Avocado-Lime Pie (T)

Tahini Lemon Bars (G)

After the Vernal Equinox—the first day of astronomical spring—the sun rises above the equator. The days begin to be longer than the nights. Nature awakes from its winter slumber. Seeds burst open with earth-splitting energy; sap stored in tree trunks circulates and brings life to the tips of branches and roots; rivers swell, coursing rapidly. Full of vitality, animals gambol and run. The Ram charges full speed ahead, jolting with energy, butting headfirst into competition and obstacles. Aries is under the fiery influence of Mars, but the sun—now getting stronger day by day—also brings its stimulating, illuminating effects to the world, both to external reality and our inner lives. Aries is a time of liveliness, enthusiasm, optimism, courage, and bright ideas, but it can also be a time of impulsivity and aggression.

April winds, like the winds of fate, can deliver seemingly insurmountable challenges. And if you go tilting at windmills, attacking imaginary enemies, you will certainly be overmatched by your own lack of common sense. The Ram, beaten, will totter like a little lamb. Mars, the God of War, has no patience for self-pity, however. Aries always moves forward, perhaps foolishly nonchalant about risk. If the warrior stops to try to understand himself, though, it would mean lapsing into fear, into immobility, into the (preceding) Piscean ocean of undifferentiated emotion. "Charge!" says the Aries's instincts, and charge the Aries will.

With the weather improved, but still too often raw, the first phase of spring is not the time to stand still—heat must still be generated as the thaw progresses. Early spring is the time to move forward, to explore, to plant seeds, germinate ideas and projects, and get moving on them. You may start many things and not finish them. This is okay. As in the garden, where plants will eventually have to be thinned, which projects you will focus on, which products you will put the finishing touches to, will be decided later, with Taurus practicality and Gemini reflection. For now, coming out of the darkness, Aries is the time for action, even if only for its own sake.

By the end of April, there is no question that the winter is over. The struggle for forward progress begins to lose its intensity. Now action for its own sake makes no sense; it's a waste of energy. The Bull's warmth and sensitivity mellow the Ram's fire and hard edge. The comforts of down-to-earth routines and sensual indulgence supplant instinctive movement and daring-do. After Aries brings the world to life, steadfast Taurus provides the Ground of Being, the theological concept that God is inherent in the structure of all matter rather than a Creator separate from creation. There is thesis and antithesis in the Zodiac. Aries turns to Taurus. Mars red becomes Venus green. Blood becomes chlorophyll. It is the time to work the soil, literally and metaphorically, the fertile medium from which things grow.

Though one can relax and enjoy the finer things in life as the striving subsides, there is still plenty of work to be done. As the daylight increases, Taurus brings a strong sense of purpose. Taurus is the time to regulate action, stabilize it, and apply it to specific ends. Of the many things started in quixotic Aries, the hard-nosed Bull decides which ones are practical and worth seeing through.

The Bull, symbol of productivity and purposefulness, plods forward slowly but surely. The symbol for Taurus is a circle with a pair of upward projections; it represents a bull with horns. Because of the implication of masculinity, the sign may seem an inappropriate one for the Earth Mother, but it comes to us from ancient days, the dawn of agriculture. It is the headdress of the Egyptian goddess Hathor, the deity the Greeks identified with Aphrodite, the Romans Venus. In it we see the Goddess of Love in her Planting Queen persona, a

APRIL WINDS, LIKE THE WINDS OF FATE, CAN DELIVER SEEMINGLY INSURMOUNTABLE CHALLENGES.

fertile Earth Mother. A physical being, she is no stranger to hard work. She has strong appetites and does not hesitate to satisfy them.

With Earth under Venus's green thumb, May is known as the merry month. It is a time of colorful blossoms, seductive shapes, sweet smells, and fruitfulness. Life is good. Everywhere, in the fields and in our beings, Mother Nature brings forth things young and tender, bursting with lush (and luscious) softness.

And with Venus comes her darling boy Cupid. Known as Eros to the Greeks, he shoots his arrows of sexual desire, concupiscence. Yes, in the merry month, there may be action for its own sake, but it's the time to make love, not war.

After thesis and antithesis comes synthesis. The twin personas of Gemini are wound together like the two snakes wrapped around the winged staff of Mercury. Gemini combines the fiery, headstrong Aries with the thoughtful, earthy Taurus and gives them an airy twist, breezing back and forth between blind instinct and calculated rationality.

Gemini is the time of partnerships and relationships. Weddings tie knots, making two one. School graduations launch individuals into new relationships with the world they live in.

As the messenger of the gods, Mercury, Gemini's ruler, is the fastest thing in the sky. His namesake planet completes its orbit around the sun in less than three Earth months. Under Mercury's influence, the steady pace of Taurus picks up considerably.

Gardens everywhere spring into their full June splendor. New generations of birds twitter in their nests. Farmers bring their first harvest to market.

Daylight is reaching its maximum span. The long days and warm nights invite us outdoors. As spring slides toward summer, the intricate design of being is on full display—the profuse overgrowth of

SPRING

ARIES

Deviled Eggs and Diablo Slaw, page 42

Opposite: Couscous and Cracked Wheat Tabbouleh, page 48

Above: Asparagus and Fresh Favas Fettucine, page 54

Left: Arancini and Ceci Arrabiata, page 60

Above: Sriracha Salmon
Cakes, page 66

Right: Merguez
Moussaka, page 72

Above: Roasted
Radishes, page 78

Left: Carrot Cupcakes,
page 81

TAURUS

Above: Baby Arugula Pesto and Baby Peas Conchiglie, page 56

Left: Spring Vegetable Quiche with New Potatoes, Arugula, and Cheddar, page 62

Opposite: Classic
Passover Brisket, page 74

Left: Mashed Baby
Limas, page 79

Below: Avocado-Lime
Pie, page 82

GEMINI

Left: Endives with Parmesan, Olives, and Walnuts, page 46

Below: Farro and Fiddleheads, page 52

Above: Linguine and Ramps al Olio, page 58

Opposite: Pan-Roasted Tomato and Kalamata Spanakopita, page 64

Left: Stir-Fried Snap Peas, page 80

Below: Tahini Lemon Bars, page 84

vegetation, the tangles of vines, the strong sun by day, the endless spray of stars we can now luxuriate in gazing upon—and it inspires wonder and corresponding growth in our minds. Like the flowers, the mind blossoms; like the sun, the mind shines; like the stars, the mind sparkles. But like the vines twisting and twining together, the mind can also become confused.

The third phase of spring brings an awareness of the interconnectedness of experience, a consciousness of the interplay of thoughts and actions, of light and dark. The mind is an organ of meaning. Its function is awareness. As we become aware of the mutability within us, the arbitrariness of our identity, the infinite regresses and the paradoxes of being, we feel a healthy need to sort things out. To keep us from losing our minds, objectivity through categorization and methodical systems goes a long way.

The basic form of categorization is language. Its invention is attributed to Mercury. Language helps us get a grip on the slippery slope of the material world, and it gives us separation from the snake pit of our thoughts. While Sagittarius, directly opposite Gemini, is a philosopher, a thinker who writes about universal things, Gemini

uses language in a more poetic way. Poetry originated in incantations, power words, and magical formulas. The poet expresses personal feelings in rhyme and rhythm. The moon in June, the dove is love. A rose is still a rose no matter what it's called, but by using an agreed-upon symbol for it, we gain a kind of power over it.

Multifaceted Mercury is also the scientist. Through science, the systematic study of nature, mind asserts itself over matter. But can it really? In fact, the mind *is* matter; it is inseparable from the fabric of existence. The mind and the universe are inextricably interlaced in an intricate design. Did the brain create the world, or did the world create the brain? The answer is simple. Like left and right, inside and out, you can't have one without the other. That is the message of the Twins.

Soon it will be summer, and these exhausting mental twists and turns will pass, artifacts of the energy necessary to launch the many activities necessary for a successful spring. For now, as spring reaches its conclusion, let the music play, let everything dance together, weaving in and out, back and forth between consciousness and unconsciousness, between form and emptiness, between mind and matter.

DEVILED EGGS AND DIABLO SLAW
ARIES

The egg, literally life in embryo, represents the mystery and magic of creation. As a blueprint for a living thing and a symbol of Resurrection, no food is more Aries than the egg: Aries is all about potential. Aries marks a new beginning. With its bright yellow yolk, the egg is a food associated with sunny mornings and breakfast, the day's first food for the Zodiac's first sign.

Mars is hard-boiled. The warrior cannot afford to drop his shield and let even a wisp of self-doubt taint his thoughts lest paralyzing fear rush in. For the soldier on the march, a hard-cooked egg or two in the backpack, purse, or pocket puts an instant fix on a sudden drop in energy or an inconvenient appetite. Independent and self-motivated, alone on a mission, Ram-bam Aries may want to gulp down an egg and run.

SERVES 4 AS A STARTER

FOR THE EGGS
4 large eggs, at room temperature
¼ cup mayonnaise
1 tablespoon Dijon mustard
1 tablespoon mustard powder
½ teaspoon onion salt
¼ teaspoon cayenne pepper, or to taste

FOR THE SLAW
1½ cups thinly shredded Savoy cabbage
½ cup minced scallions, whites only
¼ cup cilantro leaves
1 tablespoon minced jalapeño pepper, or to taste

FOR THE SLAW DRESSING
1 teaspoon hot sauce, such as Tabasco
½ teaspoon ground cumin
2 tablespoons lime juice
1 teaspoon lime zest
4 tablespoons olive oil
½ teaspoon salt
½ teaspoon freshly ground black pepper

Sweet paprika, for dusting

Make the eggs. Place the eggs in a pot large enough to accommodate them in a single layer, and cover them with cold water and a little salt. The water should be at least 1 inch over the eggs. Bring the water to a gentle boil over high heat. Turn off the heat, cover the pot, and let sit 8 to 10 minutes (a shorter time will result in a softer yolk; a longer time, a firmer yolk).

Drain the eggs and run them under cold running water. When the eggs are cool enough to handle, peel them under cold running water.

Pat the eggs dry with a clean kitchen towel, and using a knife, cut them in half lengthwise.

Using a small spoon, scoop the cooked yolks into a medium-size bowl, and set aside the egg whites. Mash the yolks with a fork until they are a smooth uniform texture. Add the mayonnaise, Dijon mustard, mustard powder, onion salt, and cayenne to the mashed yolks, and mix well. Set aside.

Make the slaw. Combine the vegetables for the slaw in a large bowl.

Make the dressing. Combine the ingredients for the dressing in a small bowl, and whisk until emulsified. Add the dressing to the slaw vegetables, 1 tablespoon at a time, tossing the slaw as you go to coat all of the ingredients. (Save a little dressing to sprinkle on top of the eggs.)

Gently spoon the yolk mixture back into the egg white halves.

Divide the slaw on serving plates. Arrange two egg halves on each. Sprinkle with any remaining dressing and a hit of paprika.

 Chili peppers vary in heat. One tablespoon of the average jalapeño should be enough to wake you up. You can add more or less, depending on how diabolical you want to be.

WATERCRESS-PARSLEY SOUP

TAURUS

Taurus, ruled by Venus, appreciates the finer things in life. But with the Bull, a male animal of substance and strength as its symbol, Taurus is more about earthiness, comfort, and support than it is about bling. Few dishes are earthier, more comforting, or supportive, though still luxurious, than potato-leek soup. This version, featuring barely cooked watercress and parsley, is the color and the taste of the season, when watercress grows wild in the beds of streams; the spring greens are jumping; and the chlorophyll is high. Drizzling in some heavy cream at the end, before you puree the soup, is traditional. It makes the soup richer and elevates it, though the potatoes make it substantial enough to begin with and the generous amount of butter at the start lends the soup a dairy-sweetness without the cream.

SERVES 6 TO 8 AS A STARTER

4 tablespoons unsalted butter

4 garlic cloves, peeled and chopped

5 leeks, trimmed, cleaned, and finely chopped

2½ pounds Yukon gold potatoes, peeled and chopped into small dice

8 cups chicken or vegetable stock

3 bay leaves

1 tablespoon fresh thyme leaves

1 teaspoon salt

1 teaspoon freshly ground black pepper

2 cups chopped watercress (well-packed), plus additional for garnish

½ cup flat-leaf parsley leaves, plus additional for garnish

½ cup heavy cream, optional

Melt the butter in a large pot over medium-high heat. Add the garlic and sauté, until golden and fragrant, 1 to 2 minutes. Add the leeks and sauté, stirring attentively, until they are fully soft, 10 to 12 minutes.

Add the potatoes to the garlic and leeks, and sauté briefly until they begin to sweat, about 3 minutes.

Add the stock, bay leaves, thyme, salt, and pepper. Raise the heat to high, and bring to a boil. Cover the pot, lower the heat, and simmer until the potatoes are thoroughly soft, about 20 minutes.

Remove and discard the bay leaves. Add the watercress and parsley to the pot, and stir. If you are adding heavy cream, pour it in to taste, and stir. Remove the pot from the heat, and use an immersion blender to puree the soup.

Return the soup to medium-low heat, and simmer for 1 to 2 minutes.

Ladle into bowls, and garnish each with a few watercress and parsley leaves before serving.

Members of the onion family, leeks tend to trap sand and dirt between their layers and need to be thoroughly washed. To prepare them for cooking, cut away the roots and the dark green tops, and discard. Peel off the outer discolored or damaged layers, and discard them too. Cut what remains in half lengthwise, separate the layers, and run them under cold tap water, gently rubbing away any grit with your fingers. Be thorough. Spin them dry in a salad spinner, and they are ready to cook.

ENDIVES WITH PARMESAN, OLIVES, AND WALNUTS

GEMINI

Multiple forces are at play when the sun is in Gemini. These endive spears are packed with a variety of flavors and a mix of colors. The Twin Pillars, symbol of Gemini, represent opposite forces that may contradict or complement one another, or do both at the same time. In the kitchen, the self-aware Gemini mind-set harmonizes tastes and textures. The meaty texture and fruity red-wine flavor of Kalamata olives pair well with the crisp, sweet sharpness of the Parmesan and the nuttiness of the walnuts. The bright citrus tang of tangerine mitigates the bitterness of the endives and radicchio and accentuates the sweetness of the fennel.

SERVES 4 AS A STARTER

FOR THE STUFFING
½ cup shaved Parmesan
½ cup pitted Kalamata olives, cut into slivers
½ cup finely chopped toasted walnuts
½ cup flat-leaf parsley leaves
½ cup thinly sliced radicchio

FOR THE DRESSING
Juice of 1 tangerine
4 tablespoons olive oil
1 teaspoon Dijon mustard
¼ teaspoon minced garlic
¼ teaspoon salt
¼ teaspoon freshly ground black pepper

1 cup shaved fennel bulb
2 Belgian endives, trimmed, outer leaves
    discarded

Make the stuffing. Combine the ingredients for the stuffing in a medium bowl, and toss to mix.

Make the dressing. Combine the ingredients for the dressing in a medium bowl, and whisk until emulsified.

Add three-fourths of the dressing to the stuffing, and toss to evenly coat the ingredients.

Toss the shaved fennel with the remaining dressing. Divide the fennel shavings among the serving plates.

Select the four largest unblemished spear-shaped leaves from each trimmed endive. Save what remains for another use.

Place two spears on each plate, arranging the fennel shavings to support the endive spears upright, forming a concave pocket. Gently spoon equal portions of the stuffing into each spear.

Serve immediately.

You can use a vegetable peeler to shave the Parmesan and the fennel. Also, endives wilt quickly so it's best to cut them right before you plan to serve them. If you cut them sooner, sprinkling them with a little lemon juice helps them stay crisp and fresh looking.

COUSCOUS AND CRACKED WHEAT TABBOULEH

ARIES

Aries is associated with adolescence. Teen-agers who leave home and the security of the family are by no means fully comfortable in their new environment, a world that seems magical and unfriendly at the same time. It is a challenging place that must be conquered. Aries goes forth with trepidation and exhilaration, insecurity and wonder, impatience and determination. Standing alone, on the straight path toward full independence, Aries is partially "cooked." Bold Aries, the Ram, charges head first. Fragile Aries, the wounded lamb, recoils. But there's no time to feel sorry. Driven by blind inner need, the Ram must charge again.

With strong notes of fresh mint and tangy lemon, tabbouleh makes a suitable accompaniment to lamb. This bolder, livelier variation on the Middle Eastern classic can stand on its own. Substituting a portion of couscous for some of the traditional cracked whole wheat makes for a lighter and sweeter tabbouleh.

SERVES 8

4 tablespoons olive oil, divided
1 red onion, peeled and minced
1 clove garlic, peeled and minced
1 cup tomato or mixed vegetable juice
1 teaspoon ground cumin
¼ teaspoon cayenne pepper
½ teaspoon salt
½ teaspoon freshly ground black pepper
¾ cup bulgur wheat
¼ cup couscous
½ cup lemon juice
1 roasted red bell pepper (facing page, Roasted Bell Peppers), chopped into ⅛-inch dice
2 plum tomatoes, peeled and seeded, chopped into ⅛-inch dice
1 stalk celery, chopped into ⅛-inch dice
20 Kalamata (or other oil-cured) black olives, pitted and quartered
1 cup chopped lightly toasted walnuts (page 199, Roasting Seeds and Nuts)
1 cup shredded basil leaves
½ cup finely chopped mint
¼ cup finely chopped flat-leaf parsley

Heat 2 tablespoons of the olive oil in a saucepan on medium-high heat. Add the onion and the garlic, and sauté until the

ROASTED BELL PEPPERS

Preheat a broiler with the rack as close to the heat as possible. Trim the peppers by cutting away the tops and bottoms. Discard the seeds and the ribs. Make an incision in the center portions of each pepper so they will lie flat. Place them skin-side up on a foil-covered baking sheet, and slide them under the broiler. Because of their irregular shapes, the tops and bottoms of the peppers don't lie flat, don't blacken uniformly, and don't peel easily. You may want to use those parts for other purposes.

Rotate the peppers under the broiler as needed. Remove them when the skins are evenly blackened.

When the roasted peppers are cool enough to handle, peel off the charred skin, and cut them according to taste or recipe directions.

Any color bell pepper can be cooked using this method. However, green ones tend to be less meaty, and their skins are thinner and more adhesive.

onion becomes translucent but is still a bit crisp, about 3 minutes.

Add the vegetable juice, cumin, cayenne, salt, and black pepper to the saucepan. Bring to a boil, and add the bulgur and couscous. Stir the grains, cover the saucepan, and turn off the heat. Let sit for 10 minutes. The grains will be only partially cooked, but the acidity of the lemon juice and chopped tomatoes will finish the cooking.

Transfer the grains to a large bowl. Add the lemon juice and remaining 2 tablespoons olive oil to the grains, and stir to combine. Allow to cool slightly, then add the bell pepper, tomatoes, celery, olives, walnuts, basil, mint, and parsley. Mix thoroughly.

Let the tabbouleh stand at room temperature for at least 2 hours before serving. Better yet, refrigerate overnight. One hour or so before you are ready to serve it, remove it from the refrigerator, and allow it to come to room temperature. Before serving, stir and taste for seasoning, adding additional salt, black pepper, cayenne, oil, or lemon juice if needed.

Serve as is or spooned into romaine, endive, or radicchio leaves.

ICEBERG WEDGE WITH GREEN GODDESS AVOCADO DRESSING

TAURUS

Mars is the Red Planet; Venus the Green Goddess. Depending on her mood, she can run hot or cool as ice. Despite being a little old-fashioned, iceberg lettuce has its place. Cut into ribbons and mixed with softer greens, it gives sensual crunch. Or it can be served on its own in wedges, covered with a bold dressing. Here it is with a Green Goddess dressing that takes a few hints from guacamole.

SERVES 4

¼ cup lime juice
¼ cup olive oil
1 tablespoon mayonnaise
2 tablespoons crème fraîche
¼ cup finely minced red onion
2 tablespoons finely chopped cilantro
1 garlic clove, peeled and minced
1 tablespoon finely minced jalapeño pepper
1 tablespoon hot sauce, such as Tabasco
¼ teaspoon salt
½ teaspoon freshly ground black pepper
2 ripe avocados, peeled, pitted, and cubed
½ cup Lemon–Olive Oil Dressing
    (facing page)
1 head iceberg lettuce, outer leaves removed,
    cut into 4 equal wedges

Whisk together the lime juice, olive oil, mayonnaise, crème fraîche, onion, cilantro, garlic, jalapeño, hot sauce, salt, and black pepper in a medium mixing bowl. Add the avocado cubes to the bowl, and mash lightly with a fork, then whisk. Add the lemon–olive oil dressing to the avocado mixture, a tablespoon at a time, and whisk until smooth. If it becomes too stiff, add more dressing.

Put one wedge of lettuce on each plate. Pour a generous amount of the dressing over each wedge, and serve immediately.

LEMON-OLIVE OIL DRESSING

This simple dressing is wonderful as is, especially on a simple green salad, but it also makes a fantastic starting point for more elaborate dressings. A few squirts of it on sizzling hot chicken or fish will give it a boost of flavor. It keeps for at least ten days refrigerated, longer if you use garlic powder instead of garlic. If some remains after that, you can use it to marinate chicken or shrimp. Celery salt, onion salt, or lemon pepper adds more interest.

Makes 1½ cups

> Zest of 1 organic lemon
> ⅓ cup lemon juice
> 1 cup olive oil
> ½ small garlic clove, minced
> 1 teaspoon Dijon mustard
> 1 teaspoon seasoned salt
> 1 teaspoon lemon pepper

Combine all the ingredients in a mason jar or other sealable container, seal tightly, and shake well until emulsified. You can also combine everything in a food processor, give it a good whiz, and store in a clean jar or other container with a tight-fitting lid.

FARRO AND FIDDLEHEADS
GEMINI

Ferns are an ancient plant. They neither flower nor seed, but reproduce by dispersing spores. When conditions are right, the spore reproduces asexually: the cell nucleus divides into two. The staff of Mercury, Gemini's ruler, is the symbol for such magic—the division of one into two and the combination of two into one. In myths, Mercury, messenger of the gods, has a transcendent gender identity. His "message" is dispersed through the mind rather than the sexual organ. Memes are spores of the mind. Ideas replicate and spread by doubling, one person transmitting to another.

In the cool dampness of early spring, fiddlehead ferns—another wild plant that eludes mass production—roll out of their winter beds. They are served as a vegetable in Japan and Korea. Native Americans introduced them to New England settlers. Old Yankee recipes have them boiled in apple cider vinegar and slathered with butter. You can get them at reliable farmers' markets or, better, go exploring with an experienced forager. Their flavor is a bit like asparagus, and they can be cooked the same way.

Farro is an ancient grain that has recently resurged in popularity. It has a nutty, earthy flavor. It is chewy, but satisfyingly so. It comes pearled (with the bran removed) and semi-pearled (with a good portion of the bran intact). The cooking time on the latter is a bit longer, and the taste is more full-bodied and down-to-earth.

SERVES 4 TO 6

1 cup semi-pearled farro
½ cup apple cider vinegar
10 basil leaves, shredded
½ cup chopped scallions, whites only
½ teaspoon salt, plus more as needed
¼ teaspoon cayenne pepper
¼ cup Lemon–Olive Oil Dressing (page 51), plus more as needed
½ pound fiddlehead ferns
Freshly ground black pepper
1 cup fresh baby peas, thawed, if frozen
½ cup roasted, salted, shelled pistachios, chopped
2 cups watercress leaves

Pour 2½ cups of water into a medium saucepot. Add the farro, apple cider vinegar, basil leaves, scallions, salt, and cayenne, and bring to a boil over high heat. Reduce the heat to low, cover, and cook until tender, about 30 minutes. If any liquid remains, drain it off.

Combine the cooked farro and lemon–olive oil dressing in a large mixing bowl, and toss to mix.

Meanwhile, bring 2 quarts of lightly salted water to a rapid boil. Combine several handfuls of ice and cold water in a large mixing bowl to make an ice bath, and set aside. While the water is coming to a boil, clean the fiddlehead ferns thoroughly. Soak them in cold water, and rinse them several times. Once the water reaches a boil, add the fiddleheads, and cook until they are crisp-tender. Cooking times will vary depending on the size and thickness of the fern. For most, 2 minutes at a boil will suffice. Give a touch-test after 1 minute. The moment they are done, remove the fiddleheads and immediately plunge them into the ice-water bath. Drain them, and pat dry.

Season the fiddleheads with salt and pepper, and toss them in a bowl with a few splashes of the lemon–olive oil dressing.

Stir the peas and pistachios into the farro. Gently fold the watercress into the farro. If it seems dry, add another teaspoon or two of dressing.

Divide onto serving plates. Top each with a portion of fiddleheads, and serve.

ASPARAGUS AND FRESH FAVAS FETTUCINE
ARIES

The slush and mush of Pisces are in the past. Aries springs forward, butting against all obstacles. The sharp sword of Mars cuts clear. On the surface, there are April showers, but on the psychic level, the Aries fire won't be doused. The energy of Aries, of spring bursting forth, permeates this dish, a greener take on pasta primavera. *Primavera* is Italian for spring. Classic pasta primavera is a soupy, rich dish: pasta and vegetables swimming in a creamy butter and cheese sauce. This Aries version is lighter and brighter, studded with fresh fava beans, a spring delicacy, and the delicate tang of goat cheese.

Very young favas can be eaten raw, out of the pod, skin and all. The skin of most fava beans, however, is tough and must be removed. Prepping fresh favas, although not difficult, can be time-consuming. Tear open the pods, and remove the beans. Bring a couple of quarts of water to a boil. Drop the beans in. Wait for the water to come back to a boil, and drain. Immerse the beans in ice water. Use a knife or pinch the bean with your fingernail to slit the translucent skin. Applying gentle pressure, squeeze the bean out. Discard the skin.

Bucheron is a goat cheese from the Loire Valley in France. Tangy and smooth-textured, it does not crumble like the vacuum-sealed logs of chèvre widely available in the supermarket dairy section. When heated, it melts into the pasta like butter, but it is not quite so fatty.

SERVES 4 AS A MAIN COURSE OR 6 TO 8 AS A PASTA COURSE

1 bunch large asparagus, washed and dried, woody ends removed

5 tablespoons olive oil, divided

1 teaspoon minced garlic, divided

½ teaspoon salt, divided

½ teaspoon freshly ground black pepper, divided

2 cups chicken stock

¼ teaspoon crushed red pepper

2 cups peeled fava beans (about 2 pounds fava pods)

3 plum tomatoes, seeds and pulp removed, julienned

3 ounces goat cheese, preferably Bucheron, crumbled

1 pound fettuccine

Grated Parmesan, for the table (optional)

Preheat the oven to 400°F.

Slice the heads (the top inch or so) from the asparagus, setting aside the remaining spears. Place the asparagus heads in a large bowl, and toss them with 1 tablespoon of the olive oil, half the minced garlic, and a little salt and pepper. Spread them on a baking sheet, and place them in the preheated oven. Roast, shaking often, until they are soft and slightly browned, about 3 to 4 minutes. Remove from the oven, and set aside.

Slice the headless asparagus spears into long, thin strips, generally imitating the fettuccine in shape and length. In a medium pot, bring the stock to a boil. Add the asparagus, and cook until the ribbons soften, about 3 minutes. Strain, reserving the stock.

Heat the remaining 4 tablespoons olive oil in a medium saucepan over high heat. Add the crushed red pepper and the remaining garlic to the oil, and stir. When the oil is hot enough to shimmer, but not smoking, add the asparagus ribbons. Stir for 1 minute or

so, then add the favas. Stir for 1 minute, then add the tomatoes. Stir to coat. Season with the remaining salt and black pepper, stir, and add the goat cheese to the pan. Cover and remove from the heat.

Bring 6 quarts of salted water to a rapid boil. Add the fettuccine. Drain when the pasta is just short of al dente, about 6 to 7 minutes. Return the pasta to the pot, and place over medium heat. Add the asparagus and fava mixture to the fettucine, and toss to incorporate. Add the reserved stock a little at a time, as needed to make the mixing easier and to finish cooking the pasta. (Save any stock that remains for another purpose.) Continue tossing until the cheese is thoroughly melted and well-distributed and the fettuccine is cooked to your liking. Ideally, the tomatoes will be undercooked.

Garnish each serving with the roasted asparagus heads, and serve immediately, passing the Parmesan at the table, if you like.

BABY ARUGULA PESTO AND BABY PEAS CONCHIGLIE

TAURUS

Taurus, ruled by Venus, is represented by the Bull, a definitively masculine animal. Muscular plow-pullers of ancient days, the Bull and the Ox are associated with agricultural productivity. In May, life is good on Venus's green Earth. Mother Nature's femininity is not the delicate, passive kind. The Goddess of Love is also the Green Goddess. For all her softness and tenderness, she has a bull-like sense of purpose and determination. An effective nurturer, she is warm and tender, but fixed and enduring.

Venus is at work in May. Before the full heat of summer dries roots and wilts and bleaches tender leaves, when the heat of the day can be counted on, when nights still have a bit of chill and mornings are dewy, the new young greens and early peas are ready for the taking. The arugula is nutty, peppery, and bright-tasting; the peas are sweet, crisp, and tender.

**SERVES 4 AS A MAIN COURSE,
6 TO 8 AS A PASTA COURSE**

FOR THE PESTO

½ cup roasted, salted pistachios

4 cups baby arugula, washed and dried

10 basil leaves

¼ cup flat-leaf parsley leaves

½ cup chopped scallions, whites only

2 garlic cloves, peeled

½ cup grated Parmesan cheese, plus extra for the table

½ teaspoon salt

½ teaspoon freshly ground black pepper

¼ teaspoon crushed red pepper flakes

6 tablespoons olive oil

1 pound conchiglie

2 cups baby peas, thawed if frozen

Conchiglie are shell-shaped pasta, whose hollows will capture the pesto and the peas. Cavatelli, orecchiette, and other concave pasta are suitable substitutes.

Combine all the ingredients for the pesto in the bowl of a food processor. Process to a near-smooth paste. If the mixture is stiff, slowly drizzle in more oil as you run the processor. Scoop the pesto into a medium bowl, cover, and set aside in a warm spot. (You can spin a cup of water in the food processor bowl to clean it out, then add it to your pasta water.)

Bring 6 quarts of salted water to a rapid boil. Add the conchiglie. Drain when the pasta is just short of al dente, 8 to 9 minutes, reserving 1 cup of water.

Return the pasta to the pot, and place it over medium heat. Add the peas and 1 cup of the pesto. Toss to evenly distribute the ingredients. Add more pesto and the reserved pasta water a little at a time, as needed, to make the mixing easier and to finish cooking the pasta. Continue tossing until the conchiglie is cooked to your liking. Serve hot with grated Parmesan on the table.

PASTA

The recipes in this book call for dried pasta, which is typically southern Italian. Properly cooked, pasta should not be swimming in sauce. It should be distinctly firm and have absorbed the flavor of its sauce. Save a cup or two of the salted cooking water, and drain the pasta when it is still just short of al dente. Return the drained pasta to the empty pot, set it back on the stove over medium heat, and toss it with some of the sauce, as you would cook the stock into risotto, letting the pasta absorb the sauce before adding more, a little at a time. Add some of the reserved water as necessary, to finish cooking. Unless you have access to artisan pasta, please use a good-quality Italian import. Cooking times given for quality products are approximate.

LINGUINE AND RAMPS AL OLIO
GEMINI

Ramps, also called wild leeks, must be harvested in the wild, usually at higher elevations, and are only available during the spring. While they have a hint of scallion green, their main flavor is that of dark, tough, earthy garlic. They are not for everyone. This is fortunate. As civilization grows, wide open spaces shrink. Wild and wooly Nature is replaced by lawn order. Ramps have a mischievous Mercurial spirit that thumbs its nose at the straight, neat, genetically engineered rows of agribusiness.

Ramps have a Twin-nature. On the one hand, they are an edible weed, the food of the humble forager. On the other hand, they are in demand by fine diners who hunger for an authentic taste of quainter times when people ate things directly from Nature. The irony! Now better restaurants buy up most of the supply. You are more likely to find the little rapscallions in your backyard or on the side of the road than at the grocery store, but you can usually snag some at a good farmers' market.

 Gemini takes what's handy. If you can't lay your hands on ramps, you can substitute a half dozen or so garlic cloves and a bunch or two of scallions.

Using ramps instead of garlic, this recipe borrows from one of the simplest of southern Italian peasant dishes: *pasta aglio e olio*. The long, slow cooking takes some of the bite out of the ramps, and the addition of tomato and grated zucchini lends the dish some soft body that balances out the somewhat chewy texture of the ramps.

To clean ramps, trim the roots and thoroughly wash and rinse the (white) bulbs and the (green) leaves. Gently pat them dry.

SERVES 4 AS AN ENTRÉE,
6 TO 8 AS A PASTA COURSE

6 tablespoons olive oil
½ teaspoon crushed red pepper flakes
12 ounces ramps, trimmed and cleaned, bulbs chopped and leaves thinly sliced, separated
1 small zucchini, grated
1 plum tomato, peeled and chopped
10 basil leaves
½ teaspoon salt
½ teaspoon freshly ground black pepper
1 pound linguine fine, or spaghettini
½ cup grated Parmesan cheese, plus more for the table

In a heavy saucepot with a tight-fitting lid, warm the olive oil and red pepper flakes over high heat. When the oil is very hot but not smoking and the pepper is starting to infuse, add the ramp bulbs, and sauté for 1 to 2 minutes. Add the ramp leaves, and sauté 1 minute more.

Add the zucchini, tomato, basil, salt, and black pepper, and stir to mix. Cover the pan and lower the heat to simmer. Allow the sauce to simmer for at least 15 minutes to marry the flavors or up to 1 hour for a more concentrated, yet gentler, flavor.

Bring 6 quarts of salted water to a rapid boil. Boil the linguine fine until just short of al dente. Drain, reserving 1 to 2 cups of the water.

Return the pasta to the pot, and place it over medium heat. Add the ramps sauce to the pasta, and toss to incorporate. Add the reserved pasta cooking water a little at a time, as needed, to finish cooking the pasta, continuing to toss, to incorporate the sauce. When the pasta is cooked to your liking, add the Parmesan and a drizzle of pasta water. Mix thoroughly and serve.

THE GEMINI TWINS

As the legend goes, Castor and Pollux, twin brothers, were the children of Zeus and Leda, Queen of Sparta. Helen of Troy was their sister. Born of god-seed in flesh-and-blood woman, Pollux was immortal but lacking in insight, while Castor was mortal, but ingenious and intelligent. Like many twins, they were two in body, but one in spirit. Averse to being separated, Pollux offered to share his immortality with his brother in return for the mental illumination Castor provided. The myth is a parable of the benefits of mutuality and cooperation. It teaches that, when one hand washes the other, the whole is more than the sum of the parts.

ARANCINI AND CECI ARRABIATA

ARIES

Play ball! It's fitting that baseball's opening day takes place when the sun moves into Aries. Aries gets the ball rolling. Arians are balls of fire. While Aries naturally wants to lead or go it alone, it's important for the Ram to modify this tendency, to learn to fit in and become a team player. Effective leadership comes from recognizing the team's needs and following one's place on it. It's just a game, Aries. Don't take it too seriously. But don't drop the ball.

A Sicilian staple, *arancini,* stuffed rice balls that are coated in bread crumbs and deep fried, are fun food, sometimes sold by street vendors. You can eat one when you are on the go or, served as suggested with spicy chickpeas adding Aries fire, sitting down for a satisfying vegetarian meal. Their name means "little oranges." This is because of their size, shape, and color after cooking—the saffron and tomato render them a beautiful golden orange hue.

**MAKES 12 ARANCINI,
TO SERVE 4 TO 6**

FOR THE CHICKPEAS ARRABIATA

¼ cup olive oil

2 garlic cloves, minced

1 teaspoon red pepper flakes

¼ cup tomato paste

2 cups diced tomatoes, drained if canned

½ teaspoon salt

2 cups cooked chickpeas, drained and well-rinsed if canned

FOR THE ARANCINI

1 tablespoon olive oil

1½ cups Arborio rice

1 cup tomato juice

1 tablespoon unsalted butter

¼ teaspoon saffron

½ teaspoon salt

½ teaspoon freshly ground black pepper

4 eggs, beaten, divided

1 cup grated Parmesan

1 cup shredded provolone

6 ounces mozzarella cut in very small cubes

All-purpose flour, for dusting

Unseasoned bread crumbs or panko, for coating

Vegetable oil, for frying

Make the chickpeas arrabiata sauce. In a medium saucepan, warm the olive oil over medium heat. When the oil is warm, add the garlic and red pepper flakes. Cook until the garlic is fragrant, about 3 minutes. Raise the heat to high. When the oil is very hot but not smoking, add the tomato paste, tomatoes, and salt, and simmer for 5 minutes. Add the chickpeas, and simmer an additional 5 minutes. Keep warm on low.

Make the arancini. In a medium saucepot, warm the olive oil over medium-high heat. When the oil is warm, add the rice, and stir, coating the grains. Toast the rice for 2 to 3 minutes, until it gives off a nutty aroma. Add the tomato juice, 1 cup water, the butter, saffron, salt, and black pepper. Bring to a boil, cover the saucepan, lower the heat to a simmer, and cook for 15 minutes. Remove from the heat, and let sit covered for 10 minutes. Transfer to a mixing bowl, and let sit until cool enough to handle.

Once the rice has cooled, prepare the arancini. Add half of the beaten eggs, the Parmesan, and provolone to the rice, and mix well.

Wet your hands with cold water, and using a ½ cup measure, scoop up some of the rice mixture. Form the rice into a ball. Be firm. Then gently make a hole in the ball by pressing a finger into it as far as you can (without coming out the other side). Fill with a few cubes of mozzarella. Reshape the ball, sealing the cheese in.

Dust the arancini with flour, dip it in the remaining beaten eggs, roll it in the bread crumbs, and set on a floured oven sheet. Repeat with the remaining rice and cheese.

To fry, heat ½ inch of vegetable oil in a large, deep skillet to frying temperature, about 360°F. Slide the rice balls in carefully one at a time, and be careful not to overcrowd the pan, so as not to cool the oil. To get the balls uniformly golden brown and crisp on all sides, roll them gently in the hot oil every minute or so, browning each surface a little at a time. About 8 to 10 minutes total should do it. Remove them with a metal slotted spoon, and let drain on paper towels.

Reheat the chickpeas if necessary. Spoon equal portions onto serving plates. Top with two or three arancini, and serve.

 If your *arancini* do not come out as perfect spheres, no worries. They will be easier to shape, however, if you let the cooked rice mixture sit in the refrigerator for at least 1 hour and up to overnight.

SPRING VEGETABLE QUICHE WITH NEW POTATOES, ARUGULA, AND CHEDDAR

TAURUS

As the world turns and the days warm, the fight is over. The contentious Mars energy stabilizes into a solid, practical-minded Venus personality. Adolescent Aries, dynamo rushing forth in desire and need for self-expression, gives way to Taurus's steadiness and persistence. Stubborn and undeviating, full of organic power, the Bull is in physical contact with the earth and the solid nourishment the earth brings forth.

The Bull has an inner Cow. The Plow Animal's mate gives sweet milk. Since the dawn of animal husbandry, the cow has been a mother to us all. Dairy Queen, with your milk of bovine kindness, we thank the Goddess of Love for you!

Ditto lowly potato, compassion fruit of the good earth; you've saved millions from starvation.

SERVES 6 TO 8

 You will need a 10-inch pie pan in which to cook the quiche.

FOR THE CRUST
3 cups shredded uncooked Idaho potatoes
1 cup crushed potato chips
1 tablespoon onion powder
2 tablespoons melted butter
2 eggs, beaten
1 cup all-purpose flour
Butter for greasing the pie pan

FOR THE FILLING
½ pound new potatoes, cut into ¼-inch dice
1 cup coarsely cracked potato chips
1 cup coarsely chopped baby arugula
1 cup chopped scallions, whites only
½ cup finely chopped red bell pepper
1½ cups shredded sharp cheddar
6 large eggs, beaten
¼ cup half-and-half
¼ teaspoon salt
½ teaspoon freshly ground black pepper

Preheat the oven to 400°F.

Make the crust. Combine all of the ingredients for the crust in a large bowl, and stir to mix thoroughly, until you have a dough that will hold together in the pie pan. Press the dough into a lightly greased 10-inch pie plate, evenly coating the bottom and sides. Bake until browned, 30 to 40 minutes.

Meanwhile, make the filling. Combine the ingredients for the filling in a large mixing bowl, and stir to thoroughly incorporate. When the crust is ready, pour in the filling and return to the oven. Bake until the center sets (a knife inserted will come out dry), about 1 hour. If the sides of the crust start to burn, cover the quiche loosely with foil.

Let sit for 15 to 20 minutes at room temperature to set. Serve sliced into wedges, with some lemony bitter greens alongside.

PAN-ROASTED TOMATO AND KALAMATA SPANAKOPITA

GEMINI

The Ram charges, the Bull plows ahead. The Twins wrap their minds around things.

Gemini is multifaceted. Phyllo is a versatile, pliable dough. It can be flexed, bent, folded, twisted, or rolled. It can star in any recipe, appetizer to dessert. Brushed with oil or melted butter and layered, it becomes the crisp, flaky wrapper for meats, vegetables, cheeses. Sheets of it, stuffed with nut pastes, sweetened and held together with honey, make dessert.

Spanakopita is Greek spinach and cheese pie. In this version it is accompanied by a sweet and savory relish of pan-roasted grape tomatoes and Kalamata olives.

Mercury has manual dexterity, with slow and fast hand modes. Sheets of phyllo dough are paper thin and delicate. Be gentle, but if you break the sheets, no worries. The layers are meant to be flaky. They will come together when you bake them.

SERVES 6 TO 8

FOR THE SPANAKOPITA

¼ cup olive oil

3 garlic cloves, minced

1 onion, chopped

2½ pounds spinach, washed, dried, and coarsely chopped

12 ounces feta cheese, crumbled

1 cup ricotta

2 eggs, lightly beaten

¼ cup finely chopped parsley

2 tablespoons finely chopped dill

¼ teaspoon ground nutmeg

⅛ teaspoon cayenne pepper

½ teaspoon salt

½ teaspoon freshly ground black pepper

¼ cup butter, melted (or olive oil, or a mixture)

1 pound phyllo sheets

FOR THE ROASTED TOMATOES

2 tablespoons olive oil

1½ pounds grape tomatoes

1 teaspoon dried oregano

½ teaspoon salt

½ teaspoon freshly ground black pepper

½ cup Kalamata olives, pitted and halved lengthwise

Preheat the oven to 375°F.

Make the spanakopita. Heat the olive oil in a large pot over medium-high heat. Add the garlic and onion, and sauté until the onion is transparent, about 5 minutes. Add the spinach, and stir-fry until the spinach is thoroughly softened.

Set a colander over a large bowl, and transfer the cooked spinach to the colander to drain. When the spinach has cooled, press it gently to remove excess liquid. (You can use the liquid in soup stock or pasta water.)

Mix together the feta, ricotta, eggs, parsley, dill, nutmeg, cayenne, salt, and black pepper in a separate large bowl. Add the spinach to the feta-ricotta mixture, and mix well.

Brush a light layer of butter (or oil) on the bottom and sides of a deep-dish casserole. Then, lightly brushing butter on each sheet as you go, layer half the phyllo sheets on the bottom of the pan.

Gently layer the spinach and cheese mixture on top of the phyllo layer. Use a soft rubber spatula to smooth it out into an even layer. Layer the other half of the phyllo sheets on top of the spinach mixture, lightly brushing with butter again, as you go.

Place the casserole in the oven until the pastry turns golden brown, 35 to 40 minutes. Allow to cool before cutting for serving.

Meanwhile, make the roasted tomatoes. Heat 1 tablespoon of olive oil in a large skillet over high heat to smoking hot. Add the tomatoes, and sear, shaking the skillet, just until their skins begin to crack, 30 to 45 seconds. Put a lid on the skillet, and remove from the heat. When the tomatoes have wilted a bit, add the oregano, salt, pepper, and olives, and stir.

Serve the spanakopita in squares, rectangles, or triangles, with a generous spoonful or two of the tomato-Kalamata relish on the side.

 Use a 9 × 13-inch casserole, preferably 3 inches deep. Most brands of phyllo dough come in 9 × 13-inch sheets. If you find otherwise, cut to suit.

SRIRACHA SALMON CAKES
ARIES

April's spring thaw brings mating season. The birds sing; the bees buzz; the Ram charges; the Salmon runs. Fresh wild-caught salmon, with its deep, rich flavor, elevates these simple croquettes. Before forming it into cakes, however, you must cook the fish, at least partially. You may poach it, but for a firmer croquette, searing is best. Sriracha is an explosive Thai-inspired hot sauce. A tablespoon of it will add zip to the Ram-charge, the Salmon-run. Bold Aries may want to wake up taste buds with a bit more. Serve on a bed of lightly dressed salad greens or alongside Farro and Fiddlehead Ferns (see page 52).

**MAKES 12 CAKES,
TO SERVE 4 TO 6**

FOR THE SALMON
1¼ pounds skinless salmon fillet(s), cut into 6 pieces
2 teaspoons salt
2 teaspoons freshly ground black pepper
2 tablespoons olive oil
2 tablespoons lemon juice

FOR THE CAKES
1 tablespoon butter
1 tablespoon olive oil
1 garlic clove, peeled and minced
1 cup finely chopped scallions, whites only
1 cup finely chopped red bell pepper
1 cup finely diced ciabatta bread
1 tablespoon sriracha sauce
1 tablespoon lemon juice
1 tablespoon Dijon mustard
1 tablespoon finely chopped dill
2 teaspoons salt
2 teaspoons freshly ground black pepper
1 cup tartar sauce
1 teaspoon baking powder
2 eggs, beaten

FOR FINISHING
2 eggs
2 tablespoons half-and-half
Panko bread crumbs (approximately 2 cups)
Lemon wedges

Preheat the oven to 425°F.

Make the fish. Season the salmon with salt and pepper. In a large, ovenproof skillet, heat the oil over high heat to smoking hot. Add the salmon fillets, and sear until they start to brown on the bottom, about 2 minutes. Place the skillet into the oven, and roast about 5 minutes or so, depending on the thickness of the fish. The fish should be barely cooked through. Transfer to a plate, flake it apart a bit with a fork, drizzle with the lemon juice, and set aside to cool. Lower the oven temperature to 400°F.

Make the cakes. Return the skillet, un-washed, to the stove. Add the butter and olive oil to the skillet, and melt over medium heat. Add the garlic, scallions, and red bell pepper to the pan, and sauté until just soft, about 5 minutes.

Transfer the sautéed vegetables to a large mixing bowl. Add the diced bread, sriracha, lemon juice, mustard, dill, salt, and pepper to the bowl, and stir to mix thoroughly.

Let the mixture cool for a few minutes, then add it to the bowl of a food processor, along with the tartar sauce, baking powder, and eggs. Carefully pulse to a rather coarse chop.

Add the salmon and pulse again, scraping the sides of the bowl back into the center after each pulse. You want a medium-coarse chop, with shreds of salmon meat, not a paste. Transfer this mixture back to the mixing bowl. Gently shred any large lumps of fish with your fingers to break them up.

Line a baking sheet with parchment paper. Use a cup measure to scoop the salmon mixture, and form into cakes, patting the mixture into rounds between your palms. Set each cake on the lined baking sheet, and then freeze the whole batch for 15 to 20 minutes—this will make it much easier to handle the cakes when you dip them in the egg wash before cooking.

Finish the cakes. Combine the eggs with the half-and-half in a medium-size bowl, and beat till frothy. Gently dip each cake into the wash, covering on all sides. (You may want to use a slotted spoon to lower them into the egg wash.) Dust each cake with panko, and set on a separate well-oiled baking sheet.

Bake the salmon cakes for 10 minutes. Turn them and bake until uniformly browned, another 20 to 25 minutes or so. Serve immediately, with lemon wedges for squeezing on the side.

ROASTED BLACK COD AND SESAME SPINACH

TAURUS

In spring, when Venus's gentle touch comes to soften and sweeten the earth for the plow and the bull goes to work, the Alaskan black cod, with its snow-white meat, starts running wild in the deep, icy-cold waters. Like the Goddess of Love, lying on her bed of soft green velvet, the black cod is luscious, luxurious, distinctive, delicate, and smooth.

Mirin is a kind of Japanese rice wine. A naturally fermented complex carbohydrate, it has a lower alcohol content than sake, and it is sweeter. Its syrupy flavor is balanced by the miso with its rich salt-of-the-earth persona.

SERVES 4

 The cod must be marinated overnight, so start the dish the day before you plan to serve it.

FOR THE COD

½ cup mirin

¼ cup fresh orange juice

½ cup light miso paste (shiro or shinshu)

1 tablespoon sugar

1 tablespoon orange zest

1 tablespoon grated ginger

4 black cod fillets (approximately 6 ounces each), skin on

3 tablespoons sesame oil

FOR THE SPINACH

2 tablespoons sesame oil

1 pound spinach, washed, dried, and chopped

½ teaspoon salt

2 tablespoons sesame seeds

Make the cod. Bring the mirin to a simmer in a small saucepot over medium heat. Add the orange juice, miso, and sugar to the simmering mirin, and stir until the sugar is dissolved. Add the orange zest and ginger, and stir. Remove from the heat, and pour into a large mixing bowl. Allow to cool.

When the mirin mixture has cooled completely, add the cod fillets, making sure they are submerged in the marinade, and cover the bowl with plastic wrap. Refrigerate overnight.

When ready to cook the cod, preheat a broiler with the oven rack on the second rung from the top. Remove the cod from the marinade, and set aside on a clean plate.

Heat the sesame oil in a large, ovenproof, nonstick skillet over high heat to smoking hot. Carefully add the cod fillets skin-side down, and sear until the skin is golden brown and crisp, about 1 minute. Place the skillet under the broiler to crisp the top and finish cooking, another 4 or 5 minutes. The fish is done when it flakes easily in the center.

Meanwhile, make the spinach. Heat the sesame oil in a large pot or skillet over medium-high heat. Add the spinach and salt, and stir until the spinach starts to wilt. Lower the heat, cover, and cook briefly to soften, about 2 minutes. Stir in the sesame seeds.

Arrange a bed of spinach on each plate, and nestle the cod atop. Serve immediately.

SWEET AND SOUR SNAPPER WITH MANGO-CITRUS RELISH

GEMINI

As right cannot exist without left, we could not know sweet without the taste of sour. Reconciling opposites is the genius of Gemini. The Mercurial leaning toward intellectual independence seeks choice and the experience of a variety of possibilities. Think of this recipe as primarily a method. The specific fish you use is of secondary importance. Instead of snapper, try any other white, lean, flaky fish, such as flounder, sea bass, or rainbow trout. Lemon or lime juice? Using both provides the virtues of each!

SERVES 4

FOR THE RELISH

⅓ cup lemon and/or lime juice
1 tablespoon cornstarch
¼ cup sugar
3 cups chopped ripe mango
1 tablespoon lemon and/or lime zests
2 tablespoons minced pickled ginger
1 teaspoon hot sauce, such as Tabasco

FOR THE FISH

1½ pounds snapper fillets, cut into strips, or other white flaky fish of your choosing
2 tablespoons cornstarch
1 cup all-purpose flour
1 teaspoon baking powder
½ teaspoon salt
6 ounces cold beer or sparkling water (approximately)
2 egg whites, beaten

Vegetable oil, for frying

Make the relish. Combine the lemon and/ or lime juice with the cornstarch in a small bowl, and whisk to make a slurry. Add the slurry to a small saucepan, and heat over medium heat. Add the sugar to the slurry, and stir continuously, cooking until the sugar has fully dissolved. When it comes to a simmer, add the mango, zests, ginger, and hot sauce to the pan, and simmer until the sauce has thickened. Set aside in a warm spot.

Meanwhile, make the fish. Combine the fish and cornstarch in a mixing bowl, and toss, distributing the cornstarch evenly.

Stir together the flour, baking powder, and salt in a separate large mixing bowl. Add beer or sparkling water a little at a time, whisking until a thick, smooth batter is formed. Fold in the egg whites.

Deep-frying the fish is best. But a generous ¼ inch of vegetable oil in a skillet heated to frying temperature, about 360°F, will suffice. (The oil must be very hot, or the batter will stick to the skillet rather than the fish. Before frying, toss a cube of bread into the hot oil. It should float and sizzle violently.)

Dip the fish strips in the batter, and fry in batches (do not overcrowd the skillet) until crisp and golden on both sides, about 4 to 5 minutes. Drain on paper towels.

Reheat the relish if necessary. Spoon some onto each serving plate. Add a portion of the fish, and top with the remaining relish. Serve immediately.

MERGUEZ MOUSSAKA
ARIES

Sheep are symbolic of resurrection and regeneration. Their fleece, when shorn, will promptly grow back. Since ancient days, the Vernal Equinox has been celebrated with the sacrifice of a young sheep. The sins of humanity are cleansed in the blood of the lamb. There's a bit of the martyr in Aries. Moussaka is a classic Greek lamb casserole. This version is enlivened with the spicy, earthy North African lamb sausage called merguez. Kefalotyri is a traditional Greek sheep's milk cheese. Aged and hard, with a sharp, salty flavor, it grates and melts well. If you can't find it, use another sheep's milk cheese such as caciocavallo, Manchego, haloumi, or pecorino.

SERVES 10 TO 12

FOR THE MERGUEZ
1 pound merguez sausage, sliced into 2-inch pieces
¼ cup chicken stock
1 to 2 tablespoons olive oil

FOR THE LAMB
2 tablespoons butter
3 garlic cloves, minced
1 onion, chopped
2 tablespoons olive oil
1 pound ground lamb

6 ounces tomato paste
2 cups red wine
¼ cup parsley
½ cup mint leaves
½ teaspoon cinnamon
½ teaspoon salt
½ teaspoon freshly ground black pepper

FOR THE EGGPLANT
2 pounds eggplant, trimmed and peeled, sliced lengthwise into ¼-inch-thick pieces
Coarse salt
Vegetable or light olive oil, for frying
Flour, for dredging
2 eggs, beaten with ¼ cup water

FOR THE CHEESE SAUCE
2 tablespoons butter
2 tablespoons olive oil
2 tablespoons flour
1 cup half-and-half
3 cups grated kefalotyri, or other sheep's milk cheese
½ teaspoon nutmeg
½ teaspoon freshly ground black pepper

FOR BAKING
1 cup bread crumbs
1 cup grated pecorino
¼ cup dried oregano
¼ cup olive oil

A deep 9 × 13-inch baking dish, or thereabouts, is a necessity. Moussaka benefits from sitting and can be made a day ahead.

Preheat the oven to 400°F.

Make the merguez. Spread the sliced merguez on a rimmed baking sheet. Pour the stock and the olive oil over the merguez. Roast for 10 minutes in the preheated oven, and then set aside. Lower the oven heat to 350°F.

While the merguez is cooking, prepare the lamb. In a large saucepan, melt the butter over medium heat. Add the garlic and onion, and sauté until the onion is transparent, about 6 minutes. Using a slotted spoon, remove the onion, and set aside. Add the olive oil and ground lamb, and sauté until brown, about 10 minutes.

In a large bowl, combine the tomato paste and wine. Whisk with a fork to mix. Stir the mixture into the lamb in the skillet. Add the parsley, mint, cinnamon, salt, and pepper, and stir to combine. Lower the heat to a simmer, cover, and cook for 15 minutes. Set aside.

Meanwhile, prepare and make the eggplant. Generously salt the sliced eggplant slices, and let them sit in a colander to drain for 30 minutes, turning them over several times. Rinse the salt from the eggplant slices, and pat them dry with a paper towel. Add enough vegetable oil to the skillet to come up about a ¼ inch depth. Bring the oil to a shimmer over medium-high heat—until it is almost but not quite smoking.

Dredge each eggplant slice in flour, dip in the egg wash, and carefully place in the oil. Do not crowd the pan—cook in batches if necessary. Fry each slice until it is golden brown on both sides. Drain on paper towels.

Make the cheese sauce. Heat the butter and olive oil in a medium saucepan over medium heat. Stir in the flour, a little at a time, whisking continuously to prevent lumps, until the mixture is smooth and golden. Drizzle in the half-and-half, continuing to whisk. Add the cheese a little at a time, continuing to whisk. Stir in the nutmeg and black pepper. Continue whisking the cheese sauce over medium heat until it thickens, then set aside in a warm spot.

For baking, in a medium bowl, combine the bread crumbs, pecorino, oregano, and olive oil.

Sprinkle one-third of the bread-crumb mixture in an even layer in the baking dish. Layer half the eggplant, overlapping as necessary, half the cheese sauce, half the merguez, and half the lamb mixture. Repeat. Finish with the final one-third bread crumbs sprinkled on the top. Bake uncovered until bubbly and golden, 45 to 60 minutes. If the bread-crumb top browns before the moussaka is cooked through, cover with a baking sheet or some foil. Let sit at least 20 minutes before serving.

CLASSIC PASSOVER BRISKET

TAURUS

For every action, there's a reaction. While Aries is the pioneer, Taurus is the homebody. The warrior gives way to the settler. Taurus is our home, Sweet Mother Earth. Brisket is a dish that embodies both the comforts of home and the renewal of spring. It is a favorite for Passover—the Jewish spring holiday celebrated in the home. An inexpensive, chewy cut from the cow's front forequarter, brisket is transformed by slow braising, rendering it melt-in-your-mouth tender. Every family has its own treasured brisket recipe—there are spicy variations made with harissa, and sweet laced with honey, versions where the braising liquid includes beer and others wine. The following is a classic recipe that, once you have mastered it, you can experiment with accordingly. Whichever way you flavor it, brisket is best made a day in advance of when you plan to serve it. The flavor and texture improve, and it slices more easily after overnight refrigeration.

SERVES 6 TO 8

3 pounds beef brisket
Salt
Freshly ground black pepper
6 tablespoons olive oil
4 garlic cloves, minced
3 cups chopped onion
2 carrots, peeled and grated
2 cups beef stock
1 cup chopped tomato
2 tablespoons tomato paste

Preheat the oven to 350°F.

Sprinkle the brisket with a generous amount of salt and pepper. If it is too large for you to handle comfortably, cut it in half.

Heat the olive oil over medium-high heat in a heavy casserole or Dutch oven with a tight-fitting lid, large enough to hold the brisket. When the oil is hot, add the brisket, and brown on all sides, 4 or 5 minutes per side. Remove the browned meat from the pot, and set it aside.

Add the garlic, onion, and carrots to the pot, and sauté until the onion is very soft, about 10 minutes.

Add the stock, tomato, and tomato paste to the pot, and season with additional salt and pepper. Return the meat to the pot, rolling it this way and that to moisten thoroughly. Cover the pot.

Roast until the meat offers no resistance to a fork, 2½ to 4 hours. For even cooking, after 1½ hours, uncover the casserole, and turn the meat. Cover it again, and place it back in the oven. Repeat every 15 minutes or so.

Remove the pot from the oven, allow the brisket to cool to room temperature, and refrigerate overnight.

Two hours before serving the brisket, remove it from the refrigerator. Preheat the oven to 200°F.

Skim off and discard any accumulated fat that has risen to the surface. Take the brisket out of the pot, and place it on a cutting board. For neat slices, slice the brisket against the grain while the meat is cold. For presentation purposes, as much as possible, try to hold the slices together to resemble the original shape of the brisket.

Using an immersion blender, puree the onions and carrots with the braising liquid in the pot. Return the brisket to the Dutch oven, spooning some of the braising liquid over it, and warm in the oven for 45 to 60 minutes.

TAGINE OF CHICKEN WITH POTATO, PRESERVED LEMON, AND APRICOT

GEMINI

Thesis and antithesis: Aries moves in a straight-ahead line, while Taurus is round-about, pulling the plow back and forth in the field. Then synthesis! Gemini moves in a spiral. Working together, the Twins combine and reconcile the line and the circle. The final phase of spring: the Summer Solstice approaches, the sun is high, the days are long and getting longer. Fueled by the maximum energy of the lengthening days, the growing spurt of June is on. The vegetation grows wild; creepers and crawlers intertwine in expanding coils. When the Mercurial mind is at the peak of power, the Twins—one straightforward, sharp, and swift, the other shrewd, circuitous, and unpredictable—reach out together. This chicken stew has the Twins in mind. On one hand, it's a no-nonsense comfort food; on the other hand, it's zesty and spicy and full of surprises.

SERVES 4 TO 6

FOR THE SPICE RUB
1 tablespoon paprika
1 teaspoon ground coriander
1 teaspoon ground cumin
1 teaspoon ground turmeric
1 teaspoon garlic powder
1 teaspoon onion powder
1 teaspoon salt
1 teaspoon freshly ground black pepper
1 teaspoon lemon zest
¼ teaspoon cayenne pepper
4 tablespoons olive oil

FOR THE STEW
8 chicken thighs, halved, or 4 breasts, quartered, on the bone, skin on, approximately 3 to 4 pounds
4 to 5 tablespoons olive oil
2 garlic cloves, minced
1 cup diced yellow onion
1 pound new or baby potatoes, scrubbed and halved
2 carrots, peeled and diced
1 cup chicken stock
1 cup peeled, seeded, and diced tomato
2 tablespoons tomato paste
½ teaspoon salt
½ teaspoon pepper
2 preserved lemons, chopped
24 dried apricots
24 oily green olives, such as cerignolas, pitted and halved
10 ounces grape tomatoes

Preheat the oven to 325°F.

Make the rub. Mix together the paprika, coriander, cumin, turmeric, garlic powder, onion powder, salt, pepper, lemon zest, and cayenne in a small, ovenproof skillet. Toast them in the oven until they give off a nutty aroma, about 5 minutes. Transfer the spices to a large mixing bowl. Add the olive oil to the toasted spices, and whisk with a fork to stir.

Make the stew. Dip the chicken pieces in the spiced oil mixture, and roll to coat. Massage the oil mixture into the chicken, and set the pieces on a plate.

Raise the oven temperature to 375°F.

Heat 2 tablespoons of the oil in a large casserole, Dutch oven, or tagine pot over medium-high heat (if using a clay tagine, you may need to use a flame diffuser). Add the garlic, onion, potatoes, and carrots, and sauté until the onion is soft and the potatoes and carrots are sweating, about 5 minutes. Scrape the sautéed vegetables into a bowl, and set aside.

Add another 1 tablespoon of oil to the pot. Once the oil is shimmering but not smoking, add the chicken, skin-side down, to the pot, and brown, 4 to 5 minutes per side. Cook the chicken in batches if necessary, adding another 1 tablespoon of oil between batches if needed. Set the browned chicken aside.

Discard the fat in the pot, along with any larger, loose browned bits, leave the fond, the browned bits and caramelized drippings of meat and vegetables that are stuck to the bottom of the pan, alone. Return the pot to the stove over medium-high heat. Add the chicken stock to the pot, deglazing it by scraping up the fond with a wooden spoon.

Add the tomato and tomato paste to the stock, and stir. Add the browned chicken and sautéed vegetables to the pot. Season to taste with the salt and black pepper, raise the heat to high, and bring to a boil. Immediately cover the pot and place in the oven, cooking for 45 minutes.

Remove the pot from the oven, and add the preserved lemons, dried apricots, and olives. Turn the chicken. Cover again, and return to the oven, cooking until the chicken is very tender, an additional 15 minutes or so. Add the grape tomatoes to the pot, cover it again, and return it to the oven for another few minutes, allowing the tomato skins to crack open.

Serve atop cooked couscous, either family-style on a large platter or in individual portions.

ROASTED RADISHES

ARIES

In the first month of spring, as we emerge from the time of Pisces, the Light just barely overcomes the Darkness. Feeling the night at his back, the Aries is driven to charge forth into the day. Aries balances nostalgia with impatience. Aries cuts through any lingering ambivalence with a sharp passion and a sense of urgency. The radish—crisp, red, peppery-piquant root of early spring—has the bite of Aries. Radishes are usually eaten raw, but roasting them concentrates their sharpness, and the wasabi dressing hones their edge.

SERVES 6

1 pound red radishes, washed, dried, and trimmed
2 tablespoons olive oil
¾ teaspoon salt
1 teaspoon wasabi paste
1 tablespoon melted butter
1 tablespoon rice wine vinegar
1 teaspoon sugar

Preheat the oven to 425°F.

Slice the radishes in half lengthwise, or quarter them if they are large.

Toss the radishes in a mixing bowl with the olive oil and salt. Spread the radishes on a rimmed baking sheet, and roast until they are tender but still retain a bit of crispness. After 12 minutes, gently poke one with a thin paring knife. The radish should offer only a hint of resistance. Check regularly. Cooking time should be about 15 minutes.

Combine the wasabi paste, melted butter, rice wine vinegar, and sugar in a bowl large enough to hold the radishes, and whisk until emulsified.

While the radishes are still hot from the oven, add them to the wasabi butter mixture, and toss to combine. Serve immediately.

MASHED BABY LIMAS
TAURUS

Venus is not always the glamour girl. She likes her comfort and enjoys simple pleasures too. In the merry month, with its soft colors and luxurious greenery, its gentle breezes and relaxing warmth, fertile nature abounds with tender, young things. The ordinary is fancy; the unpretentious is voluptuous. Creamy baby lima beans, also known as butter beans, are the embodiment of homey luxury.

This easy side dish begs for fresh limas, but fresh beans are not easy to come by, even in farmers' markets and gourmet food stores. If you can't find them, you will have to go with frozen. If you find fresh, about 3 pounds in the pods will yield approximately 4 cups of beans.

In any case, the nutmeg should be freshly ground. It's not only nutmeg's pleasant association with holiday eggnog that makes you feel cozy and warm. There are chemicals in it that bring on subtle feelings of well-being.

SERVES 6 AS A SIDE

1 pound shelled baby lima beans
½ teaspoon ground nutmeg, or to taste
2 tablespoons unsalted butter, melted
¾ teaspoon salt

Bring a large pot of lightly salted water to a boil over high heat. Boil the baby lima beans until they are fully tender, about 3 to 4 minutes (taste-test after 2 minutes), then drain. To ensure green color, blanch them in an ice-water bath.

Combine the cooked limas, nutmeg, melted butter, and salt in the bowl of a food processor, and process until smooth.

Serve immediately.

These limas are a great accompaniment for grilled lamb or beef or a pork roast.

STIR-FRIED SNAP PEAS
GEMINI

Open sesame! The origin of the magical command comes from the perception that sesame plants grew near hidden treasures and concealed doorways. The sealed and sacred was opened with the right incantation. There is magic in words.

Gemini is ruled by Mercury, the Roman counterpart of the Greek god Hermes. Although Mercury is associated with conscious communicative ability, he has access to the subconscious realms and can bring us messages from deep within. The word *hermetic,* derived from Hermes, denotes something sealed, not for general consumption, open only to those who know the formula.

Similarly, a recipe is a formula. Here is a simple preparation for a spring-harvest favorite. It can be made in a snap. In this formula, the secret is in the surface. "Open sesame" is not needed for a pea with an edible pod. And Gemini, you like to have alternatives. If you like, change the formula from Chinese to Italian by using olive oil instead of sesame oil, substituting pine nuts for sesame seeds, and finishing with a drizzle of balsamic vinegar instead of a dash or two of soy sauce.

SERVES 6 AS A SIDE

3 tablespoons sesame or olive oil
2 garlic cloves, minced
1 pound snap peas, stems and strings removed
¾ teaspoon salt
2 tablespoons sesame seeds or ¼ cup pine nuts, toasted
Soy sauce or balsamic vinegar

Heat the oil in a large skillet over high heat. Add the garlic, and sauté briefly to infuse the oil. Don't let the garlic burn. Add the snap peas and the salt, and stir-fry until the pods are crisp-tender, keeping them moving in the pan, about 3 minutes.

Remove from the heat. Add the seeds, and give the pan a good shake or two.

Transfer the peas to a serving bowl, and dress with the soy sauce. Serve immediately.

CARROT CUPCAKES

ARIES

In Aries season, movement is instinctive. Zippy spices such as ginger, cinnamon, and nutmeg say "come hither" to the Aries. A kid at heart, adolescent Aries is not quite over childlike inclinations and childhood dreams. A small portable cake, designed to feed just one person, feeds the inner child of the Ram on the run.

MAKES 12 CUPCAKES

FOR THE CUPCAKES

2 cups almond flour

4 tablespoons coconut flour

½ tablespoon baking soda

¼ teaspoon salt

2 teaspoons cinnamon, plus extra for garnish

1 teaspoon powdered ginger

½ teaspoon nutmeg

3 medium eggs

½ cup coconut oil, melted

½ cup honey

3 teaspoons vanilla extract

2 cups peeled, grated carrot

1 cup chopped walnuts, plus extra for garnish

FOR THE FROSTING

8 ounces cream cheese, room temperature

3 tablespoons maple syrup

1 tablespoon vanilla

⅛ teaspoon salt

Preheat the oven to 350°F. Line a muffin tin with 12 cupcake liners.

Make the cupcakes. Combine the flours, baking soda, salt, cinnamon, ginger, and nutmeg in a medium mixing bowl.

Beat the eggs, oil, honey, and vanilla in a large bowl until frothy.

Working quickly, create a well in the center of the bowl of dry ingredients, and pour in the wet ingredients. Mix well, then fold in the carrot and walnuts. The batter should be thick, but not stiff.

Divide the batter evenly among the liners. Bake for 17 to 20 minutes or until a toothpick inserted in the middle comes out clean. Let the cupcakes cool for 5 minutes in the pan, and then remove to a wire rack to cool. Do not frost until completely cool.

Make the frosting. Beat the cream cheese, maple syrup, vanilla, and salt in a large bowl until smooth. Use an offset spatula to spread a layer of frosting on top of each cupcake. Sprinkle them with a little bit of cinnamon, and top with a walnut piece.

AVOCADO-LIME PIE

TAURUS

Taurus loves foods that are creamy, soft, and sensual, and this pie does the trick. This is a no-bake pie and easier to whip up than you might imagine. The crust is made of finely ground almonds, coconut, and figs, which complement the avocado-lime combination. Because of their high fat content and buttery texture, avocados make a grand player in dairy-free desserts.

SERVES 8

FOR THE CRUST

1 cup raw almonds

1 cup unsweetened shredded coconut

12 Calimyrna dried figs

1 teaspoon vanilla extract

Dash of salt

3 tablespoons maple syrup

FOR THE FILLING

4 ripe avocados, halved, pitted, and peeled

1 teaspoon vanilla extract

Dash of salt

½ cup lime juice

¼ cup lime zest plus 1 tablespoon for garnish

½ cup coconut nectar

½ cup coconut oil, melted

Lime slices, cut in half circles

Make the crust. Combine all the ingredients for the crust in the bowl of a food processor, and blend until dough-like. The stickiness of the figs will hold the crust together.

Lightly grease a 9-inch pie dish. Scoop the crust mixture into the pan, and use your hands to press the dough evenly into the pan and up its sides.

Make the pie filling. Combine the avocados, vanilla, salt, lime juice, lime zest, and coconut nectar in the (cleaned) bowl of the food processor, and blend until smooth and creamy, stopping occasionally to scrape down the sides. Add the coconut oil, and blend until combined.

Pour the filling over the crust, and smooth it out with the back of a spoon or an offset spatula. Garnish with lime slices and zest.

Chill in the refrigerator or freezer for at least 3 hours or overnight in the fridge, until firm. Cut and serve.

TAHINI LEMON BARS
GEMINI

With summer on the way, there is June excitement; with the increase in heat and humidity, there is June lethargy. Though the Twins symbolize Gemini, they are anything but identical. One Twin, energized by the upcoming Solstice, may be restless and talkative. The other half, victim of the increased heat and humidity, may be prone to moon-in-June ennui.

Maca, a plant that grows in the high plateaus of the Andes, might be new to us, but it has been used in Peru for more than three thousand years. Its nutty butterscotch flavor paired with the almonds, coconut, and spices gives enough variety and tang to lift the spirit on a lazy, hazy June day.

The nutty texture of these bars—from almonds and sesame—gives the overactive Twin something to chew on. The syrupy sweetness suits the moody Twin.

Take two. They're small!

MAKES 16 SQUARES

FOR THE CRUST
1 cup almond meal
2 tablespoons coconut oil
2 tablespoons rice malt syrup

FOR THE FILLING
3 cups shredded coconut
¼ cup coconut milk
2 tablespoons coconut oil
3 tablespoons pure maple syrup
2 tablespoons tahini
2 teaspoons maca powder
1 teaspoon cinnamon
½ teaspoon nutmeg

FOR THE GLAZE
3 tablespoons rice malt syrup
2 tablespoons coconut oil
1 tablespoon lemon juice
1 tablespoon tahini

Line an 8-inch square cake pan with parchment paper.

Make the crust. Mix together all the crust ingredients in a large bowl. Add the mixture to the lined cake pan, and press it evenly across the bottom. Refrigerate for 1½ hours.

Make the filling. Add the shredded coconut into the bowl of a food processor, and pulse-chop a few times. Add the remaining ingredients for the filling to the bowl of the food processor, and pulse until smooth.

Pour the filling over the chilled crust, and smooth with the back of a spoon or offset spatula into an even layer. Freeze for 2 hours.

Make the glaze. Whisk together all the glaze ingredients in a small bowl until fully incorporated and smooth. Using a silicone pastry brush or the back of a spoon, smooth the glaze over the filling.

Cut into 2-inch squares, and serve at room temperature or slightly chilled. The bars will keep in the refrigerator for several days, or they can be frozen for several weeks.

SUMMER

CANCER

LEO

VIRGO

STARTERS

Cucumber Pistachio Soup (C)

Watermelon Gazpacho (L)

Chorizo-Stuffed Figs (V)

SALADS

Peaches and Boston Lettuce (C)

Baby Spinach and Radicchio Salad (L)

Haricot Verts and New Potato Salad (V)

PASTA

Lobster and Roasted Corn
Orecchiette (C)

Clams and Cockles Linguine (L)

Bucatini alla Norma (V)

VEGETARIAN

Zucchini Barzini (C)

Frittata Caprese (L)

Oven-Roasted Ratatouille Spiral (V)

SEAFOOD

Fried Soft-Shell Crabs (C)

Grilled Branzino (L)

Lemony Grilled Shrimp with
White Beans (V)

MEAT

Grilled Magret and Frisée (C)

Spiced Beef Tenderloin with Scallions
and Horseradish (L)

Golden Turmeric Chicken (V)

SIDES

Dilled Zucchini and Scallions (C)

Saffron Rice (L)

Polenta Bites with Sage-Hazelnut
Pesto (V)

DESSERTS

Coconut-Peach Crisp (C)

Kiwi Ricotta Stacks (L)

Berry Mascarpone Tart (V)

The high sun brings sweet blessings to the Earth and all its living things. The first day of summer marks the passage of the sun into the sign of Cancer, whose symbol is the Crab. With the summer sun heating land and sea, everything is growing. Just as the branch, pushing forward with new soft growth, drops its blossoms, the Crab, her tender inside grown, drops her hard shell to develop a roomier one. Like the Crab, we have our shells: physical shelters such as our homes, emotional shelters such as our families, and spiritual shelters, such as church, yoga, or the natural world, which nurture and protect the tender parts of our psyches.

June is the time for family celebrations and reunions. Graduations and weddings, rites of passage for individuals, have familial implications. Feelings of tenderness and togetherness radiate, as we gather to share food and feeling, hopes and memories.

It may seem incongruous that the time of Cancer—when the sun is brightest, the days are longest, and the nights shortest—is ruled by the moon and is a water sign. In due time, the sun and its fire will be glorified in Leo, but with the first phase of summer comes a crab-like sideways step. No matter how high Father Sun, Mother Moon had her push and pull in our deep-sea origins. The Queen of Tides, with her monthly ebb and flow, is evident in every woman's phases. At the beach, we plunge into the ocean, back into the womb whence we came.

As our earth mothers were the first and most important things in our lives, the foundation of our homes and our families, the providers of warmth, safety, security, comfort, and sustenance, Cancer is the Cosmic Source, the Goddess as the Nourisher and Sustainer of Life. She comes to us in the balmy summer air, the coziness of home, and the succulent flesh of fresh fruits and vegetables.

SUMMER

CANCER

Cucumber Pistachio Soup, page 92

Above: Lobster and Roasted Corn Orecchiette, page 100

Right: Zucchini Barzini, page 106

Left: Fried Soft-Shell
Crabs, page 112

Below: Grilled Magret
and Frisée, page 118

Coconut-Peach Crisp, page 128

LEO

Opposite: Baby Spinach and Radicchio Salad, page 96

Above: Frittata Caprese, page 108

Above: Grilled
Branzino, page 114

Right: Saffron Rice,
page 125

VIRGO

Opposite: Chorizo-Stuffed Figs, page 94

Above: Bucatini alla Norma, page 104

Left: Oven-Roasted Ratatouille Spiral, page 110

Right: Lemony Grilled Shrimp with White Beans, page 116

Below: Golden Turmeric Chicken, page 122

Opposite: Polenta Bites with Sage-Hazelnut Pesto, page 126

Berry Mascarpone Tart, page 130

As the Cycle of Life rotates, we once again see thesis and antithesis. The golden sun replaces the silvery moon, and the mighty Lion replaces the lowly Crab. In Leo, the Earth fully absorbs the radiance of the sun. The protective, gentle lunar influence wanes. The Solar personality is outgoing, magnanimous, and confident. The spirit goes forth from its shell, from the home, from Mother, and becomes an independent, self-expressive personality.

In this mid-summer phase of the cycle, we feel stronger, more dominant, more optimistic, more cognizant and more adept than we routinely feel ourselves to be. We find it natural to take on a grander, more superior role on the stage of life.

The Lion is the symbol of courage, derived from the Latin *cor,* or heart. As the sun is the heart of the solar system, Leo is the heart of the Zodiac. The August Lion is in our blood, warming us and lighting us from within. He strengthens us, inspires us, and dispels our fears. The Lion is invincible and has the pluck to rise above restraints, limitations, repression, and the commonplace. In August, tomatoes, grapes, and melons are ripe on the vine. The taste of autonomy is sweet.

The sun smiles on us. Its solar energy beams down creativity and a strong sense of

THE FIRST DAY OF SUMMER MARKS THE PASSAGE OF THE SUN INTO THE SIGN OF CANCER, WHOSE SYMBOL IS THE CRAB.

IN EARLY SEPTEMBER, WITH THE COOLER WEATHER AND SHORTER DAYS, WE BEGIN TO MOVE BACK INDOORS.

ourselves. Secure, we are more likely to take a chance, feel romantic, and enjoy the games of life, sports, and recreations of the mind. On your day in the sun, it's natural and proper to strut your stuff, overdo things, make a splash, take a risk, be passionate, extravagant, spontaneous, vivacious, dramatic, social, colorful, and energetic, and to eat, drink, and be merry. But the sun may be too bright. High summer requires us to slow down. The proud King of Beasts leads his pride and inspires his fellows to bring the game to him. The Lion's share is his due. August is the time for vacation, the time to experience the generosity of Nature, to be served, the time to have one's fill and take catnaps in the sun, the shade, and under the moon and the stars.

Toward the end of August, with summer at the peak of her bounty, the tide turns. The sun is noticeably lower, and it's getting dark earlier. There's a fragrant coolness in the evenings. Our focus and our mood shift from the lazy days of summer to the prospect of moving back indoors, going back to school, back to work. Messages of caution come from within, too. We feel a need to purify ourselves of Leo's excesses and atone for his overbearing pride.

The Maiden, cool, clear, and dry as a September day, is the embodiment of purity and grace; she is the soul of diplomacy, control, discrimination, and intellect. Like Taurus and Capricorn, astrology's other two earth signs, the Maiden is grounded, practical, and realistic. Mercury's influence, however, lightens her mind and makes it more flexible than that of her fellow earth signs. Once again, there is synthesis in the Cycle of Life. The Maiden is mercurial. The hermaphroditic offspring of the silver moon and the golden sun, she is the Quicksilver One, changeable, with both masculine and feminine tendencies.

In early September, with the cooler weather and shorter days, we begin to move back indoors. The Maiden simplifies, organizes, sorts, and disposes of clutter, attending to details and little things. School is in session: pens are full of ink, pencils are sharpened, and the pages of the notebooks are blank, virgin. Summer vacationers are back on the job. Meeting demands and high standards, putting in long hours, and mastering one's field bring satisfaction to the meticulous Maiden.

As in dreams there is a punning reality to waking life. The fruits of late summer are ripe and ready to pick. Virgo has the reputation for being picky. The end of summer is the natural time for self-criticism, self-reflection, and purification. There are days of atonement and service to others. It is a nostalgic time, a time to think about past Septembers, a time to think about health. The harvest must be protected from insects and disease, and all human workers, too, must be prepared for the hard work ahead. In the back of their minds all know winter is coming. For some this may mean eating lightly. For others, it may mean spending time in the kitchen, learning new things, developing technique, and serving others the results.

Though Libra is the sign of the Scales, Virgo is the time to balance our diets, to balance ourselves, in preparation for the Autumnal Equinox, the equality of day and night.

CUCUMBER PISTACHIO SOUP
CANCER

Cucumbers are the metaphorical embodiment of coolness. This, along with their moist flesh, has them under the influence of the moon, which links them to the sign Cancer. The cucumber's clean flavor and water content refreshes and restores.

Rock shrimp are small prawns that taste more like lobster than shrimp. They get their name from the rock-hardness of their shells. Impenetrable casing is Cancer's defense for her underlying thin skin. If using other shrimp, chop them into ½-inch pieces.

SERVES 4

1¼ cups shelled, roasted, unsalted pistachios, divided

3 cups vegetable juice (low sodium, if you prefer)

2 medium cucumbers, peeled, seeded, and chopped

6 scallions, trimmed, whites and greens chopped

½ cup baby arugula

2 ounces feta cheese, crumbled

1 tablespoon lemon juice

½ teaspoon freshly ground black pepper

½ teaspoon onion salt

2 tablespoons olive oil, divided

2 pinches of cayenne pepper, divided

1 tablespoon butter

1 garlic clove, peeled and minced

½ pound fresh rock shrimp, peeled and deveined

2 radishes, trimmed and grated

½ teaspoon lemon zest

Combine 1 cup of the pistachios and the vegetable broth in the bowl of a food processor and puree.

Add the cucumbers, two-thirds of the scallions, the arugula, feta, lemon juice, black pepper, onion salt, 1 tablespoon of the olive oil, and 1 pinch of the cayenne to the pistachio-vegetable juice mix, and puree. Refrigerate until chilled, at least 45 minutes.

Meanwhile, prepare the shrimp. Heat the butter and remaining 1 tablespoon olive oil in a medium skillet over high heat. When the butter is melted, add the garlic, and stir. Let it cook for about 15 seconds or so. Add the shrimp, and stir-fry 20 seconds, or until they are cooked through. Transfer the shrimp to a mixing bowl.

Add the remaining pistachios and scallions, the grated radishes, lemon zest, and 1 pinch of cayenne to the shrimp, and toss to mix.

Ladle the soup into bowls, and top with the rock shrimp.

WATERMELON GAZPACHO
LEO

Quintessential summer fruit, watermelons need warm soil, hot sun, and plenty of water to be as juicy as only watermelon can be. In the heat of the summer, water becomes the number one necessity for our proper sustenance. Planted under a water sign, watermelons come in fat, succulent, and sweet under fiery Leo. How clever is Nature that the watermelon comes into its season during the most dehydrating time of the year!

SERVES 8

FOR THE SOUP
4 cups cubed seedless watermelon
4 large beefsteak tomatoes, peeled and chopped
1 cup chopped scallions, whites only
20 basil leaves, whole
1 teaspoon chopped jalapeño pepper
½ cup chopped parsley
2 tablespoons tomato paste
¼ cup lemon juice
½ cup olive oil
1 teaspoon celery salt
1 teaspoon freshly ground black pepper

FOR THE CROUTONS
2 cups ½-inch cubes of focaccia
¼ cup olive oil

2 garlic cloves, minced
½ teaspoon onion salt
Pinch of cayenne pepper

Mint leaves, for garnish

Preheat the oven to 400°F.

Make the soup. Combine all of the ingredients for the soup in the bowl of a large food processor or blender, and puree. Refrigerate until chilled, at least 45 minutes.

Make the croutons. Combine the bread cubes, olive oil, garlic, onion salt, and cayenne in a large mixing bowl, and toss to mix. Spread the bread cubes on a baking tray, and bake, shaking frequently, until crisp and evenly golden brown, about 5 to 7 minutes.

Ladle the soup into bowls, and top each with a scattering of croutons and mint leaves.

CHORIZO-STUFFED FIGS
VIRGO

In late summer, figs are at their sweetest. With the excesses of Leo in the past, the Maiden phase of the cycle brings self-consciousness. After Adam and Eve ate the forbidden fruit and recognized their nakedness, it was the large leaves of the fig tree that they used for modesty. Virgo is *mutable* earth. She changes, adapts, blends, fixes, and transforms. Dedicated to the service of others, in the kitchen the Maiden is free to use this talent for handling ingredients toward sensual ends. These little bites tickle the palate with a mix-and-match blend of earthy flavors and textures: sweet, salty, nutty, spicy, creamy, juicy, cheesy, meaty, herbaceous, crisp, yet soft.

Goat cheese comes in many forms. A soft, smooth Spanish *cabra* mates nicely with the chorizo.

SERVES 4

4 tablespoons olive oil, divided
1 fresh Mexican-style chorizo sausage link
½ cup crumbled goat cheese
½ cup finely chopped pecans
1 tablespoon fresh thyme leaves
¼ teaspoon salt
¼ teaspoon freshly ground black pepper
12 fresh figs, stem ends trimmed

Preheat the oven to 425°F.

Heat 2 tablespoons of the olive oil in a medium skillet over high heat. Remove the casing from the chorizo, and brown the meat, breaking it apart as it cooks.

Mix together the chorizo, goat cheese, pecans, thyme, salt, and pepper in a mixing bowl.

Make an "X" in each fig, beginning at the stem end and slicing three-quarters of the way down. Gently pull the edges apart a bit, and place them on a lightly oiled oven sheet.

Gently pack the figs with the chorizo mixture. A tablespoon should do it. You should have more than enough stuffing to fill the fruit. Use what remains as topping, letting crumbles spill onto the oven sheet. Drizzle lightly with the remaining 2 tablespoons olive oil, and bake until the figs' flesh is soft, the stuffing is bubbly, and the topping is lightly browned, 10 to 15 minutes.

PEACHES AND BOSTON LETTUCE
CANCER

Water makes distinctions less distinct. Love connections to our fellow beings are typically moist: tears and kisses. Flora and fauna, we all breathe the same air, in and out, ebb and flow. Water sign Cancer is juicy. Her flow lubricates her intuition and sensitivity to the feelings of others. Like a peach, Cancer is sweet, warm, and fuzzy.

This sensual summer salad is best made when the peaches are soft, juicy, and sweet and the raspberries are firm and fresh. It makes a marvelous last course, easily taking the place of dessert.

SERVES 4

¼ cup olive oil

2 tablespoons red wine vinegar

1 tablespoon lemon juice

1 tablespoon honey

½ cup fresh raspberries

½ teaspoon salt

½ teaspoon freshly ground black pepper

2 large ripe peaches, preferably 1 white, 1 yellow

1 head Boston lettuce

1 cup shredded or torn radicchio

4 ounces Saint André, goat Brie, Explorateur, or other soft, creamy cheese

Combine the oil, vinegar, lemon juice, honey, raspberries, salt, and pepper in a small saucepot, and warm over very low heat, stirring to dissolve the honey. Allow the raspberries to break down slightly.

Bring enough water to cover the peaches by 1 inch to boiling. Immerse the peaches in the water for 10 seconds. Run them under cold water, and slip off their skins. Cut the peaches in half, remove the pits, and cut the halves into crescent slices.

Discard the outer leaves of the lettuce. Cut away the core, and wash the inner leaves. Dry them in a salad spinner, and then use paper towels to fully pat dry. Tear them coarsely. In a large bowl, toss them with the radicchio and enough of the raspberry dressing to coat, about ¼ cup.

Divide the dressed lettuce among four plates. Place a dollop or small wedge of cheese in the center. Arrange the peach slices in a circle around the cheese, alternating the yellow and white peach slices. Drizzle with the remaining dressing, and serve.

BABY SPINACH AND RADICCHIO SALAD
LEO

As the sun is the center of the solar system, the heart is the sun in our bodies. The Lion expresses himself warmly, exuberantly, and without restraint. He is sincere and unequivocal. He's, well, hearty! This robust down-to-Gaea composed salad is one that goes well at a summer cookout. It makes the perfect accompaniment to a hearty entrée such as grilled beef, or, with its rich medley of ingredients—crisp spinach, bitter radicchio, silky avocado, savory mushrooms, salty prosciutto, the comfort of hard-boiled eggs— it can be quite satisfying in itself.

**SERVES 8 AS A STARTER,
4 AS A MAIN**

FOR THE DRESSING

½ cup olive oil

2 tablespoons red wine vinegar

¼ cup chopped walnuts

1 teaspoon Dijon mustard

1 scallion, chopped

1 tablespoon chopped red bell pepper

1 teaspoon dried oregano

½ teaspoon sugar

½ teaspoon salt

½ teaspoon pepper

FOR THE SALAD

2 tablespoons olive oil

3 ounces thinly sliced prosciutto

1 tablespoon unsalted butter

4 ounces button mushrooms, sliced

½ cup chopped red onion

2 avocados, peeled, seeded, and cubed

1 tablespoon Lemon–Olive Oil Dressing (page 51)

2 hard-boiled eggs, sliced

¼ teaspoon salt

¼ teaspoon freshly ground black pepper

8 cups baby spinach leaves

2 cups thinly sliced radicchio

Make the dressing. Combine all the ingredients for the dressing in the bowl of a food processor, and blend until smooth. If you don't have a food processer, chop the scallions and walnuts finely, and whisk them together with the other ingredients. Set aside.

Make the salad. Heat 1 tablespoon of the olive oil in a skillet over medium-high heat. Add the prosciutto, and fry until browned and crisped, about 3 to 4 minutes. Transfer the prosciutto to a paper towel–lined plate. Melt the butter in the unwashed skillet. Add the mushrooms, and sauté until they just begin to soften, 2 to 3 minutes.

Mix together the red onion, avocado, and lemon–olive oil dressing in a small bowl, tossing gently to coat.

Sprinkle the eggs with the salt and pepper, and drizzle the remaining 1 tablespoon olive oil over them.

Mix together the spinach and radicchio in a large salad bowl. Add ¼ cup of the dressing, and toss thoroughly. You may want to add more, according to taste. (You will probably have dressing left over.) Arrange the eggs, mushrooms, and avocado mixture over the greens. Crumble the prosciutto, and scatter over the salad.

HARICOT VERTS AND NEW POTATO SALAD
VIRGO

This potato salad is another fresh and lively Mother Earth–bound dish that goes well at a summer barbecue. The Maiden is at the peak of her power in late summer when the harvest has begun. Vegetables grown underground, especially the mild-mannered potato, have a strong earth component and are associated with earth signs, particularly Virgo.

When the Europeans landed in the New World, they were introduced to the potato.

Feeding indigenous populations for centuries, wild potato varieties grew from the Andes to northern Canada. For this dish you may use multicolored Peruvian baby potatoes, sometimes known as cocktail potatoes or new potatoes. Or go north for the Yukon gold.

SERVES 8 TO 10

 All the components can be prepped in advance, even the day before, and assembled at the last minute.

FOR THE ALMONDS
1 cup blanched, slivered almonds
2 teaspoons olive oil
½ teaspoon very finely chopped fresh rosemary
½ garlic clove, finely minced
¼ teaspoon cayenne pepper
1 teaspoon brown sugar
½ teaspoon onion or celery salt

FOR THE SALAD
1 pound haricots verts, trimmed and halved
1 bunch asparagus, woody ends discarded, stalks halved lengthwise and sliced into 1-inch pieces, heads left whole
2 pounds Peruvian baby potatoes or small Yukon gold potatoes, cut into matchsticks
1 tablespoon Dijon mustard
20 oil-packed sun-dried tomatoes, julienned
12 scallions, halved lengthwise and sliced into 1-inch pieces
½ teaspoon salt
½ teaspoon freshly ground black pepper

FOR THE DRESSING
2 tablespoons mayonnaise
1 tablespoon tomato paste
2 tablespoons Lemon–Olive Oil Dressing (page 51)

ROSEMARY

A salt-tolerant, fragrant native to the Mediterranean area, rosemary is believed to stimulate memory. In Latin it is called *Rosmarinus,* which means "dew of the sea," the sea whence lovely Venus rose. Perhaps because of its charming scent and delicately salty tang, the herb is associated with the powers of the goddess. In England there is an old saying: "Where rosemary flourishes, the Lady rules."

Preheat the oven to 325°F.

Make the almonds. Spread the almonds on a rimmed baking sheet, and toast them in the oven until they are slightly browned, 10 to 12 minutes. Shake the pan often so they brown evenly.

While the nuts are baking, mix together the olive oil, rosemary, garlic, cayenne, sugar, and seasoned salt in a mixing bowl. Add the nuts right out of the oven, and toss. Set aside.

Make the salad. Bring 2 quarts of salted water to a rapid boil, add the beans, and cook until they are crisp-tender, about 4 to 5 minutes. Remove them with a slotted spoon or skimmer to an ice bath. Continue to boil the water. When the beans are cool, drain and set them aside.

Add the asparagus to the boiling water. Blanch for 1 minute or so, and remove to the ice bath. Continue to boil the water.

Add the potatoes to the boiling water, and cook them until they are tender, about 6 minutes. Drain the potatoes, transfer to a large bowl, and while the potatoes are still hot, toss with the mustard.

Add the cooked haricot verts and asparagus to the bowl with the potatoes. Add the sun-dried tomatoes, scallions, salt, and pepper, and mix.

Make the dressing. Whisk together the mayonnaise, tomato paste, and lemon–olive oil dressing in a small bowl.

Gently toss the potato mixture with half the dressing, adding a little more at a time, until all the ingredients are evenly coated.

Top with the toasted almonds, and serve.

LOBSTER AND ROASTED CORN ORECCHIETTE

CANCER

In Cancer, as the sun stops in his northerly motion we find a reversal of Gemini's eagerness to extend in all directions. Our awareness goes inward instead of out, and the tendency for defining boundaries becomes strong. The lobster, like the crab, is a crustacean, a Cancer at heart, at home in its shell in the watery depths. With the uprush of oceanic spiritual and emotional forces that accompany the Solstice, the individual might be washed away in the ebbtide. The shell defines, protects, and preserves the single, separate person.

In summer, when all of Nature rises up toward the sun, the corn stands tall and ripe. The husks sing sweetly in the hot breeze. Ears of corn, roasted in their husks on the summer fire, blacken on the outside while the kernels steam within. The caramelization that takes place when roasting the corn makes the kernels sweeter, but this recipe will work with boiled corn.

Many seafood counters sell cooked lobster meat. If that option is not available, drop a couple of 1½ pound lobsters into boiling water. When the water comes back to a boil, cook for 7 minutes. Allow to cool, cull the meat, and chop it.

The name *orecchiette* means "little ears." They are small, ear-shaped pasta. Their ingenious shape will automatically pick up the corn kernels and pine nuts in their little hollows.

Saffron, the stiles and stigmas of a Mediterranean crocus, is associated with Venus, the sun, and Mercury. In ancient Egypt and India, it was a symbol of status and wealth, used by noble ladies to tint their skins and scent their baths. The Sumerians associated saffron with the fire of the sun and used it in their remedies and magical potions. According to Greek myth, Hermes, the Greek counterpart of Mercury, created saffron when he accidentally wounded his friend Crocus, whose blood dripped to earth and sprouted as the flower that bears his name.

SERVES 4 TO 6

6 ears of fresh corn, yellow, white, or bicolor

4 tablespoons olive oil

2 tablespoons butter

¼ teaspoon crushed red pepper flakes

½ cup chopped scallions, whites and greens

1 cup Summer Tomato Sauce (page 107)

Pinch of saffron

¼ cup toasted pine nuts (page 199, Roasting Seeds and Nuts)

½ pound cooked lobster meat, cut into small cubes

1 pound orecchiette

½ cup grated Parmesan cheese

1 cup quartered grape tomatoes

Preheat a grill or the oven broiler. Place the corn, husks still on, directly on the grill. Turn regularly, until blackened on all sides, but not burned, about 8 minutes. Set aside to cool. Remove the husks and as much silk as you can. Using a sharp knife, carefully strip the kernels off the cobs.

Heat the olive oil and butter in a large skillet over medium heat. When the butter is melted, add the crushed red pepper. Add the scallions, and sauté until they soften, about 2 minutes. Add the tomato sauce and saffron, and stir. Lower the heat, cover, and simmer for about 5 minutes.

Remove the tomato sauce mixture from the heat, and add the corn kernels, pine nuts, and lobster meat. Cover and set somewhere warm.

Meanwhile, bring 6 quarts of well-salted water to a rapid boil. Add the orecchiette, and cook until just short of al dente. Reserve 1 to 2 cups of the cooking water, and drain.

Return the orecchiette to the pot, and add the corn-lobster mixture. Over low heat, toss the pasta and the sauce. Add the grated Parmesan, and continue to toss, adding small amounts of the reserved water, if necessary, to finish cooking the pasta.

Divide the pasta into bowls, and garnish each with a scattering of the grape tomatoes.

CLAMS AND COCKLES LINGUINE

LEO

The Greeks called the Goddess of Love and Beauty Aphrodite; the Romans, Venus. She was worshipped as the Morning Star. The birth of our nearest planetary neighbor is often depicted as a beautiful woman rising from the sudsy sea on a shell. The foamy, briny clam nectar in this dish is a reminder that the ocean is the Mother of Beauty. Complex life-forms though we are, we carry her mineral-rich womb in our blood and in the cockles of our hearts. In the Leo phase of the cycle, Beauty emerges. We are aware and rightly proud of what a wonder we are.

Leo rules love affairs. Aphrodite had all sorts of affairs. A Superwoman with powers far beyond those of mortal women, she ruled both the pleasures and pains of love, its salutary effects as well as its untoward emotions. Herbal lore tells us basil soothes stressful emotions and replaces them with feelings of tenderness. Oregano and parsley, too, have reputations for mood brightening. It is no coincidence that this trio is the classic seasoning of sunny southern Italy. For Goddess's sake, love and let love!

SERVES 4 TO 6

4 dozen shucked littleneck clams with their juice (1½ cups juice)
¼ cup finely chopped flat-leaf parsley, plus extra for garnish
½ cup shredded fresh basil leaves
1 tablespoon dried oregano
½ teaspoon freshly ground black pepper
6 tablespoons olive oil
2 garlic cloves, finely minced
¼ teaspoon crushed red pepper flakes
1 pound linguine
2 pounds cockles

 Have your fish seller shuck 4 dozen littleneck clams and put them in a container with their juice. This should yield about 1½ cups of juice. If it's a little short, add some white wine.

Stir together the clam juice, parsley, basil, oregano, and black pepper in a large bowl.

In a heavy saucepot with a tight-fitting lid, heat the olive oil over high heat. Add the garlic and red pepper flakes. When the flakes just begin to sizzle and the garlic begins to turn golden and has a nutty aroma, add the clam juice mixture. It should hiss a little.

Cover, and reduce the heat to low. Simmer very slowly, just below a boil, for at least 30 minutes, preferably 1 hour for all the flavors to meld. Be attentive. Don't let the juice evaporate.

Bring 6 quarts of salted water to a rapid boil. Add the linguine. While the pasta cooks, rinse the cockles under cold running water, making sure to rinse away all grit and any shell fragments.

In a separate skillet, warm a generous ½ cup of the clam sauce over low heat.

Drain the linguine when it is just short of al dente, and reserve 1 to 2 cups of the cooking water.

Return the linguine to the pot. Add the remaining clam sauce to the pasta, and gently toss over medium-low heat. Add small amounts of the reserved pasta water a little at a time to finish cooking the pasta, if necessary.

Meanwhile, raise the heat up to high beneath the warming clam sauce. Add the cockles, and stir. After about 30 seconds, add the clams. As they cook, the clams and cockles will give up delicately scented white froth. After a minute or so, the cockles will open and the clams will firm up. Cook just until they firm up, but no more (overcooking will make the clams rubbery). Discard any unopened cockles.

Divide the linguine among four bowls. Top each with some of the clam and cockle mix, garnish with a pinch or two of parsley, and serve immediately.

BUCATINI ALLA NORMA
VIRGO

The Maiden loves the familiar. A creature of habit, she is conservative, guarded. She learns by rote and finds if something worked once, it will work again, and again, and again.

Throughout Sicily, Pasta alla Norma is on almost every restaurant menu, and whether in a local eatery or a white-table dining room, there is little variation in ingredients or preparation. Some sources try to add false glamour to the name by linking it to Bellini's opera, citing the composer's partiality to eggplant. The legend goes that the dish was named in tribute to Bellini's nineteenth-century opera *Norma,* considered his masterwork. The Italian phrase *una vera norma*—"a real Norma"—is used to compliment something of high quality. But *norma* also shares a root with the Italian word *normale*—the Latin for "norm," which means the rule or pattern of things, that which is *normal*. And pasta alla norma is the epitome of all that is normal or regular, simple and comforting, predictable in its normalcy—the perfect dish for a Virgo.

The typical way to prepare the dish is to fry half the eggplant in cubes—which are mixed into the pasta at the end or served on top—and sauté the other half until creamy and dissolving into the tomatoes. If you have a summer grill lit, however, you can grill half the eggplant in slices instead of frying and roast the other eggplant whole on the grill, instead of sautéing. The smoky hint of fire this adds to the dish captures the essence of summer.

A member of the nightshade family, eggplant must be thoroughly cooked in order to be palatable. Prepared correctly, eggplant is mild and sweet, but it naturally has a bitter aftertaste. Salting the eggplant before cooking it removes this bitterness.

Ricotta salata, or "salted ricotta," is the aged, dry, crumbly version of the milky, spoonable fresh ricotta most people are familiar with. It's similar to feta, but milder and less moist.

SERVES 4 TO 6

2 medium eggplants (1½ to 2 pounds total), washed and trimmed, one eggplant cubed into ¾-inch squares; one eggplant small diced

1 to 2 tablespoons kosher salt, or other coarse salt

1 cup olive oil

1 garlic clove, minced

¼ teaspoon crushed red pepper flakes

1 cup Summer Tomato Sauce (page 107)

1 pound bucatini (also called perciatelli)

1 cup ricotta salata, grated or crumbled

½ cup thinly sliced fresh basil

If using a grill, slice one of the eggplants into ½-inch-thick rounds; salt them as in the recipe; then grill until they are tender, flipping the pieces to char evenly, about 2 minutes per side. Slice the cooked rounds into cubes. Place the other eggplant whole on the grill, and roast it, turning occasionally, until it is thoroughly soft. Slice the grilled eggplant in half lengthwise, scrape out the flesh, and mix it with the tomato sauce.

Place both the cubed and diced eggplant in separate colanders, and salt liberally. Allow the salted eggplant to sit for at least 30 minutes, tossing occasionally. The eggplant should be limp and releasing liquid by the end of the set time. Gently squeeze the eggplant pieces with your hands to release more of the bitter liquid, then rinse them well to remove the salt. Pat the pieces dry with a paper towel.

In a sauté pan or skillet large enough to hold the eggplant cubes in a single layer, heat the olive oil over high heat until it shimmers but before it smokes. Add the cubed eggplant to the hot olive oil, and fry until crisp and golden brown on all sides. Remove with a slotted spoon to a paper towel–lined plate or baking sheet, and set aside.

Pour off most of the oil that is left in the pan, except for about 2 tablespoons, and lower the heat to medium-high. Add the garlic to the pan, and sauté for 1 to 2 minutes, until fragrant. Add the diced eggplant, and sauté until it is quite soft and breaking down, crushing it with a wooden spoon as it cooks. Once the eggplant is fully softened, add the crushed red pepper and tomato sauce, and cook, covered, until creamy smooth, stirring occasionally, 15 to 20 minutes.

Meanwhile, bring 6 quarts of well-salted water to a rapid boil. Add the bucatini, and cook until just short of al dente, about 8 minutes. Drain the pasta, reserving 1 cup of the cooking water, and return the pasta to the pot. Add the sauce to the pasta a little at a time, tossing to coat. Add the reserved cooking water as necessary to facilitate mixing the sauce and pasta.

Serve topped with the fried eggplant cubes, ricotta salata, and basil.

ZUCCHINI BARZINI
CANCER

Easy-going, fluid, and moony, Cancer sails a dreamboat. Like a Moon Child, zucchini's watery, soft sweetness is its strength. But too much of a good thing is not necessarily better. Best not to drift away entirely. Smaller zucchini have more earth in them; they are firmer and less spongy. In Italy, this dish is known as *barzini,* little boats. Their cargo is their own carved-out pulp combined with whatever cheese, meat, herb, or vegetable you have on hand. Serve on a bed of lightly dressed greens.

SERVES 4

4 medium zucchini, 6 to 8 inches long
4 tablespoons olive oil, divided
½ teaspoon salt, divided
2 garlic cloves, minced
4 scallions, whites and greens chopped
½ cup finely chopped celery
½ cup grated carrot
1 cup peeled diced tomato
¼ cup panko bread crumbs
¼ cup finely chopped flat-leaf parsley
12 basil leaves, chiffonade sliced
½ teaspoon freshly ground black pepper
1 cup feta cheese, crumbled, divided

Preheat the oven to 375°F.

Wash and dry the zucchini, and trim the ends. Halve them lengthwise. Peel the bottoms as necessary to make them lie flat. Use a small spoon to scrape out the pulp in the center of each. Reserve the pulp and the peelings. Rub the zucchini hulls all over with 1 tablespoon of the olive oil, and sprinkle with half the salt. Place them on a baking sheet.

Heat the remaining 3 tablespoons olive oil in a skillet over high heat. Add the garlic and scallions. Sauté for 1 minute. Add the celery, carrot, tomato, and zucchini pulp and peelings. Sauté 3 or 4 minutes. Add the remaining salt, lower the heat, and cover. Cook for about 10 minutes, until all the vegetables have thoroughly softened. Remove from heat, and add the panko, parsley, basil, black pepper, and ¼ cup of the feta. Stir to mix thoroughly.

Stuff the zucchini boats with the filling. Top each with a portion of the remaining feta.

Bake until the hulls have softened but still retain their shape and a bit of their crunch, about 30 to 35 minutes.

SUMMER TOMATO SAUCE

When summer life gives you an abundance of tomatoes, make tomato sauce. The recipe below is for 4 quarts of chopped and pureed fresh tomatoes in whatever portions your garden has provided. A combination of fresh tomatoes—plum or Roma tomatoes for body; beefsteak or heirloom tomatoes for juice; cherry and grape tomatoes for sweetness—imparts the virtues of each.

Sauce is best without the tomato skins. Before cooking, puree cherry and grape tomatoes in a food processor. Cut an "X" in the nonstem-end of plum, beefsteak, and heirloom tomatoes, and drop them in boiling water for 15 seconds. Remove the tomatoes, and slip off the skins as soon as they are cool enough to handle. Chop the peeled tomatoes.

Start by gently heating 2 or 3 cloves of crushed garlic and ½ teaspoon chili pepper in several tablespoons of high-quality olive oil. Add the tomatoes, along with a generous handful each of chopped fresh basil, flat-leaf parsley, and oregano. Season with salt and pepper and simmer slowly uncovered for 1 to 3 hours, until the sauce thickens. Stir every so often.

Depending on what you prefer, you can leave the sauce chunky or use an immersion blender to puree.

FRITTATA CAPRESE
LEO

Enjoy those "Lazy Lion" Leo summer Sundays with brunch, a late, leisurely breakfast that is also a square meal. The frittata is an Italian omelet, an egg and "whatever there is in the house"—meat, cheese, or vegetable—pie. Cooked slowly over low heat, then passed under a broiler, it is satisfying to make and satisfying to eat. It is quite versatile. It can be made ahead of time, even the day before. It can be eaten plain, or as filling in a sandwich. It may be served hot or at room temperature and can be eaten for breakfast, lunch, or light supper. It travels well. Usually, the pie is cut into wedges. But occasionally it appears cut up into cubes and tossed in a green salad.

Caprese salad originated on the sunny isle of Capri in the Tyrrhenian Sea off Naples. It is typically made with basil or arugula leaves, sliced tomatoes, and fresh mozzarella. This version puts the warm-weather favorite *into* the eggs.

Use only the fleshy outer layer of the tomatoes. Cut a slice from each side, the top, and the bottom. Scrape out the seeds and discard them along with the stem scar. Save the rest of the tomato for another use, such as sauce. For a creamy frittata, use fresh mozzarella. However, since the tomato fillets will release water, dry, packaged mozzarella will help keep the finished result firm instead of runny.

SERVES 4

10 large eggs
25 large basil leaves, chiffonade sliced
½ cup flat-leaf parsley leaves
½ teaspoon salt
½ teaspoon freshly ground black pepper
1 tablespoon butter
2 tablespoons olive oil
¼ teaspoon crushed red pepper flakes
4 scallions, whites and greens chopped
4 ounces mozzarella, shredded
   or cubed
2 cups julienned tomato fillets

Preheat a broiler, and set the oven rack in the middle position.

Beat the eggs with the basil, parsley, salt, and black pepper in a large bowl.

Heat the butter and olive oil in a 10-inch ovenproof, nonstick skillet over low heat. When the butter is melted, add the crushed red pepper and the scallions to the pan. Raise the heat under the skillet to high. When the oil and butter are bubbly hot, but before they burn, add the beaten egg mixture. Tilt the pan to distribute the eggs evenly. Scatter an even layer of the cheese over the eggs, then scatter the tomatoes. Lower the heat, and cover, cooking the frittata until the bottom is set, about 15 minutes.

To cook the top, remove the lid, and place the skillet under the broiler for about 1 minute, until firm and golden. Remove and let sit for 5 minutes to set fully. Shake the skillet to loosen the frittata from the sides. It should slide out of the skillet onto a platter.

Cut into four portions, and serve each wedge with lemony greens, crusty bread, and a dollop of fresh butter.

OVEN-ROASTED RATATOUILLE SPIRAL
VIRGO

In late August, eggplants, squash, tomatoes, and peppers are in abundance. The herbs are at their full fragrance and flavor. Ratatouille is the perfect dish to take advantage of this bounty. Though native to Provence, there are many ratatouille-like dishes that appear across the Mediterranean. The Spanish have *pisto,* Sicilians *caponata,* and the Greeks and Turkish *tourloú,* to name a few.

The quick approach to ratatouille is to sauté all the vegetables together. In a Maiden frame of mind, you think about order and purity of method. Here is a layered approach with the eggplant, peppers, squash, onions, and tomatoes overlapping in a colorful spiral.

The spiral, a curved plane that winds around a center, continuously increasing or decreasing in a methodical way, is the cosmic fingerprint on the mundane; it is the shape of galaxies and snails, storms and eddies, and the logarithmic spirit that forms the ancient protein strings of our genetic code.

Herbes de Provence is a combination of herbs native to the Mediterranean basin. It usually includes summer savory, fennel seed, thyme, basil, rosemary, and lavender. You can buy it in jars. But if you have an herb garden and a food processor (or, better yet, a mortar and pestle), it doesn't take long to make your own. Summer savory, a key ingredient, is not nearly as popular as it ought to be. The name tells you something. It has a touch of spice and a light bright fragrance that is similar to marjoram and thyme but a bit subtler.

SERVES 4

6 tablespoons olive oil

¼ cup herbes de Provence

3 garlic cloves, minced

¼ teaspoon crushed red pepper flakes

½ teaspoon salt

1 teaspoon freshly ground black pepper

1 red bell pepper

1 yellow bell pepper

1 orange bell pepper

4 medium beefsteak tomatoes

1 Italian or Japanese eggplant (about 1 pound), sliced into ⅛-inch-thick rounds

1 zucchini, sliced into ⅛-inch-thick rounds

1 yellow squash, sliced into ⅛-inch-thick rounds

1 red onion, sliced into ⅛-inch-thick rounds

Preheat the oven to 400°F.

Combine the olive oil, herbes de Provence, garlic, crushed red pepper, salt, and black pepper in a small bowl.

Trim the bell peppers by cutting away the tops and bottoms. Save them for another use. Discard the seeds and the ribs. Make an incision in the center portion of each pepper so it will lie flat. Use a cookie cutter or mold to cut the flesh into rounds the same size as the squash rounds. Save what remains for another use.

Slice the tomatoes into rounds about ¼ inch thick. Use the most similarly sized rounds from each tomato. You will get 4 to 6 per tomato, depending on the size of the tomato and how you slice it.

Chop up the insides of the tomatoes, discarding as many of the seeds as possible. You should have about 2 cups. Mix this with 2 tablespoons of the oil and herb mix, and spread it in an even layer across the bottom of a heavy-duty 12-inch skillet.

Starting in the center of the skillet, build layers in a tight spiral, overlapping and coiling out, moistening each vegetable slice lightly in the oil and herb mixture before setting it in place thus: eggplant, bell pepper (alternate colors as you go), squash (alternate zucchini and yellow squash as you go), red onion, and tomato. Repeat until the skillet is full. Drizzle with the remaining oil and herb mixture.

Bake until all the vegetables are cooked, about 30 to 45 minutes. It will be soupy. Turn off the oven, and leave the ratatouille in there for about 1 hour. This will dry it out and enable you to serve it in neat, colorful wedges. Best served slightly warm or at room temperature.

FRIED SOFT-SHELL CRABS
CANCER

In early summer, soft-shell crabs come into full season. The Crab, symbol of Cancer, moves sideways, getting through life in a hard shell. The shell is shelter, a home for the crab, a place to be comfortable, a place to nest, a place to rest. When the water is warm, the crab temporarily sheds last year's shell to form a new, larger shell. Unable to protect itself from predators and now more appealing to them, upon molting, the crab will become less active, stop eating, and start looking for a place to hide.

Serve the soft shells, slathered with spicy, lemony mayonnaise, on a bed of lightly dressed salad greens, or on toasted ciabatta rolls.

SERVES 4

Seafood markets that sell the crabs will remove the head, the gills, and the small flap on the underside. Once cleaned, the crabs should be cooked as soon as possible.

FOR THE MAYONNAISE
1 cup mayonnaise

1 tablespoon prepared mustard, Dijon or whole grain

¼ cup Lemon–Olive Oil Dressing (page 51)

2 garlic cloves, minced

½ teaspoon cayenne pepper

FOR THE CRABS
8 soft-shell crabs, cleaned

4 cups vegetable oil, for frying

2 large eggs, beaten

¼ cup beer

2 tablespoons tartar sauce

1 tablespoon cracked fennel seeds

½ teaspoon salt

1 teaspoon freshly ground black pepper

2 cups flour, for dredging

2 tablespoons salt-cured capers, unrinsed

2 tablespoons finely chopped parsley

Make the mayonnaise. Whisk together all the mayonnaise ingredients in a small bowl until silky. Cover and refrigerate.

Prepare the crabs. Cut the crabs in half down the center from head to tail. Place the halves in a salad spinner, and spin them very gently once or twice. Discard whatever small amount of water or loose innards separate. (This will help prevent them from spitting hot oil at you when you fry them, and it will tighten up their texture, too.)

Heat ⅓ inch of vegetable oil in a suitable pot or skillet to frying temperature, about 360°F.

Whisk together the eggs, beer, tartar sauce, fennel seeds, salt, and pepper in a bowl large enough to fit the crab halves. Dredge the crabs with flour, then dip them in the egg mixture.

Without crowding the pot, fry the crabs until they are a deep golden brown, and drain them on a paper towel–lined plate. Sprinkle the crab with the capers and parsley while hot.

Serve hot with the mayo, either on greens or as a sandwich.

GRILLED BRANZINO
LEO

The sea is the realm of Neptune, the Roman counterpart of Poseidon. Neptune is also the god of fresh water. The sun and Neptune were rivals. They quarreled over areas of influence: which lands the sun dried, which Neptune rained upon. During the height of the summer, as the sun goes into Leo, the heat and dryness are most intense. The rivers and lakes are at their low points. In the hope that Neptune would shower his blessings on the parched fields, the Romans celebrated the Neptunalia, a wild, wet festival of water and wine, feasting and boisterous celebration.

Now that we have water from taps and bottles for our bodies and sprinkler systems for our lawns and gardens, the vital importance of rain is minimized in our minds. We may show a little Neptunian devotion by conserving water, or at least not taking it for granted. And when the temperature climbs, we may want to dispense with the Leo feasting in favor of some lighter fare. We can thank Neptune for that, too!

Branzino is a Mediterranean seabass with delicate white flesh. Combined with a side of zucchini medallions (page 124), this makes a light, simple meal for a hot summer night.

Capers are the unopened, pickled flower buds of *capparis spinosa,* or caper bush, a plant indigenous to the Mediterranean. Their savory mustard-like tang is a wonderful enhancement for seafood.

SERVES 4

¼ cup olive oil
1 teaspoon salt
1 tablespoon pepper
4 branzino fillets, skin on
   (about 1½ pounds)
¼ cup Lemon–Olive Oil Dressing
   (page 51)
1 teaspoon salt-cured capers, unrinsed
2 lemons, cut into wedges

Preheat the oven to 425°F. Heat a gas, charcoal, or wood grill.

Pour the olive oil onto a rimmed baking sheet, and sprinkle with the salt and pepper. Coat each fillet with the mixture.

Combine the lemon–olive oil dressing with the capers in a small bowl, and set aside.

Make sure the grill is hot and clean and the flesh sides of the fillets are well-oiled. Place them flesh-side down on the grill for about 30 seconds. Gently lift with a spatula to see if grill marks have appeared. If so, they should slide off the grill intact.

Return them skin-side down to the baking tray, and pour the dressing-caper mixture over them. Finish cooking in the oven, about 2 or 3 minutes. Serve with lemon wedges.

GRILLING FISH

Putting fish on the grill is quick and easy. Fish with firm flesh, such as swordfish and monkfish, can be cooked entirely on the grill. Fish with medium-firm flesh, such as bass and salmon, will tend to flake apart if cooked entirely on the grill. They are best started on the grill and finished in a hot oven or under a broiler. When putting fish fillets or steaks on the grill, it is essential that the grill be hot and well-cleaned with a sturdy, stiff wire grill brush.

LEMONY GRILLED SHRIMP WITH WHITE BEANS
VIRGO

The Maiden is a clear thinker. Her conceits are intellectual. A skilled analyst, with a practical earth-element mind, Virgo can reduce complexity to black and white, breaking large problems down into small solvable pieces. When little things are attended to properly and efficiently, the whole is more than the sum of the parts. In this seafood and salad entrée—a quick yet elegant and satisfying meal—the Maiden exercises her sense of simplicity and harmony attending to the details.

You can use any size shrimp. Larger varieties need not be skewered. But this dish works best with smaller shrimp. Cleaned, with the shells off, "medium" shrimp will number somewhere between 30 and 35 shrimp per pound. They can be served on or off the skewers.

Supporting these little nibbles from the sea is a black and white salad.

SERVES 4 (MAKES 8 SKEWERS)

FOR THE BEANS

2 cups cooked cannellini beans, rinsed well
    and drained if canned
1 cup pitted Kalamata olives, cut in half
    lengthwise
¼ cup finely chopped red onion
½ cup grated fennel
½ cup grated radish
12 ounces grape tomatoes, halved
¼ cup olive oil
2 tablespoons white wine vinegar
2 tablespoons dried oregano
2 teaspoons prepared mustard
⅛ teaspoon cayenne pepper
½ teaspoon salt
½ teaspoon freshly ground black pepper

FOR THE SHRIMP

1½ pounds shelled, deveined medium
    (30/35 count) shrimp
½ cup olive oil
Juice of 1 lemon
¼ cup white wine vinegar
2 tablespoons dried oregano
⅛ teaspoon cayenne pepper
2 garlic cloves, minced
½ teaspoon salt
1 teaspoon pepper
Lemon–Olive Oil Dressing, for drizzling
    (page 51)

Heat a gas or wood grill.

Make the beans. Mix together the beans, olives, onion, fennel, radish, and tomatoes in a large mixing bowl.

Whisk together the olive oil, vinegar, oregano, mustard, cayenne, salt, and pepper in a small bowl until emulsified. Pour over the bean mixture, and toss to coat evenly. Set aside.

Make the shrimp. Using two skewers side-by-side, impale the shrimp so they will lie flat. In a shallow rectangular baking dish slightly longer than the skewers, combine the olive oil, lemon juice, white wine vinegar, oregano, cayenne, garlic, salt, and pepper. Add the skewered shrimp, and turn to coat evenly. Let them sit for about 1 hour, rotating once or twice.

Place the skewered shrimp on the hottest part of the grill. Spoon on some extra marinade, and close the grill lid; this will give them a smoky flavor. Check them after 1 minute. Turn the skewers when the shrimp are just beginning to char. Baste again. Continue grilling until the shrimp are pink and slightly charred, no more than 5 minutes total.

While the shrimp are still sizzling from the grill, give them a few squirts of the lemon–olive oil dressing. After 1 to 2 minutes, you should be able to strip them off the skewers. Or you may want to serve them *en brochette*. To serve, divide the bean salad among four plates. Top each with a portion of the grilled shrimp, or a skewer.

 If you are using 8-inch skewers, you will need about 8 skewers to make 4 servings. If using wood or bamboo skewers, make sure to soak them in water for at least 10 minutes before grilling, to prevent them from scorching.

GRILLED MAGRET AND FRISÉE
CANCER

In astrological anatomy, the moon rules the breast, the center of feminine softness and responsiveness to the feelings of others; at the same time, the moon is the ruler of the Cancer phase of the Zodiac cycle. The beginning of summer is soft and moist. The warm weather, like sweet cosmic milk, nourishes the spirit.

Magret is the breast of a Moulard duck, which is a cross between a Muscovy male and a Peking Hen. It is larger than other ducks and has a thicker and juicier breast. Tasting more like beef than poultry, magret is the rare bird you can eat rare. Don't be put off by all the fat. It is actually leaner than other ducks. When cooked, most of it is rendered and the skin will be brown and crisp. If your grill allows for indirect heat, you may cook the breasts entirely on it. If not, it is best to sear the breasts on the grill and then place in a preheated oven.

SERVES 4 TO 6

FOR THE DUCK
2 boneless Moulard duck breasts, about
    2 pounds
2 tablespoons orange juice
2 tablespoons soy sauce
2 ounces Cointreau or other orange-flavored
    liqueur

2 tablespoons thyme
2 tablespoons olive oil
2 garlic cloves, minced
½ teaspoon salt
1 teaspoon freshly ground black pepper

FOR THE FRISÉE
1 teaspoon sugar
¼ teaspoon salt
⅛ teaspoon cayenne pepper
1 tablespoon butter
1 tablespoon maple syrup
1 cup chopped walnuts
6 tablespoons olive oil
2 tablespoons orange juice
1 jigger (1.5 ounces) Cointreau
1 tablespoon red wine vinegar
1 tablespoon prepared mustard
1 scallion, whites only, chopped
Pinch of salt
Pinch of freshly ground black pepper
6 cups frisée, trimmed, washed, and torn
    into bite-size pieces
1 cup torn or shredded radicchio
1 cup baby arugula

Preheat the oven to 375°F.

Make the duck. Place the duck breasts meat-side down on a work surface. With a sharp knife, crosshatch the fat, being careful not to cut into the meat.

Stir together the orange juice, soy sauce, Cointreau, thyme, olive oil, garlic, salt, and pepper in a bowl. Place the duck in a large ziplock bag, and pour in the marinade. Seal the bag, and massage the marinade into the breasts, concentrating especially on working it into the slits you made. Refrigerate for at least 2 hours.

Preheat the grill to high. If your grill does not allow for indirect heat, raise the oven temp to 400°F.

Remove the breasts from the marinade, and place them fat-side down on the grill. Be careful. Because of the fat, the flame may leap. Sear until grill marks appear, about 1 minute or even less. Brush the meat side with some olive oil, flip, and sear it similarly.

If your grill allows for indirect heat, brush on some marinade and continue cooking the breasts, skin-side up, at around 400°F (if your grill lets you know such things). Otherwise, transfer the duck to the oven.

Cook the breasts for about another 8 minutes total, brushing with marinade halfway through. Use a meat thermometer to check their doneness. An internal temperature of 130°F is medium-rare. Magret is best when it is slightly pink.

Let sit at least 10 minutes before slicing. Using a sharp carving knife, slice the meat across the grain on a bias into very thin slices. Try to maintain the original shape of the breast.

Meanwhile, make the frisée. Stir together the sugar, salt, and cayenne in a small bowl, and set aside.

Combine the butter and maple syrup in a small saucepot over medium heat, and stir, bringing it slowly to a boil. Remove from heat. Add the walnuts to the butter–maple syrup mixture, and stir to coat.

Transfer the nuts to a rimmed baking sheet lined with parchment paper. Sprinkle the sugar mixture over the nuts, and toss gently to coat; spread out the nuts in an even layer. Toast in the oven until they are golden, 5 to 10 minutes. Let the nuts cool completely on the sheet.

Whisk together the olive oil, orange juice, Cointreau, vinegar, mustard, scallion, salt, and pepper in a small bowl until emulsified.

Place the frisée, radicchio, and arugula in a large mixing bowl, and toss with just enough dressing to coat. Divide evenly among four to six serving plates.

Top each portion of greens with a portion of meat, handling it carefully to keep the slices lined up. Scatter the walnuts over each plate, and serve.

SPICED BEEF TENDERLOIN WITH SCALLIONS AND HORSERADISH

LEO

Some animals are vegetarians. Some animals eat vegetarians. Bovines eat grass. Felines eat meat. They do what comes naturally. It's obvious that cows are more closely related to us than carrots. They share more DNA with us than we would like to think. While some people have reasonable reservations about eating creatures of apparent sentience, most of us follow our natural inclinations because meat from red-blood animals has certain substances that are necessary for our animal vitality, and in a truly holistic sensibility, animal vitality is the basis for spiritual well-being. Eaten with the proper grace, in a Leo frame of mind, red meat makes a consecrated centerpiece for a special occasion.

Little things mean a lot. Toasting the coriander, cumin, and fennel seeds is an extra step that adds a subtle dimension of flavor.

SERVES 6 TO 8

2 tablespoons coriander seeds
2 tablespoons cumin seeds
1 tablespoon fennel seeds
2 tablespoons granulated garlic
1 teaspoon cayenne pepper
1 teaspoon freshly ground black pepper
1 teaspoon salt
½ cup olive oil, plus more as needed
12 scallions, trimmed and left whole
3 pounds trimmed beef tenderloin, preferably center-cut
½ cup prepared horseradish
½ cup crème fraîche
¼ cup mayonnaise
1 tablespoon Dijon mustard
2 tablespoons Lemon–Olive Oil Dressing (page 51)

Toast the coriander, cumin, and fennel seeds in a medium skillet over medium heat. When they become aromatic, transfer them to a bowl to cool a bit. Place the cooled seeds in a plastic sandwich bag, and use a kitchen hammer or rolling pin to crush them. Or grind them in a clean coffee grinder.

Stir together the spice mixture, granulated garlic, cayenne, black pepper, salt, and olive oil in a small bowl. Pour the oil mixture onto a rimmed baking sheet large enough to accommodate the beef.

Roll the scallions in this mixture, and set them aside.

If the tenderloin has a tail, fold it under and tie it with butcher's twine. Set the meat in the spiced oil mixture. Coat the meat all over with the spiced mixture, and give it a gentle massage. Let the beef sit at room temperature for about 1 hour.

Meanwhile, preheat a grill to medium-high, and use a grill brush to make sure the grate is clean. If your grill does not have indirect heat, preheat the oven to 400°F.

Place the scallions on the grill for about 2 minutes, rolling them once. Return them to their plate.

Place the tenderloin on the grill, close the lid, and brown it on one side, about 1 minute. There should be some of the olive oil spice mixture left on the oven tray. Before turning, brush the top of the fillet with it. Grill the other side until it browns, about 1 minute more. Do the same with the sides, until the tenderloin is evenly browned all over. If you run out of marinade, brush with more olive oil.

Move the meat to a cooler part of the grill, and close the lid. Or, if your grill only runs hot or cold, put the meat back on the tray, and place it in the heated oven. In either case, don't go by time. After a few minutes, check for doneness by inserting a meat thermometer into the thickest part of the fillet. When it reaches about 120°F, it is medium-rare.

Place the meat on a carving board, and let it rest for 10 minutes.

Meanwhile, make the horseradish sauce. Finely chop the grilled scallions. Add the scallions to a large bowl with the horseradish, crème fraîche, mayonnaise, mustard, and lemon–olive oil dressing in a bowl, and mix thoroughly.

To serve, thinly slice the beef, and serve with a dollop of sauce on the side.

GOLDEN TURMERIC CHICKEN
VIRGO

The chicken is sacred to the planet Mercury, whose domain is everyday life. Mercury is the ruler of the earth sign Virgo, and Virgo is associated with small animals. The chicken is the food of everyday life, informal and familiar.

Giving us both eggs and nourishing protein at a reasonable price, widely popular in all age groups, the chicken is universally considered a symbol of well-being and nourishment. Soup made from it is revered as a healing restorative.

Turmeric is the ground root of the curcuma plant. It imparts a deep orange-gold color to food seasoned with it, and it has both the bittersweet bite of ginger and the heat of hot pepper. Traditionally, it had a place in rituals of purification. Recent studies show that it does indeed have significant anti-inflammatory properties.

SERVES 4 (MAKES 8 SKEWERS)

 You will need 8 skewers. If using wood or bamboo skewers, make sure to soak them in water for at least 10 minutes before grilling, to prevent them from scorching.

½ cup olive oil, divided
¼ cup lemon juice
¼ cup freshly squeezed orange juice
2 teaspoons ground cumin
2 teaspoons smoked paprika
1 teaspoon cinnamon
1 teaspoon turmeric
⅛ teaspoon cayenne pepper
2 garlic cloves, minced
1 teaspoon salt
1 teaspoon freshly ground black pepper
2 pounds boneless, skinless chicken breasts or thighs, cut into 1-inch cubes
1 large red onion, cut into 1-inch squares
1 large fennel bulb, well-trimmed, cut into 1-inch squares
1 large red bell pepper, trimmed, seeds and ribs removed, cut into 1-inch squares

Whisk together ¼ cup of the olive oil, the lemon and orange juices, the cumin, paprika, cinnamon, turmeric, cayenne, garlic, salt, and pepper in a bowl large enough to accommodate the chicken cubes. Add the chicken to the marinade, and toss to coat evenly. Cover with plastic wrap, and refrigerate overnight.

Prepare a hot grill. When ready to grill, add the onion, fennel, and pepper squares to the marinating chicken, and toss to coat.

SUMMER FIRE FESTIVAL

The first day of summer—the Summer Solstice—is the longest day of the year. But even at the moment of the sun's brightest shining, it is beginning its downward course and giving way to the longer nights ahead. In ancient times, to symbolize the sun's power and extend it into the night, ensuring the fertility of the flocks and the fields, there were open-air, torch-lit gatherings where revelers set ablaze heaps of straw, building bonfires in celebration of the sun. Offerings were thrown onto the flames. Fire also served to roast the meats and vegetables consumed at the Solstice Feast.

The Roman fire festival that led up to the Summer Solstice was called the *Vestalia.* It was in honor of Vesta, goddess of the hearth, home, and family. Fire, symbolic of the heart of the home, is sacred to her. Ironically, this Cosmic Mother is a virgin. She is a different sort of virgin than the Virgo Maiden of late summer, however, whose unattainability comes from a reluctance to enter into passions that would interfere with the practicalities of her daily routines, responsibilities, and obligations. Vestal Virginity, on the other hand, is anything but mundane. As unspent fertility, chastity concentrates the life force, makes it far-reaching, inclusive of heaven and earth. The Vestal Virgin's procreative powers are spiritual, capable of world-changing magic.

In modern times, barbecues are a popular way we can re-create the summer-fire tradition, making the night a time of light and power. One of the best parts of summer is firing up the grill. With passage through flames, meats, seafood, and vegetables nourish us with the sun's energy.

Thread each skewer with two rounds of one piece each in the following order: onion, chicken, fennel, chicken, pepper, chicken.

Grill the kebabs over medium-high heat, brushing with the remaining marinade, until the chicken meat is thoroughly cooked through and the vegetables have softened, 8 to 10 minutes.

DILLED ZUCCHINI AND SCALLIONS
CANCER

Zucchini squash, with its mild, comforting moistness has lunar qualities. Its taste is as soothing as a mother's touch. Seared, moon-shaped medallions of zucchini tossed with scallions and dill make a light summer side dish that pairs well with seafood.

SERVES 4

2 tablespoons olive oil
2 medium zucchini, cut into ½-inch-thick rounds
4 scallions, whites and greens finely chopped
⅛ teaspoon crushed red pepper flakes
¼ teaspoon salt
Freshly ground black pepper
¼ cup finely chopped dill leaves

Heat the olive oil in a skillet that has a lid on high until it is just short of smoking. Lay the zucchini rounds down flat in the pan. (If they don't all fit in your pan, do them in two pans or in batches.) Cover the pan with the lid, and cook until the zucchini rounds are golden on one side, about 1 minute. Turn them over, and repeat.

Remove from the heat. (If you seared them in two batches, return the first batch to the pan.) Add the scallions, red pepper flakes, salt, a few grinds of black pepper, and the dill leaves to the pan, and stir.

Cover the pan, and let sit for 2 to 3 minutes, allowing time for the scallions and dill to wilt, the flavors to mingle, and the zucchini to soften a bit more. The medallions should be crisp-tender, firm, and just barely cooked through to the center.

SAFFRON RICE
LEO

The Lion is sunny, cheerful, and congenial. Flowers are the sun's light solidified. Saffron imparts a luminous, golden-yellow hue and a floral aroma that turns ordinary rice into gold. Fennel, a bulb with a mild, sweet licorice taste, grows wild around the Mediterranean region. It is a digestive aid. In Italy, thin wedges of it are served in antipasti and between courses of large feasts to increase the appetite, help with digestion, and cleanse the palate.

SERVES 4 TO 6

1 cup chicken stock
¼ cup freshly squeezed orange juice
¼ cup currants or raisins
Generous pinch of saffron, crumbled
2 tablespoons butter
1 tablespoon olive oil
1 tablespoon fennel seeds
⅛ teaspoon chopped fresh chili, or to taste
½ cup minced fennel
½ cup minced onion
1 cup Jasmine rice
¼ cup toasted pine nuts (page 199, Roasting
    Seeds and Nuts)
½ teaspoon salt
½ cup frozen baby peas, thawed

Stir together the chicken stock, orange juice, and ¼ cup water in a small bowl, and add the currants and saffron. Let the currants soak for 30 minutes.

Heat the butter and olive oil in a heavy saucepot with a tight-fitting lid over medium-high heat. When the butter is melted, add the fennel seeds and the chili. Allow to infuse for about 1 minute. Add the fennel and onion, and sauté until the vegetables soften a bit, 2 to 3 minutes.

Add the rice, stirring, until it gives off a nutty aroma, about 1 minute or so. Add the currant-stock mixture, pine nuts, and salt, and bring to a boil. Stir once, reduce the heat to low, cover, and simmer for 15 minutes.

Remove the pot from the heat, and let stand, covered, for 7 minutes. Uncover, fold in the peas, fluff with a fork, and serve.

 In choosing fennel, select firm, tightly packed bulbs. To prepare: discard the stocks and most of the fronds (reserving a few fronds for garnish). Trim the woody base and discard the outer layers of the bulb. Halve the bulb vertically. Notch out the triangular cores from each half, and discard.

POLENTA BITES WITH SAGE-HAZELNUT PESTO

VIRGO

Polenta, flavor-absorbent and soul-satisfying, is nearly as versatile as pasta, and it can go on the grill and in the fryer, places pasta dare not venture. Why is it not more popular? Perhaps it's because sticklers for tradition insist you pour it into boiling water in a slow steady stream, whisking all the while for 45 minutes, enduring shoulder pain and burns as the hot mush spits on your hands. As with everything good in life, your patience, optimism, and dedication will be rewarded . . . in time. The Maiden, with her cool character and clear mind, is well aware of that. Quick-cooking polenta, which dissolves in a minute or two, may not be quite as fluffy as its more traditional counterpart, but it has an edge in the effort-reward equation. The time you save with instant polenta may help polenta become a more frequent guest at your table.

Sage is another herb native to the Mediterranean region. The Latin word for sage, *salvia,* is derived from the Latin verb *salvare,* to save. The imperative form *salvere,* "be well," was used as a parting wish. Sage is sacred to Jupiter. Its hairy gray-green leaves have a beguiling scent, earthy but uplifting.

SERVES 4 TO 6

FOR THE POLENTA
¾ cup sage leaves
3½ cups vegetable stock
1 cup quick-cooking polenta
1 teaspoon salt
2 tablespoons unsalted butter
½ cup grated Parmesan
2 tablespoons olive oil plus extra for broiling, divided

FOR THE PESTO
¼ cup sage leaves
¼ cup grated Parmesan
¼ cup olive oil
1 garlic clove, peeled
½ cup toasted hazelnuts (page 199, Roasting Seeds and Nuts)

Make the polenta. Chop ¼ cup of the sage leaves. Add the chopped sage and stock to a saucepot over high heat, and bring the stock to a boil. Gradually stir in the polenta, and add the salt. Continue to stir, cooking until all the stock is absorbed. This should take only a few minutes. Lower the heat, add the butter and cheese, and stir until the melted butter and cheese are thoroughly incorporated into the polenta.

No need to serve these addictive little bites warm. They can be made in advance and used to accompany various entrées. Sage pairs well with meat, especially poultry. But it can also bond with certain seafood. You might try serving these bites with grilled shrimp (page 116). Put a couple of bites on each plate and the rest on the table. Everyone will reach for more.

Oil the bottom of a large, rimmed baking tray with 1 tablespoon of the olive oil. Pour the polenta onto the tray, and using a soft rubber spatula, spread it into an even layer ¼ to ½ inch thick. Coat the top with another tablespoon of olive oil. If the polenta doesn't fit, use a second tray.

Let the polenta sit for 1 to 2 hours at room temperature, until it has set. Refrigerating overnight is best.

Meanwhile, make the pesto. Combine the ingredients in the bowl of a food processor, and pulse until smooth. Set aside.

Once the polenta is firm, slice it into 1½ × 1-inch rectangles.

Preheat a broiler with the rack as close to the flame or element as possible.

Heat the extra olive oil in a skillet over high heat. Add the remaining ½ cup sage leaves to the pan, and fry until crisp. Pour the contents of the skillet over the sliced polenta. Remove the sage leaves, and set them aside (they will burn under the broiler). Use a brush or your fingertips to distribute the olive oil on the polenta bites.

Put the tray(s) under the broiler. Broil until crisp and golden brown on one side, 1 to 2 minutes, then turn and crisp the other side, 1 to 2 minutes. Check at the 1-minute mark to ensure you do not burn the polenta.

While the bites are still hot, dab each piece with a small spoon of the pesto. Put them on a serving platter, scattering the fried sage leaves over them, and serve.

COCONUT-PEACH CRISP
CANCER

Cancer is the nurturer of the Zodiac. She is warmhearted, gentle, and protective. As the coconut has a hard shell to protect the sweetness within, the Crab can be thick-skinned in protecting herself and those she loves. With the moon in June, surrounded by family, she can let herself "crumble" a bit. This comforting, rustic dessert has a delicate, comforting sweetness, a fruit filling in a soft streusel shell. For a little extra coconut flavor, you may substitute coconut flour and coconut sugar for the all-purpose flour and regular sugar.

SERVES 6

FOR THE STREUSEL TOPPING
1 cup sliced toasted almonds (page 199, Roasting Seeds and Nuts)
½ cup rolled oats
½ cup all-purpose flour
¼ teaspoon salt
¼ teaspoon cinnamon
⅓ cup sugar
5 tablespoons cold unsalted butter, cut in pieces
2 tablespoons shredded coconut

FOR THE FRUIT FILLING
3 large ripe peaches, peeled, pitted, and sliced
2 cups fresh blueberries
2 teaspoons lemon juice
½ teaspoon vanilla extract
⅓ cup sugar
2 tablespoons cornstarch

Preheat the oven to 350°F.

Combine the almonds and oats in the bowl of a food processor, and gently pulse until blended. Add the flour, salt, cinnamon, and sugar, and gently pulse to combine all evenly. Add the butter, and pulse to distribute. Transfer to a large bowl, stir in the shredded coconut, and refrigerate while you make the fruit filling.

Butter a 10-inch pie dish or a 9 × 13-inch baking dish. In a large bowl, combine the peaches and blueberries. Sprinkle the lemon juice and vanilla over the fruit. Add the sugar and cornstarch, and gently toss.

Pour the filling into the pie dish. Distribute the streusel topping evenly over the top, squeezing little clumps of streusel together as you go.

Place the dish on a foil-lined cookie sheet in case the filling bubbles over. Bake for 45 minutes, watching to make sure the top doesn't get too dark.

Serve warm with ice cream or yogurt.

KIWI RICOTTA STACKS

LEO

In high summer, the fire is outside. The King of Beasts does not want to slave over a hot stove. This warm-weather dessert is a refreshing blend of light, fragrant fluff and tangy sweetness. Fruity and creamy, it cools the Lion's jets.

SERVES 4

4 to 6 green or gold kiwi, peeled and sliced into ¼-inch rounds
Zest and juice of 1 orange
8 ounces ricotta
¼ teaspoon ground cinnamon, plus more for garnish
1 tablespoon honey
½ cup shelled, roasted, unsalted pistachios

Combine the kiwi and orange zest and juice in a small bowl, reserving a bit of zest for garnish.

Combine the ricotta, cinnamon, and honey in a blender or food processor, and pulse until smooth. Transfer the cheese mixture to a mixing bowl.

Place half the pistachios in the bowl of the food processor or blender (no need to rinse it out first), and pulse into a coarse paste. Fold the paste into the cheese mixture.

On four serving plates, layer a slice of kiwi, a generous teaspoon of the cheese mixture, and some extra cinnamon if you wish. Repeat twice (kiwi-cheese-kiwi-cheese) in a stack, finishing with a kiwi slice and the remaining (whole) pistachios. Sprinkle with the reserved orange zest.

BERRY MASCARPONE TART
VIRGO

The Maiden has a reputation for being critical and having a sharp tongue. This summer dessert—sweet, creamy, and sensual—puts a bit of sugarcoating on the Maiden's sharp tongue. Earth sign Virgo's dryness limits the range of her emotional sensitivity. No one is perfect, but this is not necessarily a blemish on her character. Dispassion is necessary for mental clarity. But when dealing with others, especially when pointing out flaws, a little diplomacy helps get the point across more effectively.

While "vanilla" has popular associations with the Virgo tendencies toward conventional behavior, values, and desires, real vanilla is in fact an exotic spice. Vanilla comes from the seedpod of *Vanilla planifolia,* a type of orchid. Real vanilla has a sweet, smooth, sensual savor, a taste that conjures up the tropical paradises where it originated.

SERVES 8

FOR THE PASTRY
½ cup unsalted butter, softened, plus extra for buttering the tart pan
2 cups flour
1 tablespoon lemon zest
3 egg yolks
¾ cup sugar
¼ teaspoon salt
1 to 2 tablespoons half-and-half, as needed

FOR THE FILLING
1 vanilla bean, split lengthwise
8 ounces mascarpone, at room temperature
2 tablespoons rum
2 pints mixed berries, such as raspberries, blackberries, and strawberries (if using strawberries, quarter them)
¼ cup raspberry jam
¼ cup apple juice

Mint leaves, for garnish

Preheat the oven to 400°F.

Generously butter a 9- or 10-inch tart pan with a removable bottom.

Make the pastry. Combine the flour, zest, yolks, sugar, salt, and ½ cup butter in the bowl of a food processor, and pulse to coarse-grained crumbs, adding 1 to 2 tablespoons of half-and-half, if necessary, to bring the dough together. Transfer to a mixing bowl, and work the mixture briefly by hand. Leave it a little rough. Sprinkle it with flour, wrap it in plastic wrap, and refrigerate for 1 hour.

Roll the dough out into a 10- to 11-inch circle. Gently press it into the tart tin and up its sides. (If there is overlap, use it to form a bit of a lip around the perimeter.) Put the dough into the freezer for 30 minutes.

Bake the pastry until lightly brown, about 25 minutes. Cool on a wire rack.

While the tart shell cools, make the filling. In a mixing bowl, combine the vanilla seeds and mascarpone, and whisk until smooth. Drizzle in the rum, whisking as you do so, until you have a smooth, spreadable mix.

Use a soft spatula to spoon the mascarpone onto the pastry in an even layer. Top with the berries—use your imagination, making spokes, spirals, yin-yang, a star; the choice is yours.

Combine the raspberry jam and the apple juice in a small saucepot over medium-low

Since vanilla pods can be somewhat costly, it is best to be efficient, careful, and thorough when prepping them for use. Hold the pod tightly by the stem end on your work surface, and use a small sharp knife to split it lengthwise into two halves. Using a teaspoon, scrape the seeds from the halves. Try not to get them on your fingers. Mix half with the pastry and half with the mascarpone. Before discarding the pod, use it to spice the rum. Place it in a small saucepan with the rum, and bring it to a simmer. Cover, turn off the heat, and let cool. (If you do this after you make the dough, it will be room temperature when you are ready to assemble the tart.)

heat. Stirring to dissolve the jam, cook until the juice-jam mixture thickens, 4 to 5 minutes. Using a small spoon, drizzle this glaze over the berries.

The tart is ready to serve, or it can be refrigerated. Serve garnished with mint leaves.

FALL

LIBRA

SAGITTARIUS

SCORPIO

STARTERS

Butternut Squash Soup with Roasted Pepitas (L)

Roasted Acorn Squash with Mushrooms and Hazelnuts (S)

Rösti with Smoked Salmon and Scallion Crème Fraîche (SA)

SALADS

Waldorf Salad (L)

Roasted Golden Beets and Walnuts (S)

Persimmon Pomegranate Salad (SA)

PASTA

Broccoli Rabe, Sausage, and White Beans with Penne (L)

Linguine with Cauliflower Two Ways (S)

Linguine Fine with Broccoli and Anchovies (SA)

VEGETARIAN

Butternut Squash Lasagna (L)

Falafel with Sesame Sauce (S)

Manchego-Stuffed Peppers with Salbitxada (SA)

SEAFOOD

Scallops and Israeli Couscous (L)

Fried Oyster Po' Boys with Cajun Slaw (S)

Pan-Seared Halibut Tacos and Roasted Tomato–Poblano Salsa (SA)

MEAT

Apple-Stuffed Pork Tenderloin (L)

Pomegranate Chicken (S)

Turkey Saltimbocca (SA)

SIDES

Roasted Brussels Sprouts (L)

Roasted Rosemary Potatoes (S)

Pumpkin Risotto (SA)

DESSERTS

Apple Crumble (L)

Chocolate Chip Cookies (S)

Plum Upside-Down Cake (SA)

Fall brings the wonder of the harvest season: the apple-crispness in the air, the red and golden splendor of the falling leaves, the sunshine doing a long, slow fade from butterscotch orange to cold steel gray, and the scattering of seeds in the chill wind. Fall marks the coming of the holidays, occasions to give thanks and celebrate not only the harvest, but the miracle of being alive, of having loved ones, and those things that make living and loving possible: the earth, the air, the sun, the rain, and the spirits in the plants and in the planets!

In Libra, as in Aries, the Light and Dark forces are balanced. The days and the nights are of near equal duration, and the temperature is moderate. From the end of September and into October, being outdoors is pleasurable, but at the same time, the coziness of home is welcome, too. In Aries the days are lengthening, the nights getting shorter, and the momentum is toward discovery and the expression of the self. Aries is competitive, a rival to peers. On the opposite side of the Zodiac, in Libra, the nights are getting longer and the days are getting shorter, and the momentum is toward coming together with others. The work of the harvest is communal. Ruled by Venus, the Libra phase is a time for partnership and social cooperation, the fellowship of culture and spirit, the group effort for the general welfare. With the Horn of Plenty spilling forth, the kitchen comes to life. Meals, sharing food and prosperity, are Holy Communion.

Scales are impartial. They are used to weigh and to balance. Justice must be blind and avoid prejudices. The Libra phase is about objectivity and evaluation. We measure and assess the fundamental things in our lives. Who and what have meaning to us? How important are they to us? Scales must have mechanical precision, but can Venus be a Love Machine? In her domain, balance includes good taste, polish, beauty, order, civilization, and cultural refinement. We see her in the persona of the Homecoming/Harvest Queen, floating before us in the fresh, bright autumn air, with gentle smiles and gestures of blessing for all. But when Venus is dominant, the sun is at a disadvantage. The sense of self is diminished.

Venus needs to be loved and needs to be seen as attractive. Social graces and keeping up appearances are wonderful assets, but living is a messy business. Giving pleasure to others, being sincere, civil, considerate, agreeable, and compliant are certainly virtues, but only if the accord is genuine.

If it is in the avoidance of confrontation or in people pleasing, individuality is at risk. And like the weather, one day the lingering summer warmth, the next the incipient harshness of winter, Venus sometimes has a hard time making up her mind. With too much balance, life may go out of balance. True balance does not come from mild manners and being agreeable, but in centering our own inner equilibrium.

In any case, as the world turns, Scorpio balances Libra. Toward the end of October, the days shrink and darken. The nights lengthen. The cold creeps in. The trees are bare; the leaves lie in frosted piles. The energy shifts from Venus and her need to take others into account to Mars and Pluto whose deep, primal self-centered needs assert themselves and take precedence over social connections. In contrast to Libra, the Scorpio mind-set is private, emotional, mysterious, and intense.

We become aware of what is deep inside of us: the agricultural past in our psyches, the dread darkness approaching, the vegetation dying away and with it sustenance growing scarce. Death lurks in the shadows. Chthonic drives surface and unleash their power—that old black magic, down and down we go. And yet, seeing the Scorpion as the symbol of abiding evil is a cultural prejudice.

TOWARD THE END OF OCTOBER, THE DAYS SHRINK AND DARKEN. THE NIGHTS LENGTHEN. THE COLD CREEPS IN. THE TREES ARE BARE; THE LEAVES LIE IN FROSTED PILES.

The ancient Egyptians held the Scorpion in great reverence. They recognized a symbolic connection between the creepy crawlies dwelling beneath the earth and the Cycle of Life. Like the Beetle, a creature of the fertile sludge surrounding the Nile, the Scorpion signified initiation into sacred mysteries of the Afterlife.

Death, the breakdown of matter, leads to regeneration, fertility. The "clean" sand of the Egyptian desert was virtually devoid of life. Out of the black earth—dark, heavy, and moist mire—came the golden grain. The

Egyptians called the muck *al kimia:* black earth. Alchemy is the magic of turning dark to light, base material into gold. Pluto, co-ruler of Scorpio, is the God of Wealth and Power.

A dip into the dark side brings awareness that decay is the rich stuff of life. In our well-lit, transparent, antiseptic modern world, we don't get our hands dirty nearly enough. If life gives you piles of leaves, make compost!

The Scorpio phase is about what's going on in our guts, exploring our primal feelings and instincts and areas. Even in the best of us, there's venom, cold-heartedness, cunning, and deceit. Real communication on a soul level means breaking barriers and taboos, getting under the rock, into those dark, moist, hidden, really private places where the Scorpion thrives. In the trip to the Underworld, the line between Sacred and Sacrilegious disappears. The shameful, decadent, and socially unacceptable become noble and honest. We take personal responsibility for our dark side.

Turn, turn, turn. With Sagittarius, ruled by Jupiter, the autumn harvest comes to the final stage of plenitude. The puritanical adage "waste not, want not" does not apply when the Horn of Plenty pours forth its most sustainable abundance: the fruits of the mind

FALL

LIBRA

Butternut Squash Soup with Roasted Pepitas, page 138

Opposite: Waldorf Salad, page 144

Above: Broccoli Rabe, Sausage, and White Beans with Penne, page 150

Left: Scallops and Israeli Couscous, page 162

Above: Apple-Stuffed
Pork Tenderloin,
page 168

Right: Apple Crumble,
page 180

SCORPIO

Opposite: Roasted Acorn Squash with Mushrooms and Hazelnuts, page 140

Above: Linguine with Cauliflower Two Ways, page 152

Left: Falafel with Sesame Sauce, page 158

Opposite: Fried Oyster Po' Boys with Cajun Slaw, page 164

Above: Chocolate Chip Cookies, page 182

SAGITTARIUS

Rösti with Smoked Salmon and Scallion Crème Fraîche, page 142

Right: Persimmon Pomegranate Salad, page 148

Below: Manchego-Stuffed Peppers with Salbitxada, page 160

Opposite: Pan-Seared Halibut Tacos and Roasted Tomato–Poblano Salsa, page 166

Above: Turkey Saltimbocca, page 172

Right: Plum Upside-Down Cake, page 184

and of spirit ripen and, with festive flourish, amplify our enjoyment of the pleasures of the body. Jupiter's jovial appetite eats its fill, the Jovial mind-set is wealthy, the Jovial heart is warm and generous, and the Jovial spirit, eyes all aglow, sees nothing wrong with wanting it all and having it.

Jupiter is associated with good luck and good fortune. This makes Sagittarius a time of great expectations. Its symbol, the Centaur, shoots his arrows heavenward to the stars. Globetrotter, he represents humanity's highest aspirations: universal benevolence, reason, optimism, enthusiasm, guilelessness, and capaciousness. Our minds come out of our primal needs; our visions broaden. Under the rule of extravagant Jupiter, the King of the Mountain, we can see the Big Picture.

Fire sign Sagittarius corresponds with the liturgical season of preparation for the return of the sun at the Winter Solstice—Advent, the luckiest time of the year. The word *advent* means "coming" and carries with it the urge for going. Animals are on the move. It is time for winter migration. The underlying animal in us strives for a higher, more inclusive identity. The Centaur is an adventurer. He loves the wide-open spaces, the pleasure of cranking the horsepower and going far afield, off the beaten path, to seek things that are unusual and challenging. Away from the tribe, beyond those personal spheres of cultural, religious, ethnic, or geographical connections, the rough-and-ready galloping gourmet samples different ways of thinking, of being, of eating, and uses reasoning and abstraction to formulate Universal Principles that supersede blood-relatedness.

There's a light up ahead. The Centaur looks toward the New Year. He makes plans for the future. With the lights, bells, and decorations and the holiday cheer snowballing with every passing day, this is an easy time to let go of grudges and resentments. Think big! Jupiter does not abide boundaries or borders. At the same time, his *live and let live* attitude would not make restrictions or limitations on the freedom of others. Possessiveness and jealousy are confining, a waste of emotional energy. Life is too short for pettiness.

In the last days of Sagittarius, the fall comes to its close. It is a bright time, a time of hope, a time of peace and excited expectation that the Light will rise from its decline. Death will fade, as the Light of the World, the sun, is born on the Winter Solstice.

BUTTERNUT SQUASH SOUP WITH ROASTED PEPITAS

LIBRA

While summer squash are tender and bruise easily, squash that arrive in the fall are sturdy and tough. On Libra's scale, measured by volume, the autumn varieties outweigh their summer relatives. But cooking reveals their essentially balanced, light, moist, soft, sweet squash nature.

In the autumn wind, leaves fall and seeds are cast about. The life force of the dying plant is gathered in the seed. The seed is the source of life for the coming year. In a real sense, the seed is immortal. Until germination, it is a closed unit that contains the plant's full potential, which it will realize with a sprout when the conditions are appropriate. This soup welcomes the autumn with a scatter of pumpkin seeds, tokens of good luck and prosperity.

The beautiful golden color of the soup will appeal to the Libra's refined aesthetic and need to consume food that is as lovely to behold as it is delicious.

SERVES 6 TO 8

FOR THE SOUP

3 tablespoons unsalted butter

1 garlic clove, peeled and minced

2 tablespoons peeled, grated ginger

1 medium onion, peeled and chopped

1 medium carrot, peeled and thinly sliced in rounds

1 rib celery, thinly sliced

1 butternut squash (2 to 3 pounds), peeled, seeded, and cut into small chunks

½ teaspoon salt

½ teaspoon freshly ground black pepper

½ teaspoon nutmeg

6 cups chicken or vegetable stock

FOR THE PUMPKIN SEEDS

1 teaspoon honey

1 teaspoon olive oil

½ teaspoon onion or celery salt

⅛ teaspoon cayenne pepper

1 cup raw pumpkin seeds, shelled

Preheat the oven to 325°F.

Make the soup. In a large stock pot, melt the butter over medium-high heat. Add the garlic, ginger, onion, carrot, and celery, and sauté until thoroughly softened, about 10 minutes.

Add the squash, season with the salt, pepper, and nutmeg, and stir. Sauté the squash until it begins to soften, about 5 minutes.

Add the stock, and raise the heat to high. Bring the soup to a boil, lower the heat to simmer, cover, and cook until all ingredients are fully tender, about 20 minutes.

Meanwhile, make the pepitas. Stir together the honey, olive oil, seasoned salt, and cayenne in a medium bowl. Add the pumpkin seeds, and toss to coat evenly.

Line a rimmed baking sheet with parchment paper, and spread the pumpkin seeds on it in a single layer. Roast, shaking frequently, until they are lightly browned and aromatic, about 12 minutes.

Once the soup is ready, remove it from the heat. Use an immersion blender to puree, or blend in smaller batches in a food processor, and return to the pot. Keep the soup warm over a low flame until ready to serve.

Ladle the soup into serving bowls, and garnish each with a generous scattering of seeds.

ROASTED ACORN SQUASH WITH MUSHROOMS AND HAZELNUTS
SCORPIO

Although less celebrated today, the moon has lost none of her power. The great oceans are at her command. Physically, we are mostly water. Tugged by the moon, our emotional tides ebb and flow. Full moons are times of fruition and realization. The waxing crescent prior to it (when the rounded edge is to the right) is the time to focus on hopes and wishes and go forth. The waning crescent (when the rounded edge is to the left) is a time for retreat and self-reflection. Opposites can attract. Here is a Scorpio-Libra affair, a mating of mushrooms, with their caps, graceful stems, woodsy must, and explosive way of popping up overnight with the pure, sweet, sensible acorn squash. The wholesome and modest vegetable, spiked and reddened with cayenne and cinnamon, cut into half-moon-shaped slices, served in opposing crescents, signifies the bounty to come and the richness we glean within us. In the fall, many unusual wild mushrooms such as oysters, morels, and enokis find their way to the market. Try something new.

SERVES 4 TO 6

½ cup olive oil, divided

¼ teaspoon cayenne pepper, or more to taste

¼ teaspoon cinnamon

¼ teaspoon nutmeg

1 teaspoon salt, divided

1 cup washed and dried, well-packed fresh sage leaves

1 medium acorn squash (about 2 pounds), peeled, seeded, and sliced lengthwise into 8 to 12 wedges

1 cup finely chopped onion

2 cups thinly sliced mushrooms

1 tablespoon thyme

1 cup coarsely chopped toasted hazelnuts (page 199, Roasting Seeds and Nuts)

Preheat the oven to 400°F.

Combine ¼ cup of the olive oil, the cayenne, cinnamon, nutmeg, ½ teaspoon of the salt, and the sage on a rimmed baking sheet just large enough to accommodate the squash. Roll the squash wedges in this mixture, coating them evenly. Distribute the sage leaves over, under, and around the squash pieces, making sure to coat them with oil as well. Arrange the squash crescents so they all lie flat on the baking sheet, and place them in the oven.

Roast until the squash is thoroughly soft, the bottoms have browned, and the sage leaves are crispy, about 25 minutes.

Meanwhile, warm the remaining ¼ cup olive oil for about 1 minute or so in a skillet set over medium-high heat. Add the onion, and sauté until soft, about 5 minutes. Add the mushrooms, and continue sautéing until they sweat and wilt. Add the thyme and the remaining ½ teaspoon salt to the pan, and stir. Add the hazelnuts, toss thoroughly, and using a large spoon to hold back the veggies, strain off any excess liquid.

To serve, arrange two squash crescents on each plate, caramelized-side up, facing one another (waxing and waning). Spoon equal portions of mushrooms between them, and serve.

HARVEST, HUNTER'S, AND YULE MOONS

With the arrival of the fall, the Night Force rises. Until not so long ago, illumination from the moon was vital. Being out of doors after dark is in our psyches. Libra is the time for gathering. The Harvest Moon, big orange pumpkin, lights the fields. Scorpio is the time for hunting. The Hunter's Moon, blood-red eye, lights the bare woods, facilitating tracking. Sagittarius is the time for wonder. The Yule Moon, opposite to the low sun, has its highest arc. Its brilliance lights a midnight meditation: all is calm, all is bright, silent night on the glistening, fresh-fallen snow.

RÖSTI WITH SMOKED SALMON AND SCALLION CRÈME FRAÎCHE

SAGITTARIUS

Salmon is a fish at home in both fresh and salt water. It is hatched in a river and spends its early life there. When it is large enough to take care of itself, it gets the urge for going. Downstream with the flow, it goes to live in the open ocean. When it is fully matured, having seen the wide world, as if drawn by an inner magnet, it returns to the river of its birth, swimming upstream to spawn.

The word *salmon* is derived from the Latin verb *salire*—"to leap." Most species of salmon migrate during the late fall. The Centaur takes the world in leaps and bounds. Going against the flow, the mating salmon has challenges. With Jovian confidence and determination, the salmon does not take "no" for an answer. It battles oncoming rapids, attacks obstacles, is battered and bruised against rocks, leaps up over waterfalls, trying and trying again, until it succeeds and arrives at its destination.

The potato pancake has many different personas. This recipe follows the eggless Swiss tradition, the *rösti*. For the classic *latke,* add the optional beaten egg. The best potato pancake is thin, crisp, and crunchy on the outside and soft and moist but not oily on the inside. The tricks for success are wringing as much water out of the potatoes

as you can before cooking and controlling the temperature of the oil (i.e., keeping it good and hot) when you fry them. A neutral oil with a high smoke point, such as light olive oil, will yield the most dependable results.

SERVES 4

FOR THE CRÈME FRAÎCHE

1 cup crème fraîche
¼ cup minced scallions, whites only
1 tablespoon finely chopped dill
2 tablespoons capers, drained
½ teaspoon freshly ground black pepper

FOR THE PANCAKES

1½ pounds Yukon gold or russet potatoes, peeled
1 small yellow onion, peeled
1 teaspoon salt
½ teaspoon freshly ground black pepper
1 egg, beaten (optional)
½ cup light olive oil, for frying
6 ounces sliced smoked salmon
Watercress leaves, for garnish
Lemon wedges

Make the crème fraîche. Stir together the crème fraîche, scallions, dill, capers, and black pepper in a small bowl. Set aside.

Make the pancakes. Shred the potatoes using the large holes of a box grater.

Shred the onion using the large holes of the box grater. Finely chop what doesn't shred. Mix the potatoes and onion in a bowl. Add the salt and pepper, toss, and let rest for 10 to 15 minutes. Using your hands, squeeze as much liquid as you can out of the potato-onion mix. Dry the bowl, return the potato mixture to it, and ring out the mixture a second time, this time wrapping it in a clean kitchen towel and wringing it dry. (If using the egg, dry the bowl, return the potato mixture to it, mix in the egg, and proceed.)

Divide the mixture into four equal portions, and create 4 round cakes that are 3 to 4 inches in diameter and about ¼ inch thick.

Add about ⅛-inch depth of the oil to a large skillet, and set on high heat. When the oil is sizzling hot, use a spatula to slide in the pancakes, one at a time, letting the oil come back to sizzling temperature before adding the next pancake. When they are all in, lower the heat to medium-high. Do not let the oil burn.

Fry the cakes until they are crisp and golden on the underside, about 8 minutes. Flip them, and cook for about 8 minutes more. Drain on paper towels.

To serve, top each pancake with some of the smoked salmon and a generous spoonful of crème fraîche. Garnish with watercress leaves and a lemon wedge.

WALDORF SALAD

LIBRA

In Roman and Greek mythology, the apple is sacred to Venus and Aphrodite. Given to her by Dionysus, the God of Wine, the apple was an homage to her beauty. Later, the apple would become the symbol of the Fall—of man's eviction from paradise. The original Waldorf salad was invented in the 1890s by the maître d'hôtel at New York City's Waldorf Hotel. Originally, it consisted of apples and celery tossed in mayo, served over lettuce. Soon walnuts found their way into the mix. Over the years, there have been variations, but the core ingredients have remained. The Waldorf salad's longevity is a testimony to the remarkable interplay of its delicious mix of textures and flavors—cool and creamy, tart and crunchy. Chilled and crisp as a golden October day, this variation keeps the crunch of the original and balances it with the juicy sweetness of grapes. Using several different varieties of apple makes the dish interesting. Try one Honeycrisp and one Macoun, then, for a tart taste, Granny Smith or, for more sweetness, go with Red Delicious. Mâche is a specialty green, available at specialty grocers. In contrast to the snap of the other ingredients, this delicate lettuce, with its loose floral shapes of thin, velvety, tender leaves, adds succulence.

¼ cup mayonnaise

2 tablespoons plain yogurt

1 tablespoon honey

1 tablespoon lemon juice

¼ teaspoon nutmeg

3 apples, cored and cut into 1-inch pieces

3 stalks of celery, trimmed and sliced into ½-inch pieces

¾ cup halved red or green seedless grapes

¼ cup raisins

¾ cup lightly toasted walnuts (page 199, Roasting Seeds and Nuts)

4 cups loosely packed mâche

 To make this salad a meal, try adding diced, roasted chicken or turkey.

SERVES 4

Whisk together the mayonnaise, yogurt, honey, lemon juice, and nutmeg in a small bowl.

Combine the apple, celery, grapes, raisins, and toasted walnuts in a large bowl. Add the dressing, and toss to coat. At this point, the salad can be refrigerated until ready to serve, up to overnight.

To serve, divide the mâche among four plates, and top with some of the Waldorf salad.

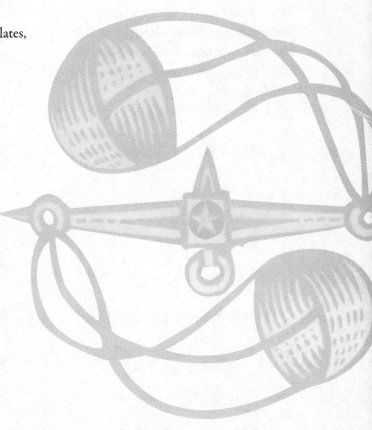

ROASTED GOLDEN BEETS AND WALNUTS
SCORPIO

In the Cycle of Life, Scorpio is the natural alchemist, turning base matter into gold. From the dark soil come rays of sunshine in the form of golden beets. Baby golden beets are best. If you can find them, you will need about 2 pounds, tops off. Red beets will suffice, but they will bleed and give a gory twist—the dark side of Scorpio—to the otherwise sunny and bright look of the Underworld in this dish. Ideally, you will make your veggie bed with beet sprouts, but realistically, any variety or combination will do.

SERVES 6

FOR THE BEETS

6 medium golden beets, washed and
    trimmed
2 tablespoons olive oil
¼ cup white wine
½ cup chicken stock
2 tablespoons lemon juice
1 tablespoon dried thyme
¼ teaspoon salt
1 cup walnuts, toasted and chopped
    (page 199, Roasting Seeds and Nuts)

FOR THE DRESSING

2 tablespoons mayonnaise
2 teaspoons Dijon mustard
¼ cup Lemon–Olive Oil Dressing (page 51)
½ tablespoon thyme
¼ teaspoon salt

FOR THE "BED"

2 cups beet sprouts or microgreens, or a mix
    of your choice
½ cup grated carrot
½ cup minced scallion, whites and pale
    greens only
1 to 2 endive heads with leaves separated

Preheat the oven to 400°F.

Prepare the beets. Quarter the beets lengthwise, and slice the quarters into ¼-inch-thick, wedge-shaped pieces. (If using baby beets, trim the ends and cut them in half across their width.)

Whisk together the olive oil, wine, stock, lemon juice, thyme, and salt in a large mixing bowl. Add the beets, and toss to coat.

Spread the beets evenly on a rimmed baking sheet, and roast until they brown and soften, about 40 minutes. Turn them halfway through their cooking time. Add a few tablespoons of stock, as necessary, if the liquid evaporates. (Baby beets will roast in 20 minutes, as they are more tender.)

Transfer the roasted beets to a mixing bowl. Add the walnuts, and toss to mix. Chill in the refrigerator for about 15 minutes.

Meanwhile, make the dressing. In a small bowl, whisk together the mayonnaise, mustard, lemon–olive oil dressing, thyme, and salt until emulsified.

Put the beet sprouts or microgreens into a mixing bowl. Add the carrot and scallion, and using two forks, toss to gently combine all the ingredients. Work in some dressing, a little at a time, until you have a fluffy mix. Reserve some of the dressing for the beets.

Add some of the dressing to the beets and walnuts, and toss to coat evenly.

To serve, fill the endive leaves with the beets. Divide the endives and beets onto separate plates, nestle some of the salad mix on the side, and serve.

PERSIMMON POMEGRANATE SALAD
SAGITTARIUS

Persimmons ripen when the leaves have fallen from the trees. They appear briefly in markets around Thanksgiving time. With their sweet taste and sensual fleshy texture, they are Jupiter's fruit. Japanese folklore has it that the persimmon seeds, which may be shaped like a fork, a knife, or a spoon, have foresight about the upcoming winter. The spoon is the shovel of a snowy winter; the knife means cutting winds and ice; the fork means a mild winter.

Fuyu and Hachiya persimmons are the ones most commonly found in the United States. Virtually seedless, the Fuyu is yellowish orange and has a flat bottom. It has a crisp texture and a moderately sweet taste. You can crunch into it, skin-on, as you would an apple. The Hachiya comes to a point at the bottom and is almost heart-shaped. It can be eaten only when it is fully ripe, and the flesh has a super-soft, almost custard or jelly-like texture. The skin is astringent and cannot be eaten. In this dish, where sliced persimmons are the order of the day, it is best to use the Fuyu variety.

This is a salad to close a late autumn meal. Sweet and savory, it will serve nicely alongside a festively roasted bird at a holiday meal.

SERVES 6

FOR THE DRESSING
2 tablespoons maple syrup
2 tablespoons pomegranate molasses or red wine vinegar
6 tablespoons olive oil
1 tablespoon minced shallot
½ teaspoon salt
½ teaspoon freshly ground black pepper

FOR THE SALAD
1 head Boston lettuce, washed, dried, and torn into bite-size pieces
3 Fuyu persimmons, sliced
1 cup pecans, chopped
½ cup pomegranate seeds
6 ounces mascarpone, Saint André, or other soft, creamy cheese

Make the dressing. Whisk together the maple syrup, pomegranate molasses, olive oil, shallot, salt, and pepper in a bowl until emulsified.

Make the salad. Place the lettuce in a large bowl, and add a few tablespoons of the dressing. Toss to coat evenly. Divide the dressed greens among six plates. Top each with the persimmon slices. Sprinkle with the pecans, pomegranate seeds, and a drizzle of dressing. Add a small dollop of creamy cheese in the center, and serve.

BROCCOLI RABE, SAUSAGE, AND WHITE BEANS WITH PENNE

LIBRA

Broccoli rabe, a cool-weather vegetable, smacks of the autumn air. Sometimes known as rapini, relative of broccoli and a descendant of mustard greens and horseradish, it has a bitter, sharp, complex green flavor. Some cooks recommend blanching it before sautéing it. This makes it milder. But why lessen such a distinctive flavor? Better to give it some Libra equilibrium. The meaty sweetness of the sausage and the smooth earthy silkiness of the cannellinis balance the broccoli rabe's brisk, zesty character.

**SERVES 4 AS A MAIN,
6 AS A STARTER**

¼ cup plus 2 tablespoons olive oil, divided

2 sweet Italian pork sausages, casing removed

½ teaspoon crushed red pepper flakes

2 garlic cloves, minced

1 bunch broccoli rabe, washed, trimmed, and chopped into ¼-inch pieces

¼ cup chicken stock

2 cups cooked cannellini beans (if canned, well-rinsed)

1 pound penne rigate

Grated Parmesan, for the table

Heat 2 tablespoons of the olive oil in a saucepot over medium-high heat. Add the sausage, and cook, breaking up the sausage with a wooden spoon until the meat is browned, about 8 minutes. Set aside.

In a large pasta pot, heat the remaining ¼ cup olive oil over medium-high heat. When the oil is hot, add the crushed pepper flakes and garlic. Once the pepper flakes start sizzling and the garlic gives off a nutty aroma, raise the heat to high, and add in the broccoli rabe. Sauté for 1 to 2 minutes to wilt.

Transfer the broccoli rabe to the pot with the sausage, and return this pot to medium-high heat. Set aside the pasta pot.

Add the chicken stock to the broccoli rabe–sausage mixture, and bring to a simmer, scraping up any bits of meat stuck to the bottom of the pan. Add the beans, and stir. Reduce the heat to low, cover, and cook until the thickest pieces of the broccoli rabe stems are tender, about 5 minutes. Remove from the heat.

Bring 6 quarts of salted water to a rapid boil in the pasta pot (no need to clean any leftover broccoli rabe juices first). Cook the penne just short of al dente, 8 to 9 minutes. Drain, reserving 1 to 2 cups of the cooking water. Return the pasta to the pot, and add the broccoli rabe mixture. Simmer over medium heat, adding some of the reserved cooking water if necessary, until the pasta is cooked to your liking.

To serve, divide among individual bowls, and top with grated Parmesan.

LINGUINE WITH CAULIFLOWER TWO WAYS
SCORPIO

Cauliflower is broccoli's next of kin. While broccoli sprouts its green head toward the sun, cauliflower forms a compact flower head surrounded by thick green leaves, which keep out the sunlight, so the flower never develops chlorophyll and remains white. Thus, even though it grows above ground, it has the chthonian spirit of Scorpio. Use the better-formed florets for roasting, the irregular ones and loose bits for creaming.

SERVES 4 AS A MAIN,
6 AS A STARTER

1 large head cauliflower (about 1½ pounds)
6 tablespoons olive oil, divided
1 teaspoon salt, divided, or more to taste
½ teaspoon crushed red pepper flakes, or
    more to taste
1 pound linguine
Grated Parmesan, for the table (optional)

You can serve cauliflower prepared without the pasta as a vegetable side dish.

Preheat the oven to 375°F.

Trim away and discard the cauliflower's leaves and lower stem. Cut the head into florets. Cut down larger florets to ¾-inch diameter.

Toss half of the florets in a bowl with 3 tablespoons of the olive oil and ½ teaspoon of the salt. Spread in one layer on a shallow baking sheet, and roast, shaking the pan occasionally, until tender and cooked through, and brown and crisp on all surfaces, about 45 minutes.

Meanwhile, combine the remaining cauliflower with about ½ cup water in a saucepot, and bring to a boil over high heat. As soon as the water boils, add the remaining ½ teaspoon salt, lower the heat to a simmer, and cook, covered, until thoroughly soft, about 20 minutes. Transfer the cauliflower and the cooking water to a food processor and blend until smooth, or transfer to a mixing bowl and puree with an immersion blender.

Heat the remaining 3 tablespoons olive oil in a medium saucepot. Add the crushed red pepper. When the pepper flakes give off a pungent aroma, but before they burn, carefully pour in the creamed cauliflower. It will spit and sputter. Cover, reduce the heat to low, and simmer for 10 minutes.

Bring 6 quarts of salted water to a rapid boil. Add the linguine. Cook just short of al dente. Reserve 1 to 2 cups of the cooking water. Drain the pasta, and return it to the pot over medium heat. Stir in the creamed cauliflower a little at a time, tossing until the sauce is absorbed and the pasta is cooked to your liking. Depending on your taste, you may need the reserved water, or you may have leftover creamed cauliflower.

To serve, divide the cauliflower linguine among individual bowls, making a nest in each mound of pasta. Fill each nest with some of the roasted florets, and serve with grated Parmesan on the table, if desired.

LINGUINE FINE WITH BROCCOLI AND ANCHOVIES

SAGITTARIUS

The anchovy, like chthonic Scorpio, is—well, let's say—controversial. Oily, fishy, fuzzy, and salty, it's more naughty than nice: that's true. But here Jupiter, Sagittarius's ruler, gets the better of Pluto, Scorpio's ruler. Benevolent broccoli, with its big green friendly head, is a Jovian vegetable. The anchovy marries well with the amiable broccoli, adding a little zip to the jolly green giant. The sweet, mild, cool ricotta cheese blesses their union.

SERVES 4 AS A MAIN, 6 AS A STARTER

2 cups chicken stock

3 cups well-trimmed broccoli florets (about ½ inch in diameter)

4 tablespoons olive oil

1 2-ounce tin oil-packed anchovies

3 garlic cloves, minced

¼ teaspoon crushed red pepper flakes

½ cup Summer Tomato Sauce (page 107)

1 pound thin linguine

4 ounces fresh ricotta

Bring the stock to a boil in a medium pot over high heat. Add the broccoli florets, and boil until just tender, 2 to 3 minutes. Strain the broccoli, reserving the stock to add to the pasta water.

Heat the olive oil, anchovies and their packing oil, garlic, and red pepper flakes in a large saucepot over medium-high heat, and stir. When the anchovies begin to disintegrate and the garlic gives off a nutty aroma and is turning golden, add the broccoli florets. Sauté briefly. Add the tomato sauce, and taste for seasoning, adding some salt if you wish. Remember, the anchovies are salty.

For al dente broccoli, remove from the heat. If you prefer it softer, continue to cook, covered, over low heat, until it is done to your liking.

Bring 6 quarts of lightly salted water plus the reserved chicken stock to a rapid boil. Add the linguine, and cook until just short of al dente. Drain the linguine, reserving 1 to 2 cups of the cooking water. Return the linguine back to its pot, add the broccoli tomato sauce, and cook over medium heat. Toss the pasta and sauce to combine, adding the reserved cooking water as necessary to finish cooking the pasta to your liking.

Divide among serving plates. Top with a generous tablespoon or two of ricotta, and serve.

BUTTERNUT SQUASH LASAGNA
LIBRA

Libra is the sign of balance and all things being equal. But Venus prefers comfort over its opposite. There are layers of reasoning that go into making up one's mind. Some things are, but at the same time they are not. Since this vegetarian entrée uses slices of squash instead of noodles, it is technically not lasagna. On the other hand, the squash holds its shape in the layering, much like lasagna noodles. Up in the air, Venus comes back to earth for comfort food. Sweet, soft, and creamy, this casserole melts in your mouth. You may substitute Swiss or Jarlsberg for the Gruyère. Or use a little of each if you can't make up your mind. Serve with lightly dressed bitter greens on the side.

SERVES 8

2 tablespoons butter

4 tablespoons olive oil, divided

3 garlic cloves, minced

6 scallions, chopped

1 cup thinly sliced mushrooms

2 cups chopped chard

½ teaspoon salt, plus more as needed

4 ounces Gruyère, coarsely grated

4 ounces pepper Jack cheese, coarsely grated

1 cup ricotta

3 eggs, beaten

⅛ teaspoon cayenne pepper

½ teaspoon ground nutmeg

1 butternut squash, peeled, halved lengthwise, seeds discarded, and cut into ¼-inch-thick slices

½ cup shelled sunflower seeds

Preheat the oven to 400°F.

Heat the butter and 1 tablespoon of the olive oil in a large skillet set over medium-high heat. When the butter melts, add the garlic and scallions. Sauté for 1 to 2 minutes. Add the mushrooms. Sauté until wilted, 3 to 5 minutes. Transfer the mushroom-scallion mixture to a bowl, and set aside.

Add another 1 tablespoon olive oil to the skillet. When the oil is hot, add the chard, and season with the ½ teaspoon of salt. Sauté until soft, about 3 minutes.

Transfer the chard to the bowl of a food processor. Pulse until roughly chopped. Add the mushroom-scallion mixture, the Gruyère, Jack, and ricotta cheeses, eggs, cayenne, and nutmeg. Pulse a few times to a coarse chop.

Combine the squash, the remaining 2 tablespoons olive oil, and a dash of salt, and toss to coat.

Layer a 9 × 13-inch baking dish with half the squash slices, overlapping as necessary. Top with half the cheese-vegetable mixture, another layer of squash, then the remaining cheese-vegetable mix. Finish with a scattering of sunflower seeds.

Cover the baking dish tightly with aluminum foil, and bake until cooked through, about 1 hour. (A sharp, pointed knife should pierce the center with no resistance.)

Best not to serve this steaming hot. Let settle for 30 minutes or so to firm up, before cutting into portions.

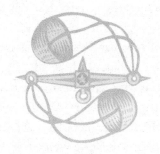

FALAFEL WITH SESAME SAUCE
SCORPIO

Scorpio is the sign of death and regeneration, metamorphosis and transformation. The Phoenix, symbol of transcendence and transformation, is associated with Scorpio. Unlike the sneaky arachnid that kills with poison, the majestic Phoenix soars like an eagle. His predation impresses and inspires. At regular intervals, he makes a funeral pyre of his own nest and goes up in flames. Then, starting as a worm in the marrow of a charred bone, he rises from the ashes and soars again.

Spiritually, we are like chickpeas. Humble beans, we must be "soaked," "seasoned," and "cooked" to be transformed into full-fledged human beings.

Since there is no egg or other binding substance, except for the chickpea's affinity for itself, in these little croquettes, they can be difficult to shape and can fall apart in the frying. To combat these tendencies, a little couscous or bulgur wheat, added to the mix, will absorb excess moisture and make for better shape and texture. Another trick to help them stick together is to make the sesame sauce first and leave ¼ cup or so in the food processor to mix with the chickpeas. The sauce's viscosity not only helps bind the falafel, but having some of the sauce on the inside adds to their flavor.

SERVES 4 TO 6

(MAKES 18 TO 20 FALAFEL BALLS)

2 cups dried chickpeas, soaked in water for about 12 hours and drained
¼ cup Sesame Sauce (facing page)
1 large garlic clove, minced
1 medium onion, chopped
½ cup chopped parsley
¼ cup uncooked couscous or bulgur wheat
1 tablespoon ground coriander
1 tablespoon ground cumin
⅛ teaspoon cayenne pepper
1 teaspoon onion salt
1 teaspoon freshly ground black pepper
2 teaspoons baking powder
4 cups vegetable oil, for frying

ACCOMPANIMENTS

4 to 6 cups arugula or other greens
1 bunch radishes, trimmed and sliced
1 to 2 red onions, sliced in rings
2 to 3 tomatoes, sliced
1 to 2 cucumbers, sliced
1 dozen pitas

Combine the chickpeas and the sesame sauce in the bowl of a food processor, and pulse to a coarse paste. Transfer to a mixing bowl.

Combine the garlic, onion, parsley, couscous or bulgur wheat, coriander, cumin, cayenne, onion salt, black pepper, and baking powder in the bowl of the food processor (no need to

SESAME SAUCE

The sesame sauce will thicken as it sits. Adding a little more water than you think is necessary will compensate for this. The recipe will make almost 2 cups of sauce. Since you're going through the trouble, you may want to make extra. It will keep up to a week in the refrigerator and can be drizzled on vegetables or mixed with cooked, pureed chickpeas or favas and cumin to make hummus.

1 cup tahini

¼ cup olive oil

1 garlic clove, peeled

½ cup lemon juice

1 teaspoon celery salt

⅛ teaspoon cayenne pepper

2 tablespoons toasted pine nuts, for garnish

Combine the tahini, olive oil, garlic, lemon juice, celery salt, and cayenne in the bowl of a food processor, and pulse to blend. Slowly drizzle in a bit of water (or more lemon juice) until the sauce has a creamy, flowing consistency. Transfer to a pretty serving bowl, and garnish with the pine nuts.

clean it first), and pulse to a coarse paste. Add this to the chickpeas, and mix thoroughly.

Transfer the chickpea mixture back to the bowl of the food processor (do this in batches if it will not comfortably fit), and pulse to a gritty paste. Transfer back to the mixing bowl.

Using a ¼ cup measure, scoop out the mixture, and use your palms to form it into a ball, slightly flattened on the top and bottom. Set the falafel on a baking sheet, and refrigerate for about 2 hours.

Pour a ½ inch or so of vegetable oil into a fryer or deep skillet, and heat over medium-high to 375°F. If you don't have a thermometer, heat until the oil is shimmering and beginning to bubble, but not smoking.

A small bit of falafel batter added to the pan should sizzle immediately. Carefully add the falafel to the pan, a few at a time, taking care not to crowd the pan and cooking in batches if necessary. Turn them until they are a deep golden brown on all sides. Transfer to a paper towel–lined plate to drain.

Put the pitas in the oven for about 1 minute or so to heat them. Be careful not to toast them; you want them pliable. Put the warmed pitas in a basket or cloth-lined serving bowl.

Serve family style. Arrange the falafel on a platter. Set it out next to a platter of vegetables, the bowl of sesame sauce, and the basket of warm pitas.

MANCHEGO-STUFFED PEPPERS WITH SALBITXADA
SAGITTARIUS

The Sagittarius quest is to dream the impossible, achieve the unachievable, touch the untouchable. You might even call the Sagittarian personality . . . quixotic. Manchego, the cheese from La Mancha, is not nearly as quixotic as the man. It is a quite sensible and practical dairy product. Manchego, with its nutty, somewhat sharp and sweet flavor, brings the quest back to earth. It grates well, and you can use it as you would Parmesan. Like Parmigiano-Reggiano, it has Denominacion de Origen status, which means it is protected. By law, it must be made in the region of Castilla-La Mancha, central Spain, entirely from the milk of Manchega sheep. Salbitxada, a Catalan sauce, somewhat similar to Romesco, is a tangy rich combination of roasted red peppers, tomato, toasted almonds, garlic, and spicy chili.

SERVES 4

FOR THE PEPPERS
4 red bell peppers
3 tablespoons olive oil
2 cups cooked brown rice
2 cups cooked black beans (if canned, rinsed well and patted dry)
1 teaspoon ground cumin
1 teaspoon finely chopped jalapeño pepper
¼ cup finely chopped cilantro
2 tablespoons lime juice
½ teaspoon salt
½ teaspoon freshly ground black pepper
1½ cups grated Manchego cheese

FOR THE SAUCE
2 garlic cloves, minced
1 tablespoon minced jalapeño pepper
½ cup toasted almonds (page 199, Roasting Seeds and Nuts)
1 red bell pepper, roasted, peeled, and sliced (page 49, Roasted Bell Peppers)
3 plum tomatoes, peeled, seeded, and chopped
1 tablespoon smoked paprika
1 tablespoon sherry vinegar
½ teaspoon salt
¼ cup olive oil

Preheat the oven to 400°F.

Make the bell peppers. Cut the bell peppers in half lengthwise. Remove the seeds and ribs, but keep the stalks on. Rub them all over with 1 to 2 tablespoons of the olive oil.

Combine the remaining olive oil, the rice, beans, cumin, jalapeño, cilantro, lime juice, salt, black pepper, and 2 tablespoons of the Manchego in a large bowl, and stir to mix thoroughly. Divide this mixture evenly among the pepper halves.

Arrange the stuffed peppers in a baking dish, and bake them until the flesh is thoroughly soft, 35 to 40 minutes.

Meanwhile, combine all of the ingredients for the sauce in the bowl of a food processor. Pulse briefly to a coarse but spoonable sauce. This will yield about 2 cups, more than you will need. Extra sauce can be used to spice up any meat or vegetable.

When the peppers are cooked, use the remaining cheese to top each pepper, and return them to the oven until the cheese melts, 1 to 2 minutes.

Spoon a generous tablespoon of the sauce on each pepper, and serve.

SCALLOPS AND ISRAELI COUSCOUS

LIBRA

For this simple preparation, the scallops must be absolutely fresh. You may use sea scallops, but if you live near a bay, the dainty autumn wonders that are bay scallops—which are a quarter the size of their deep-sea cousins—become available during the fall months. For its symmetry, the scallop shell is associated with Venus, ruler of Libra. Its link to Beauty can be seen in Renaissance art, where the goddess is depicted cutting through the waves on a scallop shell.

SERVES 4 TO 6

FOR THE COUSCOUS

1½ cups chicken stock or vegetable juice

1 cup Israeli couscous

½ cup coarsely chopped toasted almonds
(page 199, Roasting Seeds and Nuts)

½ cup slivered dried apricots

½ cup Kalamata olives, pitted and halved

⅛ teaspoon cayenne pepper

½ teaspoon ground cinnamon

1 teaspoon lemon zest

2 tablespoons olive oil

½ teaspoon salt

½ teaspoon freshly ground black pepper

FOR THE SCALLOPS

2 pounds scallops

3 tablespoons olive oil, divided

1 teaspoon (salt-free) lemon pepper

¾ teaspoon seasoned salt (onion, garlic, or celery)

⅛ teaspoon cayenne pepper

Make the couscous. Bring the stock to a boil in a saucepot set over high heat. Add the rest of the ingredients for the couscous, and stir. Lower the heat to a simmer, and cover. After 4 or 5 minutes, stir. If all the liquid is absorbed, add a few tablespoons of water. Continue cooking until the liquid is absorbed and the couscous is al dente or just short of al dente. Remove it from the heat, and let it sit, covered, while you prepare the scallops. It will cook further in its own sweet and savory steam.

Make the scallops. Add the scallops to a mixing bowl. Add 1 scant tablespoon of the olive oil, the lemon pepper, seasoned salt, and cayenne, and toss gently to coat.

Heat 1 to 2 teaspoons of the olive oil in a large nonstick skillet until it is smoking hot. Carefully add a few of the scallops at a time, searing them in small batches. To keep the oil hot, do not overcrowd the pan.

Let the scallops sit without touching them for about 2 minutes. Do not stir the scallops, or they will give up liquid and poach instead of sear. After about 2 minutes, gently turn up the edge of one of the scallops. It should have a deep brown layer of caramelization. Gently flip the scallops, and sear for another 2 minutes or so until they are well-seared on both sides. Transfer to an oven sheet, allowing each scallop room to breathe. Repeat with the remaining oil and scallops until you have seared all the scallops.

Fluff the couscous with a fork, and put a generous scoop in the center of each serving plate. Surround with a circle of scallops.

FRIED OYSTER PO' BOYS WITH CAJUN SLAW
SCORPIO

If there were ever a city that had the mystery and sexy power of Scorpio in its soul, in its infectious music, and in its spicy cuisine, it is hot, humid, jazzy New Orleans. Come, take a walk on the wild side. Oysters have their reputation. Some of the most succulent ones, sweet and soft as Dixie, come from the Gulf Coast. Shucked and flown in fresh, they are available at specialty seafood counters.

MAKES 6 SANDWICHES

FOR THE SLAW

2 cups shredded cabbage

½ cup grated carrot

½ cup grated radish

½ cup minced red onion

1 tablespoon finely minced jalapeño pepper

¼ cup mayonnaise

1 tablespoon whole-grain mustard

1 tablespoon prepared horseradish

¼ cup minced dill pickle

1 garlic clove, minced

1 tablespoon capers

1 teaspoon hot sauce

1 tablespoon lemon juice

1 teaspoon sugar

½ teaspoon salt

½ teaspoon pepper

FOR THE SANDWICHES

2 pounds shucked oysters

1 cup buttermilk

3 eggs, beaten

¼ cup beer

½ teaspoon onion salt

½ teaspoon freshly ground black pepper

⅛ teaspoon cayenne pepper

1 cup all-purpose flour

½ cup cornmeal

Vegetable oil, for frying

6 ciabatta rolls

Make the slaw. Combine the cabbage, carrot, radish, onion, and jalapeño in a large mixing bowl, and toss to mix. In a second bowl, combine the mayonnaise, mustard, horseradish, pickle, garlic, capers, hot sauce, lemon juice, sugar, salt, and pepper, and whisk until smooth. Add the mayonnaise mixture to the cabbage mixture, and toss to coat evenly. Set aside.

Make the sandwiches. Place the oysters in a colander to drain off the packing liquid. Transfer them to a bowl, and add the buttermilk. Soak the oysters in the buttermilk while you prepare the batter.

In a large bowl, whisk together the eggs, beer, onion salt, black pepper, and cayenne. In a separate bowl, stir together the flour and cornmeal.

Remove the oysters from the buttermilk to a colander. Working in batches, dip the oysters in the egg mixture, then roll them in the flour and cornmeal. Place the battered oysters on a baking sheet or several plates.

Preheat the broiler.

Pour ½ inch of vegetable oil into a heavy pot or skillet. Heat to 360°F. (If you don't have a frying thermometer, drop a small cube of bread into the oil. It should start sizzling immediately. If not, the oil is not yet hot enough.)

Fry the oysters in batches until golden brown, turning them, about 2 minutes on each side. Drain on paper towels. Repeat until all the oysters are fried.

To assemble the sandwiches, slice the ciabatta rolls in half lengthwise. Pass them under the broiler to toast them lightly. Spread a thin layer of slaw on the inside of the bottom half of each roll. Cover it with a layer of oysters, and top with another thin layer of slaw. Put the top on the roll, and press down lightly. Serve with extra slaw on the side.

PAN-SEARED HALIBUT TACOS AND ROASTED TOMATO-POBLANO SALSA
SAGITTARIUS

Chilly late fall days can use some perking up. Fish tacos and salsa say "warm" and "sunshine." They suggest the country of their origin, Mexico, temporarily sating the Sagittarian hunger for travel. When it comes to halibut, wild-caught Alaskan is the most flavorful and tender.

The technique of dry-roasting the tomatoes, onions, garlic, and peppers is typical of Mexican cooking. It concentrates flavors. Use a heavy-duty skillet. A large cast-iron one works best. If you want to be authentic, roast each vegetable separately. But with a little vigilance, you can do them all at the same time, as recommended here.

SERVES 4

10 ounces grape tomatoes, halved
2 poblano peppers, halved and seeded
1 jalapeño pepper, halved
8 scallions, trimmed
4 garlic cloves, peeled
3 tablespoons olive oil, divided
2 tablespoons chopped cilantro, plus extra
    leaves for garnishing
2 tablespoons lime juice
2 tablespoons tequila
1 tablespoon tomato paste
½ teaspoon salt, divided
1 teaspoon freshly ground black pepper,
    divided
1 pound halibut fillet, cut in 4 pieces
⅛ teaspoon cayenne pepper
½ teaspoon cumin
2 tablespoons lemon juice
8 corn tortillas
Lime wedges

Make the salsa. Place a large, heavy-duty skillet over medium heat. When a drop of water sizzles on its surface, add the tomatoes, poblano peppers, and jalapeño, skin-sides down. Do not crowd the pan—keep the vegetables as far apart from each other as possible. If you have room and they will fit without overcrowding, add the scallions and garlic cloves. Dry-roast until the tomatoes start to wilt and the skin of the peppers puckers and can be removed with a little rubbing. Turn the scallions and garlic cloves until they are lightly browned on all sides. Depending on how hot the skillet, this can take anywhere from 10 to 20 minutes. Remove the vegetables from the skillet, and remove the peppers' skins.

Chop the tomatoes and the peppers, keeping or discarding the jalapeño seeds according to your tolerance for heat—the more seeds, the hotter the salsa will be. Mince the garlic and the scallions. Combine the roasted vegetables, 1 tablespoon of the olive oil, the cilantro, lime juice, tequila, tomato paste,

¼ teaspoon of the salt, and ½ teaspoon of the black pepper in a bowl, and stir to mix thoroughly. Let sit for 10 minutes or more while you prepare the fish.

Make the fish. Wipe the skillet clean, and place over high heat until searing hot. (A pearl of oil dropped on the surface will instantly smoke.) Rub each piece of fish lightly with the remaining 2 tablespoons olive oil, and season with the cayenne, cumin, and remaining ¼ teaspoon salt and ½ teaspoon pepper. Carefully add the fish to the pan, and sear until brown on the underside, about 3 minutes. Flip and brown the other side. Remove the fish from the skillet, flake apart, and sprinkle with the lemon juice.

Assemble the tacos. Lay two tortillas on each plate. Top each tortilla with halibut and a spoonful of the salsa. Garnish with cilantro leaves, and serve with lime wedges on the side.

APPLE-STUFFED PORK TENDERLOIN
LIBRA

In early October, the Romans celebrated a harvest feast in honor of Ceres, the Goddess of Agriculture, in particular grains (it is from Ceres we derive our word *cereal*). The Cerelia was a demonstration of gratitude for all she had done in the previous six months. A pig was sacrificed, and roasted pork with a cornucopia of autumn fruits and vegetables were on the menu. The apple is the symbol of autumn. With its light, well-balanced taste and texture, it is airy Libra incarnate. Different apples can give this dish a personality change. Fuji, Gala, and Granny Smith are good candidates. Try a mixture.

Most recipes call for pork to be cooked to 160°F, but that standard need only apply to ground pork and organ meats. For pork steaks, chops, and roasts—and for moist meat—the minimal food safety temperature is actually 145°F. You can take it out of the oven when an internal thermometer reads as much and cover the tenderloin with foil. The hot sauce, poured on the medallions, will ensure that they are cooked through.

SERVES 6 TO 8

2 tablespoons olive oil

2 cups ¼-inch dice peeled and cored apple, divided

2½ cups apple cider, divided

½ cup quick-cooking polenta

½ cup minced prunes

1 teaspoon salt, divided

½ teaspoon freshly ground black pepper

6 tablespoons apple butter, divided

1 cup grated sharp cheddar cheese

1 3-pound pork tenderloin, cut into two equal lengths

8 slices bacon, plus more as needed

2 tablespoons unsalted butter

1 garlic clove, minced

⅛ teaspoon cayenne pepper

2 tablespoons all-purpose flour

2 tablespoons Dijon mustard

Preheat the oven to 375°F.

Heat the olive oil in a medium saucepot set over medium-high heat. When the oil is hot but not smoking, add 1 cup of the apple to the pan, and sauté until softened, about 2 minutes. Add 1½ cups of the apple cider to the pan. Raise the heat to high, and bring to a boil. Slowly pour in the polenta, whisking as you do so. Add the prunes, ½ teaspoon of the salt, and the pepper, and stir. Fold in 2 tablespoons of the apple butter and the cheddar, then transfer the polenta mixture to a mixing bowl to cool.

With a long, thin knife or skewer, poke a hole all the way through the center of the long length of each pork loin half, starting at one end through to the other end. Then insert the handle of a wooden spoon or a honing steel into the hole, wiggling the utensil a bit, to widen the center hole to accommodate the polenta mixture.

Fill the center holes of the pork tenderloins with the polenta mixture, a little at a time, pushing and pressing it in with whatever tool you have, so that the whole channel is filled. Don't overfill. If you have extra stuffing, panfry it in a nonstick pan, and serve it on the side.

Lay the bacon strips horizontally in a row on a rimmed baking sheet. Set the stuffed tenderloin halves down on the bacon, perpendicular to the strips. Wrap 4 bacon strips around each of the tenderloin halves. Tuck the ends under. Use extra bacon if necessary to cover the tenderloins, and secure the strips with toothpicks.

Place the tenderloin halves in the oven, and roast until the internal temperature reaches 145°F, about 30 minutes. Remove the stuffed tenderloin halves from the oven. Ideally, the bacon will be a little crispy, but if not, that's okay. The purpose of the bacon is to flavor the tenderloin and keep it from drying out. You can remove the bacon before you slice the tenderloin, or keep it if you prefer. Remove the toothpicks securing the bacon to the tenderloin. Carefully pour off the excess fat, and cover the tenderloins with foil.

Make the sauce. Melt the butter in a saucepan over medium heat. Add the garlic, cayenne, the remaining 1 cup diced apple, and the flour to the pan, and stir. Sauté to soften the apple, about 2 minutes. Add the remaining 1 cup apple cider, stirring continuously to break up and dissolve any lumps of flour. Add the remaining 4 tablespoons apple butter and the remaining ½ teaspoon salt to the pan, and stir thoroughly. Simmer, uncovered, until the sauce thickens slightly, about 3 minutes. Fold in the mustard, and keep the sauce simmering over low heat until ready to slice the tenderloins.

Slice the pork tenderloins crosswise into oval medallions about 1 inch thick, and arrange on plates. Spoon on the sauce while it is hot, and serve.

POMEGRANATE CHICKEN
SCORPIO

Scorpio is associated with both sex and death, eros and thanatos, the two facets of mortality. Pomegranates, with their numerous seeds, have served as a symbol of fruitfulness and fertility dating back to antiquity. For the Greeks and the Romans, the pomegranate was also symbolic of the underworld. Greek mythology tells us that as Persephone was leaving the underworld, Hades tricked her into eating six pomegranate seeds, condemning her to return, as the fates had declared that anyone who consumed food or drink in Hades's realm was doomed to remain there. Persephone is often depicted holding a pomegranate. The myth of Persephone—her abduction by Hades; her mother's famine-causing grief; and her triumphant return each spring—is a metaphor for the cycle of growth, dormancy, and regrowth, which governs all things in the physical realm. Birth-death-regeneration is the way of Nature.

If you don't happen to live near a Middle Eastern market, pomegranate molasses is easily available online. Its marvelous tartness makes it an exotic substitute for lemon juice or vinegar. It can be used in a simple vinaigrette. A dash gives iced tea an unexpected jolt. You can drizzle it on vegetables or whisk a bit into dips and relishes.

SERVES 6

½ cup pomegranate molasses
3 tablespoons olive oil, divided
2 tablespoons honey
1 teaspoon ground cinnamon
1 teaspoon freshly ground black pepper
1 teaspoon salt
1 teaspoon ground turmeric
½ teaspoon allspice
½ teaspoon cumin
½ teaspoon grated nutmeg
⅛ teaspoon cayenne pepper
3 garlic cloves, minced
3 pounds boneless, skinless chicken thighs and/or breasts (thighs halved, breasts quartered)
2 tablespoons unsalted butter
4 cups yellow onions, thinly sliced
2 cups coarsely chopped roasted, salted pistachios
½ cup pomegranate seeds

Preheat the oven to 375°F.

In a small saucepot, combine the pomegranate molasses, 2 tablespoons of the olive oil, the honey, cinnamon, black pepper, salt, turmeric, allspice, cumin, nutmeg, cayenne, and half the minced garlic over low heat. Cook, stirring continuously until the honey melts, 1 to 2 minutes. Set aside to cool.

Combine the chicken with the pomegranate molasses mixture in a large bowl, and toss to coat. For more flavorful, tender chicken, cover the bowl with plastic wrap, and marinate overnight in the refrigerator.

Heat the butter and the remaining 1 table-spoon olive oil in a large, ovenproof skillet with a lid over medium-high heat. When the butter melts, add the remaining garlic

and the onion to the pan, and sauté until the onion is soft and beginning to brown, about 10 minutes. Add the pistachios, and stir. Gently nestle the marinated chicken pieces into the onion mix. Use a rubber spatula to scrape all of the spicy marinade out of the bowl and on top of the chicken.

Cover the pan, and bake until the chicken is cooked through, about 30 minutes.

Remove from the oven, fold in the pomegranate seeds, and serve with rice or couscous.

TURKEY SALTIMBOCCA
SAGITTARIUS

Saltimbocca is Italian for "jump into the mouth." This specialty from Rome is usually made with veal scallopine—very thinly sliced or pounded cutlets—but in keeping with the season, this version substitutes turkey breasts. More than a symbol, the turkey is the flesh of Thanksgiving feasts, the centerpiece of our gratefulness for food and family. In the United States, it is celebrated in early Sagittarius, the beginning of the holiday season. It is a time to be jovial and thankful and a time to talk turkey. The sage speaks plainly. Words of wisdom and prayers of gratitude jump *out* of his mouth! He says "grace" before meals.

SERVES 4 TO 6

½ cup white wine

1 cup chicken stock

1 teaspoon fresh thyme leaves

1 ounce dried porcini mushrooms, broken into small bits

1 teaspoon freshly ground black pepper, divided

8 turkey cutlets, pounded to ⅛ to ¼ inch thickness

8 slices prosciutto

24 fresh sage leaves

1 cup shaved Parmesan

3 tablespoons all-purpose flour, divided

½ cup olive oil

2 tablespoons butter

¼ teaspoon salt

To pound meat cutlets at home, lay the meat between two sheets of plastic wrap. If you don't have a meat mallet, a heavy-bottomed pan will do the trick.

Combine the wine, stock, thyme, and mushrooms in a saucepot, and bring to a boil over high heat. Immediately lower the heat to a simmer, and cover. Simmer for 10 minutes, then remove from the heat and set aside.

Sprinkle ½ teaspoon of the black pepper over the turkey cutlets. Cover each turkey cutlet with 1 slice of prosciutto. Scatter a few sage leaves and a few shavings of Parmesan over the prosciutto. Roll the turkey tightly into a cylinder, and insert toothpicks on long diagonals so only the tips show along the seams to secure. Three or four toothpicks per cutlet should make the seams secure. (Note how many toothpicks you use so that when you remove them you can be assured that you've removed them all.) Dust the rolls all over with 2 tablespoons of the flour.

Heat the olive oil over medium heat in a large skillet. When the oil is hot but not smoking, place the rolls seam-side down in the pan. Brown on all sides, about 8 minutes total. Transfer the rolls to a plate, and set aside in a warm spot.

Pour off any of the oil remaining in the skillet. Add the butter to the skillet, and melt it over medium heat. Add the remaining 1 tablespoon flour, whisking continuously with a fork to prevent lumps. Once the flour has turned golden, add the porcini-stock mixture, the remaining ½ teaspoon black pepper, and the salt. Bring the sauce to a simmer.

Place the rolls in the sauce, and simmer for about 5 minutes. This will help reduce the sauce and ensure that the poultry is fully cooked.

Serve immediately.

ROASTED BRUSSELS SPROUTS
LIBRA

Brussels sprouts are like little cabbages and are delicious when roasted. No frills and easy does it, this simple side can go into the oven with your poultry entrée or pork roast. Crisp and salty on the outside, mushy and sweet within, there is a marvelous balance of tastes—Venus/Libra equilibrium—using just three ingredients.

SERVES 6 TO 8

2 pounds Brussels sprouts, trimmed, discolored outer leaves discarded
¼ cup olive oil
1 tablespoon salt

Preheat the oven to 375°F.

Combine the sprouts, olive oil, and salt in a mixing bowl, and stir thoroughly. Transfer to a rimmed baking sheet, scraping all the oil and salt from the sides of the bowl with a soft rubber spatula.

Place in the oven, shaking every 10 minutes or so, until the sprouts are soft and a deep golden brown, 35 to 40 minutes. To test for doneness, press down on one of the larger sprouts. The skin should be crisp, and the sprout should squash easily.

CORNUCOPIA

The material prosperity and spiritual abundance of a successful harvest are symbolized by the cornucopia, which is Latin for *Horn of Plenty*. Its origin lies in Greek mythology. Before the age of Olympian gods, there were the twelve primeval Deities known as the Titans. Zeus, the Greek Jupiter, was the child of Rhea and Cronos, whom the Romans call Saturn. Father Time, he was the original Grim Reaper. Knowing her husband's obsessive jealousy and his fear of being replaced by his offspring, Rhea bore Zeus in secret and hid him on Earth with Amalthaea, a nymph who wet-nursed him in a she-goat's guise. As Zeus grew, so did his power to bestow blessings. When his nanny's horn broke off, he filled it with all the good things heaven and Earth had to offer. The Horn of Plenty is symbolic of everything one's heart could desire.

ROASTED ROSEMARY POTATOES
SCORPIO

The potato is a member of the *Solanaceae,* or nightshade, family. The Underworld cousin of the tomato and the eggplant, it has eyes but cannot see. Is its external Plutonian/Scorpio character balanced or masked by the bland white flesh inside? Similarly, these roasted potatoes come from the oven crisp and brown on the outside, downy soft and white within.

Soaking the peeled, cut potatoes in acidulated ice water helps bring out their inner fluff.

Using some seasoned salt (onion, garlic, or celery) adds a savory note.

Potatoes and rosemary have an affinity for one another. In Rome, rosemary was the herb of choice for the Romans' household gods. In the fall, large bunches of it were cut and brought into the house to bless it with its peaceful, protective fragrance.

The potatoes pair nicely with the Apple-Stuffed Pork Tenderloin (page 168) or any roasted poultry.

SERVES 8 TO 10

8 russet potatoes
¼ cup white wine vinegar
½ cup light olive oil
½ stick butter, softened
½ cup very finely chopped fresh rosemary leaves
1 teaspoon seasoned salt, plus extra for sprinkling
1 teaspoon freshly ground black pepper

Preheat the oven to 425°F.

Place each potato on a cutting board, and use a knife to take thin slices from all 6 sides, removing most of the skin and the round edges so that the potato is roughly rectangular and will lie flat on all sides. Use a peeler to remove any remaining skin. Cut each potato lengthwise into 3 flat pieces, then cut each piece in thirds. You will have 9 long, roughly rectangular fingers from each potato.

Fill a large bowl with ice and cold water. Add the vinegar. Soak the potatoes in the vinegar mixture for about 1 hour.

Drain the potatoes, and pat them dry with paper towels.

Dry the bowl, and return the potatoes to it. Add the oil, softened butter, rosemary, seasoned salt, and black pepper, and mix thoroughly.

Transfer to a rimmed baking sheet. If there is not enough room for all the strips to lie flat, use a second sheet.

Place the potatoes in the oven. Begin checking them after 15 minutes. As they begin to brown, flip them over. Continue baking them, flipping and rotating as necessary, until they are brown and crisp on all sides, like potato fries. This will take about 45 minutes to 1 hour.

Pour off any oil, drain on paper towels, and serve hot, sprinkled with additional seasoned salt.

PUMPKIN RISOTTO
SAGITTARIUS

No vegetable captures the imagination more than the humble pumpkin. In recent years, when fall comes, it appears as an ingredient in everything from coffee to muffins to pancakes to ale. Its bland flavor and unpretentious demeanor allow it entrance wherever it wants to go. It has a psychological power that far outreaches its taste appeal. Perhaps because it was the food of the poor, it links us to our agricultural past. Or perhaps as a potential jack-o'-lantern it has Scorpio charm, a little frightening yet a herald of sweet things to come. Trick or treat? To Scorpio, they may be one and the same.

But there is no good reason for the pumpkin to be relegated to All Hallows' Eve. Sagittarius sees the big picture. The Centaur knows it is more than that. Appearing in pies, soups, and sides, its season carries all through the November Thanksgiving celebration into the December Festival of Light.

Risotto is the typical dish of northern Italy. It refers to a method of cooking rice rather than a specific list of ingredients, which vary according to locality and season. Carnaroli rice is used in northern Italy. If you use another type of rice, you will have to adjust the amount of stock by ½ cup or so, more or less.

Pumpkin seed oil (*Kernöl* or *Kürbiskernöl* in German) is a specialty item, a European Union Protected Designation of Origin product that comes from Austria and Slovenia. You can get it online or at specialty gourmet and health-food shops. It has a strong nutty flavor and a full array of polyunsaturated fatty acids. Combined with cider vinegar and some olive oil, it makes a tasty salad dressing. A little bit goes a long way. A finishing drizzle gives this risotto a distinctive flavor.

SERVES 6 TO 8

4 cups chicken or vegetable stock
½ teaspoon salt
3 cups ¾-inch dice peeled pumpkin
2 tablespoons unsalted butter (plus 1 to
    2 tablespoons extra, optional)
2 tablespoons olive oil
1 cup minced onion
1½ cups carnaroli rice
½ cup white wine
1 cup grated Parmesan cheese
Freshly ground black pepper
1 teaspoon pumpkin seed oil

Bring the stock to a boil in a large saucepot over high heat. Add the salt and pumpkin. Lower the heat to simmer, and cook until the pumpkin is fully tender, 10 to 15 minutes. Using a skimmer or slotted spoon, transfer the pumpkin to a bowl. Cover the stock, and keep it warm over low heat.

In a separate pot set over medium-high heat, combine the butter and olive oil. When the butter melts, add the onion, and sauté until it has lost all its crunch, about 10 minutes. Add the rice, and raise the heat to high. Cook, stirring constantly, until the grains just start to toast and give off a nutty aroma, about 2 minutes.

Raise the heat on the stock to medium-high, bringing it to a gentle boil.

Add the wine to the rice, and let the alcohol evaporate. Lower the heat under the rice to medium-high, and start adding the simmering stock, ½ cup or so at a time. Stir continuously. When the rice absorbs the stock, add another ½ cup. Continue to add more stock as the rice absorbs it, and continue to stir.

After about 8 minutes, add half of the cooked pumpkin, letting the cubes melt into the rice.

Total cooking time is usually around 16 minutes, but this depends on the rice type and brand and how much stock it has absorbed. The best way to know when it is ready is to taste a grain. Properly cooked risotto is starchy (al dente) on the inside and creamy on the outside.

Add the grated Parmesan and, if you wish, more butter. Stir and cover. Let sit for 2 to 3 minutes to soften a bit more and absorb the cheese and butter.

Serve in bowls garnished with the remaining pumpkin, a few grinds of black pepper, and a healthy drizzle of the pumpkin seed oil.

APPLE CRUMBLE

LIBRA

While the apple has a reputation for providing good health, long life, and youthful appearance, the lore around it is also shaded by hints of scandal, risk, and dark magic. The Fall is the falling leaves and the Fall from grace. An innocent couple, tempted by a serpent, breaks a taboo, loses their innocence, and acquires the knowledge of good and evil through the eating of an "apple." Romans and Greeks associated the apple with Venus and Aphrodite, respectively. The forbidden fruit is the fruit of love, the fruit of knowledge, and the fruit of death. It is the fruit of the day that keeps the doctor away and the Evil Queen's poison apple that put Snow White to sleep until love's awakening kiss. If cut horizontally, the apple reveals the pentagram pattern, a symbol for the gateway to mystical powers. Merlin's gift of prophecy came from eating one of the Faerie Queen's apples. The Druids' *Day of the Apple* is on November 1, which corresponds to All Saints' Day in the Christian Liturgy.

Apples that can take the heat, such as Cortland, Empire, Fuji, Gala, Golden Delicious, Granny Smith, Honeycrisp, Honey Gold, and Winesap, will all work well in this recipe. Using several different types provides a range of tastes and textures. The addition of chopped cranberries and sunflower seeds to the topping lends it a granola-like twist. You may want to serve this dessert as part of an autumn Sunday brunch.

SERVES 6

3 pounds apples, peeled, cored, and cut into ¼-inch-thick slices
2 tablespoons lemon juice
1 cup sugar, divided
1 tablespoon grated ginger
2 teaspoons ground cinnamon, divided
¼ teaspoon salt
2 tablespoons cornstarch
¼ cup apple cider
1 stick unsalted butter, cut into 16 cubes
1 cup fresh cranberries
½ cup shelled sunflower seeds
1 cup rolled oats
1 cup all-purpose flour

Preheat the oven to 375°F.

Combine the apple slices and lemon juice in a large bowl, and toss. Add ½ cup of the sugar, the ginger, 1 teaspoon of the cinnamon, and the salt, and toss again. In a small bowl, whisk together the cornstarch and the apple cider until the cornstarch dissolves. Add the cornstarch slurry to the apples, and toss to coat.

Use a bit of one of the butter cubes to grease a 9 × 13-inch baking dish. Transfer the apples to the baking dish, using a soft rubber spatula to scrape the mixing bowl clean.

Combine the cranberries and the sunflower seeds in the bowl of a food processor, and pulse-chop a few times, breaking them down slightly. Add the rest of the butter, the oats, the remaining ½ cup sugar and 1 teaspoon cinnamon, and the flour to the cranberry mixture, and pulse-chop into coarse crumbs.

Sprinkle the crumbs on top of the apples. Use your fingers to break up any large pieces. Bake until the topping is browned and the apples are bubbling, about 50 minutes.

Allow to cool before serving. Serve warm or at room temperature with crème fraîche, whipped cream, or ice cream.

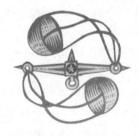

CHOCOLATE CHIP COOKIES
SCORPIO

In November, on dark nights with the wind piping its cold, mournful music through the bare trees, Scorpio energy is at its most intense. Perhaps Scorpio may be self-indulgent. Scorpio loves secrets and getting lost in sensations. Pluto's child will willfully precipitate a breakup or a crisis, or fall into a fast and furious love affair. Perhaps there will be an attraction to the occult. Psychic Circle talking board session or Tarot reading, anyone?

Water sign Scorpio develops emotional relationships with specific foods and may associate them with intense times. Scorpio is a time for sensitivity. Things that normally agree with us might temporarily not. Using almond flour and oat flour instead of the usual all-purpose flour not only makes these cookies easier to digest, they give a boost of robust protein to the crunch and gooey sweetness expected of a good chocolate chip cookie.

When you need something to munch during a séance, something to comfort you because one of your schemes has gone awry, or some wholesome communion to share at a midnight ramble, try one of these cookies!

You may just develop an infatuation with these cookies themselves and need them for all of the above.

MAKES 24 COOKIES

1 cup almond flour
½ cup oat flour
½ cup tapioca flour
1 teaspoon baking soda
½ teaspoon salt
¼ teaspoon nutmeg
¼ teaspoon cinnamon
5 ounces dark chocolate chips
¼ cup coconut oil, melted
¾ cup coconut palm sugar
2 eggs

In a large mixing bowl, using a fork, stir together the almond, oat, and tapioca flours, and the baking soda, salt, nutmeg, and cinnamon. Scoop about 1 tablespoon of the dry mixture into a separate large bowl. Add the chocolate chips to this second bowl, and toss to coat.

Beat the coconut oil and palm sugar in a third bowl, until light and fluffy. Add the eggs, and beat until thoroughly combined.

Make a well in the flour mixture, and add the wet mixture. Using a soft rubber spatula, fold the wet ingredients into the dry ingredients. Add the chocolate chips, and mix to distribute throughout the dough.

Cover the bowl with plastic wrap, and refrigerate. Chill the dough for at least 1 hour, and up to several days.

When ready to bake, preheat the oven to 325°F. Line a cookie sheet with parchment or a silicone mat.

Roll 1 tablespoon into a round between your palms, and place it on the prepared baking sheet. Repeat with the remaining dough, placing the balls about 2 to 3 inches apart from one another.

Bake until browned around the edges, about 15 minutes. Allow to cool a bit before eating.

 If you can't find oat flour, grind regular old-fashioned or quick-cooking oats in a blender or food processor. You may do similarly with the almonds, but try to process them as silky smooth as possible.

PLUM UPSIDE-DOWN CAKE

SAGITTARIUS

Because of the difficulty in obtaining the dye used to produce the color purple, it has long been associated with royalty and wealth. Sagittarians, Jupiter's children, are at home at that lofty end of the spectrum. This cake is rich, dark, and moist and supports the contrasting textures of the gooey caramel and the silky smooth plums. The rosemary and juniper infusion adds an exotic fragrance and an unexpected taste.

At an afternoon tea where looks count, this cake would be the one to serve. Or have a piece for breakfast. If you like, you can use regular dairy milk in this recipe. However, almond milk adds interest, even if you are not dairy-free.

SERVES 6 TO 8

3 tablespoons butter

½ cup plus ⅓ cup agave syrup, divided

4 purple-skinned plums, halved lengthwise, pitted, and each half cut into 3 wedges

⅔ cup almond milk

1 tablespoon apple cider vinegar

¾ cup all-purpose flour

½ cup fine cornmeal

½ cup almond flour

2 teaspoons baking powder

1 teaspoon baking soda

1 teaspoon xanthan gum

1 teaspoon salt

⅓ cup apple butter

2 teaspoons vanilla extract

¼ cup olive oil

Preheat the oven to 325°F. Position a rack in the middle of the oven.

Butter a 10-inch round cake pan, and line the bottom with parchment paper.

Combine the butter and ½ cup of the agave syrup in a small saucepan over medium heat, and bring to a brisk simmer, stirring continuously until the mixture caramelizes, about 3 minutes. Be careful not to burn it. Pour the syrup, bubbling hot from the stove, into the parchment-lined cake pan. Use the bottom of a spoon to smooth it out in an even layer. Work quickly, before the syrup begins to cool and harden. Arrange the sliced plums in a radial or spiral pattern on top of the syrup.

Stir together the almond milk and apple cider vinegar in a mixing bowl. Set aside and allow to curdle, about 10 minutes.

Stir together the all-purpose flour, cornmeal, almond flour, baking powder, baking soda, xanthan gum, and salt in a separate bowl.

Add the remaining ⅓ cup agave, the apple butter, vanilla, and olive oil to the almond milk–vinegar mix. Whisk to combine thoroughly.

Pour the liquid ingredients into the dry ingredients, and mix with a wooden spoon.

Spoon the cake batter over the plums, and spread it evenly.

Place the pan on a baking sheet, and bake for about 40 minutes. To ensure even baking, rotate the pan after 20 minutes.

When done, the cake will pull away from the sides of the pan, and a toothpick inserted in the center will come out clean.

To unmold, let the cake rest at room temperature for 15 minutes. Make sure the cake will come away from the sides by running a thin sharp knife along the edge. Place a serving platter or cutting board face down on the pan, and in one smooth, quick motion, invert the pan. If necessary, tap lightly to loosen the cake. Carefully lift up the pan.

Cut the cake into wedges, and serve.

WINTER

CAPRICORN

PISCES

AQUARIUS

STARTERS

Cauliflower Sformati (C)

White Bean–Parsnip Dip (A)

Sage Pea Soup (P)

SALADS

Kale Salad (C)

Brussels Sprouts and Chestnut Slaw (A)

Lentil Salad (P)

PASTA

Angel Hair with Fennel Pesto (C)

Pappardelle alla Cacciatora (A)

Spaghetti alla Carbonara (P)

VEGETARIAN

Toshikoshi Soba (C)

Cauliflower-Potato Curry with Spaghetti Squash (A)

Eggplant Parmigiana (P)

SEAFOOD

Steamed Mussels (C)

Oyster Stew with Gruyère and Potatoes (A)

Flounder Almondine (P)

MEAT

Roasted Ducklings in Orange Sauce (C)

Choucroute Garni (A)

Beef Bourguignon (P)

SIDES

Cranberry Relish (C)

Wild Rice Pilaf (A)

Hazelnut Sweet Potatoes (P)

DESSERTS

Cheesecake and Cherry Sauce (C)

Chocolate Chestnut Mousse (A)

Poached Pears in Maple Syrup (P)

On the Winter Solstice, the Night Force comes to the apex of its strength, and it immediately begins to recede. Every ending is a new beginning. The Day Force rises.

But before we see the tangible signs of spring, there are three months of slowly fading darkness and cold. On the physical level, the steam of the summer, the water of the spring and fall, has hardened into ice. On a psychological level, our inner lives also tend to solidify. Winter is the time of crystallization, materialization, and organization—for planning, for lofty dreams and learning, for submergence into the depths of our beings.

Cooler weather increases our need for meat, fish, and other proteins that fuel the fire of life. In temperate zones, the vegetation is dormant. Back to our roots and seeds, root vegetables and legumes appear on the menu. Slow cooking, standing over a hot stove, breathing in the flavorsome warmth, is a sensual pleasure of the season.

The long hard climb out of darkness begins as the sun enters Capricorn. The sign starts out with a bang, a week of eating and drinking, of good company, good cheer, and giving. The satyr in Saturn, the Lord of Capricorn, revels in the celebrations. Then comes the post-holiday lull: the greater part of Capricorn is the time to get down to business.

The symbol for Capricorn is the Goat, an animal at home treading the rugged, rocky cliffs and the icy, windswept, and precipitous mountain heights, sustaining itself by grazing on whatever cold-hardy wild weed it can find. Tapping our inner Goat, we tread, slowly but sure-footedly, into the New Year. Taking deliberate and firm steps into the future, with whatever austerity is necessary, we solidify our objectives; we think before we set our plans in motion, and we learn from the past and acquire the wisdom of age and experience.

Getting through the winter months no longer involves the deprivations our ancestors faced, but Saturn never forgets: conservation of resources, if not a matter of survival, is still key to expanding our awareness. When the holiday feasts are over, Capricorn remains a frugal gourmet. The true high cooking is a regimen balanced by common sense, sound economics, "waste not, want not" principles, and self-discipline.

Saturn molds us to what has been proven to work. In tune with the heavens, we follow the relentless taskmaster's recipe for success: earthbound persistence mixed with stamina and fortitude.

Capricorn is a time to make executive decisions about our lives. Good life management, like good cooking, takes skillful mixing of physical circumstances and personal tendencies, the raw ingredients of destiny. The practical philosopher Capricorn observes the way in which those ingredients react when mixed and develops a well-grounded understanding of the Art of Living. Capricorn prepares the Light for the service-minded Aquarius to decant.

The earthbound Goat gives way to the celestial Water Bearer: a servant kneels modestly as he freely pours forth a wavy flow. While both Capricorn and Aquarius are associated with the faculty of reason, Capricorn is the conformist, the conservative, the pragmatist. Aquarius is the nonconformist, the reformer, the visionary. While Capricorn values what is old, material things, and the lessons learned by experience, Aquarius has a passion for the new, for things that have never been, things that might never be, and the innovation of things that already are. Under the influence of Uranus, the God of the Upper Air, Aquarius dreams of utopias, political and social paradises, of advanced technologies, science facts segueing into science fictions.

In Aquarius, life gets more exciting with

COOLER WEATHER INCREASES OUR NEED FOR MEAT, FISH, AND OTHER PROTEINS THAT FUEL THE FIRE OF LIFE.

each passing day. Spring is on the way. Or at least the Aquarian vision looks ahead and sees it. While the word *aquarius* means "of water," Aquarius is an air sign. The water-symbolism of Aquarius is different from that of the true water signs, for whom water represents the ocean of the collective psyche, the past, the womb, the realm of nondifferentiation. The stream poured by the Water Bearer, on the other hand, is the light of ingenuity, the solving of humanity's problems through science and fellowship, the gift of heaven, the hope for the life of smooth sailing, and the dream of a bright future.

February takes its name from the *Februa*, a Roman purification ritual held on the full moon in February. Libations of wine were poured out as offerings to the gods. In ritual magic outer signs indicate inner states. Wine

is the water of the spirit. Consecrated and properly used, in wine there is truth, mental hygiene, and spiritual hydration. Sacramental imbibing was accompanied by a hot bath. Nothing takes the bite out of winter air more effectively than a long, steaming hot soak. Communal feelings are intrinsic to Aquarius. Baptism, the rite of spiritual hydrotherapy, includes us in the community. Raise the cup of communion. Salute!

The winter is long, and a certain amount of withdrawal from the cold and the darkness is a quite reasonable strategy for coping with it. The Aquarian tendency toward independence, detachment, being "different," cool calculation over emotional rashness, goes well with this time of year. With restrictions imposed by the weather, physical activity may be at an all-year low. Instead of sailing off to Candyland, the in-tune appetite hankers for nourishment for the soul rather than over-feeding a body less in need of sustenance.

The rebel, the reformer, the inventor has a tendency to see food as a social statement. Humanitarian service, the ideal of nourishing others, is a vital part of the Aquarian psyche. It is a time to consider not only what we can put in our mouths, but also what we can put in the mouths of others.

In Pisces, the days are noticeably longer, the sun clearly stronger, but the spring has not yet sprung. Neptune, God of the Deep Blue Seas, is at work in Pisces. While Capricorn conforms and Aquarius reforms, Pisces pre-forms. Our mother is Mary, she of the same name as *mare,* the Latin word for "sea." Pisces is the womb from which the rest of the Zodiac is born. In Pisces there is a strong sense of all the other signs. Strands from every one of them swirl around one another in the Neptunian depths.

The coming spring has a bewildering number of options and possibilities. Indecisiveness is natural. The symbol of Pisces is two fish swimming in opposing directions. This represents Pisces's tendency toward vacillation. Even though fish may go in opposite directions, in the psychic liquidity that underlies our seemingly solid existence, every movement we make creates ripples that affect the movements of others. Pisces is a time to join in this marvelous dance, to go with the flow of spiritual interdependence. Fish darting here and there remind us that the energy that separates us also binds us. It is all around us, inside and outside of us.

Pisces is impressionable. With the sense of individual self at its lowest point in the Zodiac, we are more responsive to the pushes and pulls of others. There are fluctuations in our moods similar to the fluctuations in the weather. There is compassion, and there is oversensitivity. There is no intrinsic harm in being unpredictable and changeable, except if this lack of structure and control expresses itself in intemperance, such as eating and drinking as a means of escape. Proper eating requires self-imposed discipline and a command of the appetite.

Unlike Virgo's self-imposed austerity, Pisces's fasting is organic. With winter stores depleted, March is a naturally lean month. You can't eat what you don't have. The month leading up to the Vernal Equinox has traditionally been a period of fasting and repentance as a Christian observance in preparation for the miracle of the Resurrection. We may want to abstain because we just want to look trim when spring weather calls for lighter clothing. A regime of self-imposed mortification of the flesh, foods that restore balance, that lift the spirits, the modest diet once upon a time imposed by Nature puts us in touch with heaven and earth.

The end of winter can be a difficult time, but it can also be an emotionally uplifting and spiritually nourishing time. The re-emergence of a stronger sun, a time of more light than darkness, of more ego, more action and less subconscious, is just around the bend.

CAULIFLOWER SFORMATI
CAPRICORN

Taskmaster Saturn, ruler of Capricorn, poses problems and challenges, the things in life that mold us into who we are. A *sformato* is a molded Italian egg dish. It's something like a soufflé, light and soft, but not as airy. The name comes from the Italian verb *sformare,* "to unmold." Saturn is the God of Irony. You are not truly molded until you are unmolded.

Sformati can be sweet or savory. They often have a béchamel sauce as a base, but here is an example using creamy-soft cauliflower and ricotta and fontina cheeses. Served with lemony arugula or watercress, it makes a light, lively starter for a dark winter's evening.

SERVES 6

3 tablespoons olive oil
1 cup minced onion
2 cups ½-inch cauliflower florets
1 cup chicken stock
3 tablespoons unsalted butter
2 tablespoons flour
½ teaspoon grated nutmeg
¼ teaspoon cayenne pepper
¾ teaspoon salt
½ teaspoon freshly ground black pepper
1 cup ricotta cheese
1 cup grated fontina
4 eggs, beaten
4 cups arugula or watercress
2 to 3 tablespoons Lemon–Olive Oil
    Dressing (page 51)

Saturn doesn't like surprises. A safe plan to ensure that the custards will part from the molds easily is to not only butter the ramekins, but also line the bottoms of the ramekins with buttered parchment papers. You will need six 1-cup ramekins.

Preheat the oven to 400°F.

Heat the olive oil in a medium saucepot with a lid over medium-high heat. When the oil is hot, add the minced onion, and sauté until it is thoroughly soft, about 10 minutes. Transfer the onion to a mixing bowl to cool.

Combine the cauliflower and the chicken stock in the pot you used to sauté the onion (no need to clean it first). Raise the heat to high, and bring to a boil. Cover the pot, and boil until the florets are soft, about 10 minutes or so. Strain the cauliflower, reserving the stock. Add the florets to the onion, and mash them up a bit with a fork.

Using the same pot, melt the butter over low heat (no need to clean the pot first). Use a pastry brush to swirl some of the melted butter around the insides of the ramekins. Cut circles of parchment paper to fit the bottoms of the ramekins. Butter the circles, and set them in place. Set the ramekins aside.

Add the flour to the remaining butter in the pan, whisking with a fork as you add to prevent lumps. Add the reserved stock a little at a time, whisking as you pour. Raise the heat to medium-high, and bring to a boil. Simmer for about 5 minutes to thicken, whisking to prevent and break up any lumps. Add the stock mixture to the cauliflower and

onions, and toss to coat. Add the nutmeg, cayenne, salt, and black pepper to the bowl, and stir, mixing thoroughly. Let cool for 5 minutes.

Once the cauliflower mixture has cooled a bit, fold in the cheeses. Add the eggs, and fold them in as well. Spoon the mixture into the ramekins. Pour a cup or so of hot water into a 9 × 13-inch casserole, and place the ramekins in the baking dish.

Bake until the sformati are set and the tops are browned, about 40 minutes. (If the water evaporates during baking, add more hot water.) Remove the ramekins from the casserole, and let sit until they are thoroughly cool. (Since they are served at room temperature, you can make the sformati well in advance.)

When ready to serve, toss the salad greens with the lemon–olive oil dressing. Unmold the sformati by running a thin knife around the edge of the ramekins. Place a small plate on top of each ramekin, and invert it, tapping lightly if necessary. The sformati should come out of the mold in one piece. Peel and discard the parchment. Serve, browned side up, with the greens on the side.

WHITE BEAN-PARSNIP DIP
AQUARIUS

Feelings of community are as important to Aquarius as they are to Capricorn. But while Saturn, ruler of Capricorn, complies and acts in accord with tradition, Uranus, ruler of Aquarius, does not go by the book. Aquarius changes what is written or reads it differently. This is a different twist on classic hummus. Parsnips' long shelf life makes them a good choice for the dead of winter. They have a sweetness that is similar to carrots, but a more tongue-tickling flavor. Their savoriness makes them suitable mates for the white bean, with its creamy mild flesh.

This dip, served with crudités and pita chips, can be an hors d'oeuvre at a social gathering or a starter for the table. It is best made in advance of serving, giving some time for the flavors to come together.

MAKES ABOUT 4 CUPS

FOR THE DIP
1 pound parsnips, peeled and julienned
3 tablespoons olive oil
½ teaspoon salt, or to taste
2 garlic cloves, chopped
1 cup canned white beans, rinsed and drained
⅓ cup tahini
¼ cup lemon juice
1 teaspoon cumin
1 teaspoon ground coriander
⅛ teaspoon cayenne pepper, or to taste

FOR THE GARNISH
1 cup shelled pumpkin seeds
3 tablespoons olive oil
1 garlic clove, minced
¼ teaspoon cayenne pepper
½ teaspoon salt
2 tablespoons lemon juice

Preheat the oven to 425°F.

Make the dip. Combine the parsnips, oil, and salt in a large bowl, and toss to coat. Turn out the parsnips onto a rimmed baking sheet, and roast, turning them over once or twice, until tender and brown, about 25 minutes.

Lower the oven temperature to 325°F.

Combine the remaining dip ingredients in the bowl of a food processor, and pulse a few times until roughly chopped. Add the parsnips and pulse until smooth, or leave it slightly chunky, according to your preference. Taste for salt, and season as necessary. Transfer to a decorative bowl.

Make the garnish. Spread the pumpkin seeds on a rimmed baking tray, and place them in the oven, shaking occasionally, until they are slightly toasted, about 12 minutes. Meanwhile, combine the olive oil, garlic, cayenne, and salt in a small bowl. Divide this mixture in half, so you end up with two bowls of seasoned oil. Add the lemon juice to one of the bowls. When the seeds are hot from the oven, add them to the bowl that does not include lemon juice, and stir to coat.

When ready to serve, drizzle the lemony oil over the dip. Garnish with the pumpkin seeds, and serve with pita chips and crudités such as fennel wedges, celery sticks, radishes, and carrot sticks.

Refrigerate any leftover dip for up to one week.

SAGE PEA SOUP
PISCES

Neptune, Lord of the Deep, rules Pisces. Herb lore has sage as a memory enhancer. Its flavor takes us back to our origins in the primeval soup. In Pisces, the Aquarian excitement, idealism, and vision of a glorious kingdom come progress from pie in the sky to something substantial, what the truly spiritual call the "poverty" of spirit.

Sage has been held in high regard throughout history for its culinary and medicinal properties. Its reputation as a panacea is even present in its scientific name, *Salvia officinalis*, derived from the Latin word *salvere,* which means "to be saved."

Want some sage advice? The naked reality of the Divine is best experienced in the simple pleasures of life. This hearty peasant soup of dried legumes and lively herbs and spices will save you on a cold day. The lack of oil in the soup itself, and the small amount in the garnish, makes this low-fat, low-calorie, and appealing to the ascetic in Pisces. But served with hot bread and butter or soft cheese, this starter can take you all the way home.

SERVES 8 TO 10

FOR THE SOUP

4 quarts chicken or vegetable stock
2 pounds dried, green split peas, rinsed
2 onions, chopped
4 carrots, peeled and quartered
3 ribs celery, chopped, leaves reserved
1 tablespoon dried sage
1 tablespoon dried marjoram
1 tablespoon garlic powder
6 bay leaves
4 tablespoons Worcestershire sauce
1 tablespoon Tabasco
2 tablespoons smoked paprika
1 teaspoon freshly ground black pepper
1 teaspoon salt, or to taste

FOR THE GARNISH

¼ cup olive oil
1 cup fresh sage leaves
4 ounces prosciutto, thinly sliced
1 cup yogurt, optional

Make the soup. Combine all of the ingredients for the soup in a large stock pot set over high heat. Bring to a boil, then reduce the heat to low and cover, simmering and stirring occasionally, until all of the ingredients are thoroughly tender, about 1½ hours. Once the peas and vegetables are tender, skim off any foam, and discard the bay leaves.

Remove the soup from the heat, and use an immersion blender or puree in batches in a food processor. Return the pureed soup to the stock pot. Taste for salt, and season as needed. Keep the soup warm over low heat.

Make the garnish. Heat the olive oil in a skillet over medium-high heat. Once the oil is hot, add the sage leaves to the pan, and fry them until crispy—do this in batches, if necessary. Remove the sage leaves with a slotted spoon, draining as much oil as possible, and dry on a paper towel–lined plate. Make sure the remaining oil in the pan is still hot before adding the prosciutto. Fry until brown and crisp.

To serve, ladle the soup into individual bowls, and crumble some sage leaves and prosciutto over each. Add a spoonful of yogurt, if you wish.

KALE SALAD
CAPRICORN

This salad is dead simple to put together, but it does require foresight and planning—you need to start it the day before you plan to serve it. The flavor develops from the touch of Saturn, also known as Father Time. Speaking of Father Time, the tradition of giving gifts at the Winter Solstice comes from the ancient Roman Saturnalia, a Festival dedicated to Saturn. Saturn, who rules Capricorn, can be a bit of a scrooge, but when he gives, he gives with all his heart.

The Hero with a Thousand Faces—the one who dies and is reborn—is incarnated in different cultures all over the earth. Represented in this salad are the colors of the season: white (grain), red (fruit), and green (leaves). These traditional hues come from Celtic woods-lore and are linked with ancient tree rituals that used mistletoe, holly, oak, and pine. For the Yule festivities, the White Goddess takes the Holly King, with his red berries, as her consort. The King is then sacrificed, and three days later, as the light begins to increase, he is reborn green, as the Oak King.

SERVES 4

3 cups baby kale, washed and dried, large stems removed (if using regular kale, cut the leaves to bite-size pieces)

6 tablespoons Lemon–Olive Oil Dressing (page 51)

1 cup quinoa, rinsed

½ cup dried cranberries

1 tablespoon orange zest

½ cup toasted pine nuts (page 199, Roasting Seeds and Nuts)

Chopped parsley

The day before you plan to serve the salad, in a large mixing bowl, combine the raw kale with 3 tablespoons of the lemon–olive oil dressing. Toss it with your hands to make sure all pieces are covered, and work it into the leaves a bit, massaging the greens. Cover the bowl of kale with plastic wrap, and refrigerate overnight. The dressing will break down the leaf fiber into a chewy texture.

Bring 2 cups water to a boil in a medium saucepan over high heat. Add the quinoa, and stir. Cover, lower the heat, and cook, simmering, until all the water is absorbed, about 15 minutes. Remove from the heat.

Add the cranberries and orange zest to the quinoa, and stir. Cover with the lid again, and let sit for about 5 minutes or so, allowing the cranberries to plump up. Remove the lid, and let the quinoa come to room temperature, then add the pine nuts and stir. Add the remaining 3 tablespoons lemon–olive oil dressing a little at a time, stirring each time, taking care not to overdress it. Cover the saucepan with its lid again, and refrigerate overnight.

The next day, assemble the salad. Combine the kale and the quinoa in a large salad bowl. Add the parsley, and toss to mix. Serve the salad either at room temperature or chilled, according to your preference.

ROASTING SEEDS AND NUTS

Roasting seeds and nuts is best done in the oven. They roast more evenly when the heat can get at them from all sides. Spread them on a baking sheet, and place them in a preheated 325°F oven, shaking frequently, until they are lightly brown and aromatic, 12 to 15 minutes.

BRUSSELS SPROUTS AND CHESTNUT SLAW
AQUARIUS

The Water Bearer pours clarity of thought and expression, good cheer, reason, and logic. But, oh, those February days can be dark! Spirits can be at an all-Zodiac low! Will the winter never end?

Some holiday cheer can help to make the season bright. Snow on the way? Dreaming of a white February? Look forward to a couple of days stuck in the house. Go on a pre-storm shop. Roast a turkey with all the fixings.

While roasting chestnuts on an open fire may not be practical, you can still get a whiff of the Feast of Light by roasting them in the oven. Cut crosses in the rounded face of the shells, place them on a baking sheet, and roast them in a 400°F oven until the corners of the crosses curl up, 25 to 30 minutes. They are easiest to peel when they are warm. Roast extra. Like many perishables, not every fresh chestnut is a winner. (Vacuum-packed shelled roasted chestnuts are available, however, if you're feeling a little less ambitious— understandable after a long winter's day.) For the Brussels sprouts, use the sharpest knife you have or, better yet, a mandoline or food processor.

SERVES 4

1 pound Brussels sprouts, trimmed, outer
    leaves discarded, and shaved paper thin
2 carrots, peeled and shredded
16 chestnuts, roasted and roughly chopped
¼ cup Lemon–Olive Oil Dressing (page 51)
1 tablespoon honey or raw sugar
½ teaspoon salt
1 cup grated Parmesan

Combine the sprouts, carrots, and chestnuts in a large salad bowl, and toss to combine.

Whisk together the lemon–olive oil dressing, honey, and salt in a small bowl, until emulsified, making sure the honey is thoroughly dissolved. (Or, you can combine the dressing ingredients in a small saucepot set over low heat, stirring until the honey is just dissolved, but take care not to allow it to get too hot.)

Add the dressing to the Brussels sprouts mixture, and toss to coat evenly. Add the Parmesan cheese, and toss again. Serve immediately.

WINTER

CAPRICORN

Cauliflower Sformati, page 192

Opposite: Kale Salad, page 198

Above: Angel Hair with Fennel Pesto, page 204

Left: Toshikoshi Soba, page 210

Above: Steamed Mussels,
page 216

Right: Roasted
Ducklings in Orange
Sauce, page 222

Opposite: Cheesecake
and Cherry Sauce,
page 236

AQUARIUS

Brussels Sprouts and Chestnut Slaw, page 200

Right: Pappardelle alla Cacciatora, page 206

Below: Cauliflower-Potato Curry with Spaghetti Squash, page 212

Opposite: Oyster Stew with Gruyère and Potatoes, page 218

Above: Choucroute Garni, page 225

Right: Chocolate Chestnut Mousse, page 238

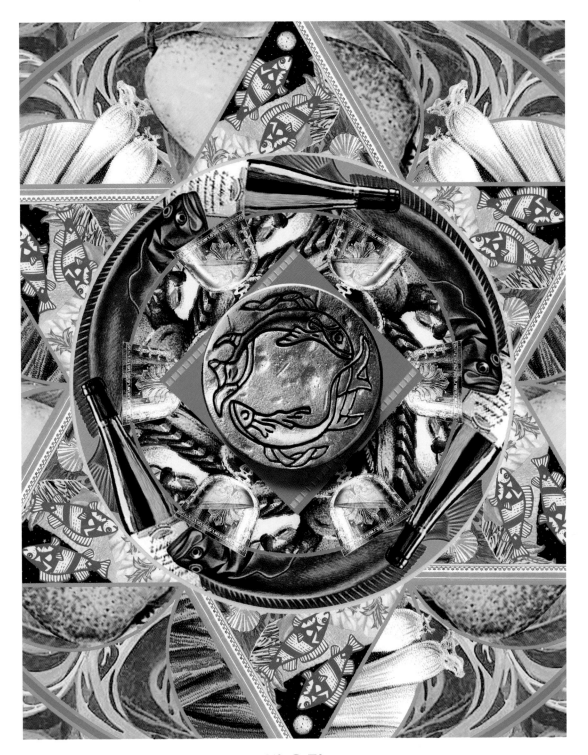

PISCES

Opposite: Sage Pea Soup, page 196

Above: Lentil Salad, page 202

Left: Eggplant Parmigiana, page 214

Above: Flounder
Almondine, page 220

Right: Beef
Bourguignon, page 228

SPROUTS

All through the dead of winter, the energy of rebirth is stored in seed form. Seeds are potential life. They store sustenance to come. In its initial stage as a sprout, the stored nutrients in the seed are unlocked. Those carbohydrates, proteins, vitamins, and minerals necessary for growth are transferred into the sprout and are in turn transferred into you! Growing sprouts from pulses—seeds, peas, and beans—during the long months when you are waiting for the sun and little grows on farms or in gardens, is rewarding physically and psychologically. Besides their nutritional value, many sprouts, especially the most common ones like alfalfa and clover, contain a chemical called coumarin. Coumarin has a sweet fresh scent that reminds one of growing grass, which in a real sense is exactly what sprouts are. This scent brings out the inner Aries in Capricorn, Aquarius, and Pisces by stimulating the areas of the brain in touch with that green time of year when the grass grows, perennials pop up their heads, and trees and shrubs push out soft green shoots and leaves. In addition to the psychological contentment of having the smell of a new-mown lawn in your salad, soup, or sandwich, coumarin has been shown to create a sensation of fullness, reducing the inclination to overeat. Perhaps these plants evolved this appetite-suppressing substance to deter rampant overeating by grazing animals.

Sprouts of many varieties are available at most markets. But there is something wonderful about growing your own food, especially if you live in an apartment or town house. Alfalfa, clover, and radish are the easiest ones to start with and the most versatile, but any grain, seed, or legume can be sprouted. Information on sprouting and equipment for it are both readily available online.

LENTIL SALAD
PISCES

Astrology is the study of the rhythm of the heavens and earth and the awareness of pulse points in the yearly cycle. The pulse that is the dried edible yield of certain pod-bearing plants comes from a different root than that of the beat of cardiac contraction and expansion. But for Pisces, life can be a dream, and in dreams there is a punning nature to reality. The Pisces rains of March add water to the dry seeds. Peas, beans, and lentils are low in fat, high in fiber, protein, and vitamins, and have no cholesterol. Compassion for others is admirable. But have a heart for your own heart, and sprout some lentils!

SERVES 6

FOR THE CROUTONS
2 cups ¼-inch cubes of focaccia bread
2 garlic cloves, pressed
2 tablespoons olive oil
⅛ teaspoon cayenne pepper
⅛ teaspoon onion salt

FOR THE SALAD
1 cup chicken stock
1 cup vegetable juice
1 onion, peeled and halved
2 garlic cloves, peeled
2 ribs celery, halved
⅛ teaspoon cayenne pepper
1 parsley sprig
1 rosemary sprig
1 thyme sprig
1 cup lentils, rinsed
¼ cup Lemon–Olive Oil Dressing (page 51)
1 carrot, peeled and cut into ¼-inch dice
3 radishes, cut into ¼-inch dice
½ cup chopped scallions, whites and pale greens only
2 cups lentil sprouts (or any variety of sprout or microgreen)
4 ounces provolone cheese, cut into ¼-inch cubes
1 head romaine, outer leaves removed (and saved for another use)

Preheat the oven to 375°F.

Make the croutons. Toss the bread cubes with the garlic, olive oil, cayenne, and onion salt. Place them on a baking sheet, and toast them, turning occasionally, until they are lightly browned and crisp on all sides, about 8 minutes.

Make the salad. In a pot with a lid, combine the chicken stock, vegetable juice, onion, garlic, celery, cayenne, parsley, rosemary, and thyme over high heat, and bring to a boil. Add the lentils. Once the liquid has returned to a boil, cover the pot and lower the heat to a simmer. Cook until the lentils are tender, 30 to 40 minutes. Discard what is left of the onion, garlic, celery, and herbs. If there is still liquid left, strain well. (You can save any leftover liquid to add to soup or to flavor rice or pasta.)

Put the lentils in a large mixing bowl, and pat them dry with a paper towel. While they are still warm, add the lemon–olive oil dressing, and toss to coat. Let the lentils come to room temperature. Add the carrot, radishes, scallions, sprouts, and provolone to the lentils.

Split crisp romaine leaves in half along the spine (so that they will lie flat). Arrange them on a platter or individual plates. Spoon the salad onto the leaves. Garnish with croutons, and serve.

ANGEL HAIR WITH FENNEL PESTO
CAPRICORN

When the holiday excesses are over and the lights are low, the time comes for quiet, simple dinners. This light, lively pasta is a welcome relief from the weeks of heavy protein.

In mythology, the Goat is a satyr, a devil devoted to the pleasures of the flesh. In Nature, there's a bit of the upcoming Aquarian angel in the Capricorn Goat. Billy is pure vegan. He would eat the fries, the bun, and the napkin and turn up his nose at the burger.

For hot fun there's Fra Diavolo in the Angel's Hair. The amount recommended is for medium heat. This is Sicilian peasant food. If you want authenticity, double it. The garnish, a "halo" of bread crumbs, is poor man's Parmigiana.

"Waste not, want not" Capricorn, child of winter, is instinctively economical and finds a use for everything. To get the most flavor out of the fennel, boil the cores and outer layers in the water in which you will eventually cook the pasta. Save the feathery tops to use in the "halo."

SERVES 4 AS A MAIN,
6 AS A STARTER

2 tablespoons fennel seeds

½ teaspoon crushed red pepper flakes

6 tablespoons olive oil, divided

1 yellow onion, finely chopped

2 fennel bulbs, trimmed, cored, and finely chopped (core, outer layers, and fronds reserved; stalks discarded)

½ cup Summer Tomato Sauce (page 107)

½ cup white wine

½ teaspoon salt

½ cup currants

½ cup unseasoned bread crumbs, lightly toasted

½ cup finely chopped fennel fronds (from fennel above)

1 tablespoon dried oregano

1 pound angel hair pasta (capellini)

Preheat the oven to 375°F.

Dry-roast the fennel seeds in a heavy-duty saucepot over medium-high heat, until they become slightly browned and give off a nutty aroma, 30 seconds to 1 minute. Add the crushed red pepper, and give a stir or two. Don't let the flakes burn.

Add 4 tablespoons of the olive oil and the onion. Sauté until the onion begins to soften, 3 to 5 minutes. Add the chopped fennel. Sauté for another 5 minutes. Add the tomato sauce, wine, and salt, and stir. Cover, and transfer to the oven. Bake for 20 to 30 minutes.

Meanwhile, place the fennel cores and outer layers in 6 quarts of salted water, and bring to a boil.

Remove the pot from the oven (the vegetables should be thoroughly soft), and coarsely puree the sauce with an immersion blender. Add the currants, stir, return the pot to the stovetop over low to medium-low heat, and simmer, uncovered, for another 10 minutes.

Meanwhile, make the garnish. Combine the remaining 2 tablespoons olive oil, the bread crumbs, fennel fronds, and oregano in a bowl, and toss to mix.

When the water has come to a boil, remove and discard the fennel, and add the angel hair. Drain the pasta after about 1 minute, when it's just short of al dente, reserving 1 cup or so of the cooking water. Return the angel hair to the pot, and set it over medium heat. Add the fennel sauce to the pasta, and toss to incorporate. Add some of the reserved cooking water if needed to help incorporate the sauce and finish cooking the pasta.

Serve in shallow bowls, topping each with a "halo" of garnish.

PAPPARDELLE ALLA CACCIATORA

AQUARIUS

Alla cacciatora, "in the style of the hunter," is a method of braising rabbit, fowl, or other small game with onions and herbs. Aquarius hunts for what is new and different. With long, slow cooking, this fills the midwinter kitchen with a reassuring aroma, a spirit that nourishes the soul. Alla cacciatora is similar to the French coq au vin. Aquarius is a nonconformist but likes things to be authentic nonetheless. The following recipe, without tomatoes, is faithful to its roots in Italy and France. If you want to be different, use white wine instead of red.

**SERVES 4 AS A MAIN,
6 AS A STARTER**

8 bone-in chicken thighs, with skin
1 teaspoon salt, divided
2 teaspoons freshly ground black pepper, divided
2 to 3 tablespoons all-purpose flour, for dusting
6 tablespoons olive oil, divided
2 garlic cloves, minced
2 medium yellow onions, chopped (about 2 cups)
1 fennel bulb, trimmed and chopped
4 to 6 medium carrots, peeled and grated (about 2 cups)
6 ounces button mushrooms, sliced (about 2 cups)
½ cup Cognac
2 cups red wine
3 cups chicken stock
1 tablespoon dried thyme
1 tablespoon dried oregano
3 bay leaves
2 tablespoons capers (optional)
1 pound pappardelle
Grated Parmesan, for the table

Preheat the oven to 275°F.

Season the chicken with ½ teaspoon of the salt and 1 teaspoon of the pepper. Dust the chicken with the flour.

Heat 3 tablespoons of the olive oil in a Dutch oven (or other suitable casserole) over medium-high heat. Brown half the thighs, about 4 to 5 minutes per side. Set them aside. Add more oil if needed, and brown the remaining thighs similarly. Set aside.

Heat the remaining oil in the pot over medium-high heat. Add the garlic, onions, and fennel, and sauté until soft, about 5 minutes. Add the carrots and mushrooms, and sauté another 5 minutes.

Add the Cognac, wine, and stock to the vegetables, and stir. Add the thyme, oregano, bay leaves, and capers (if you wish). Add the remaining ½ teaspoon salt and 1 teaspoon black pepper.

Nestle the browned chicken thighs into the vegetables. Cover the pot, and bake for 1 to 1½ hours until the meat is falling off the bone. When it is cool enough to handle, shred the chicken. Put the meat in a separate pot or skillet with 1 to 2 cups of the sauce. Discard the bones and the bay leaves.

Bring 6 quarts of salted water to a rapid boil. Add the pappardelle, and cook until just short of al dente. Pappardelle cooks quickly. For most brands, 2 or 3 minutes should do it. Drain the pasta, return it to the pot over medium heat, and add a ladleful of the wine sauce a little at a time, tossing it through to incorporate, until the pasta is cooked to your liking.

Meanwhile warm the pulled chicken over medium heat until it is heated through.

To serve, divide the pasta among individual bowls, and top with the remaining sauce and the pulled chicken meat. Pass the Parmesan at the table.

SPAGHETTI ALLA CARBONARA

PISCES

After the fatness of Tuesday comes the ashes of Wednesday. What to make when the cupboard is bare, and there's nothing left to hunt, Pisces?

There are many explanations for the name *carbonara,* literally "coal miner's pasta." The liberal use of black pepper in the finish looks like coal dust. And there are historical recipes linking it to Abruzzo, where coal miners made meals underground using nonperishable ingredients. But the general sense is that it is an American-Italian concoction that originated during the final days of World War II. When the Allies rolled into Italy, the country was in a Pisces state of mind. The larder was nearly empty. Pisces digs deep! Pasta carbonara was the result of the marriage between durable Italian staples—dried pasta, cured meat, olive oil, hard cheese, and black pepper—and American soldiers' ration of powdered eggs (and perhaps their homesickness for bacon and scrambled eggs).

Except for the parsley garnish, sign of the green soon to come, below is the classic, no-frills recipe. To make an official version, you would use the rendered bacon fat to cook the eggs. How much, if any, of the fat you use is up to you. You can use olive oil instead.

**SERVES 4 AS A MAIN,
6 AS A STARTER**

4 tablespoons olive oil, or bacon fat, or a mix
6 ounces pancetta, minced
1 pound spaghetti
4 eggs, beaten
1 teaspoon freshly ground black pepper, or to taste
1 cup grated Pecorino, plus more for the table
Fresh parsley, for garnish

Heat 1 tablespoon of the olive oil in a skillet over medium-high heat. Add the pancetta, and cook, stirring frequently, until crisp, 5 to 7 minutes.

Bring 6 quarts of salted water to a rapid boil. Add the spaghetti, and cook until just short of al dente. Drain, reserving 1 to 2 cups of the cooking water. Place the pot back on the stove over medium-high heat. Add the remaining 3 tablespoons olive oil (or 3 tablespoons of the rendered pancetta fat, or a little of both), then the eggs, and give them a quick swirl to start them cooking. Add the pasta and the pancetta, stirring constantly to cook the eggs and incorporate them with the pasta. Add a few tablespoons of the reserved cooking water as you stir and toss the pasta, both to keep the eggs from sticking to the pot and to finish cooking the pasta.

Add the black pepper and Pecorino, and toss one last time to mix. Serve immediately, garnishing each serving with parsley and passing more cheese at the table.

TOSHIKOSHI SOBA
CAPRICORN

A traditional Japanese New Year's dish of buckwheat noodles (soba) in a dashi, mirin, and soy broth, toshikoshi soba is a simple, sustaining bowl of warmth that encourages the slow but sure-footed Capricorn crossing of the threshold from one year to the next. The word *toshikoshi* itself refers to the crossing of a threshold.

Because the buckwheat plant can hold up to the elements, soba noodles, made from buckwheat, are the symbol of long life, good luck, strength, and adaptability.

The custom, preparation, and toppings of New Year's Noodles vary according to area. The dish is often garnished with shrimp tempura. This recipe offers crispy tofu instead and uses vegetable stock and shiitake mushrooms instead of *dashi,* which is made from bonito flakes. Mirin is a rice wine used in Japanese cooking. It is similar to sake but quite sweet. Adding sugar is really not necessary, but the extra sweetness is symbolic of the sweet life, of letting go of the troubles and cares of the past.

This is an easy dish, but a little Saturnian organization goes a long way. When it's go-time, have the broth hot, the soba cooking water at a low boil, and the tofu ready to fry.

SERVES 4

2 tablespoons sesame oil
6 shiitake mushrooms, stems discarded, caps sliced
8 cups vegetable stock
½ cup mirin
1 tablespoon sugar
5 tablespoons soy sauce, divided
1 teaspoon ground ginger
2 tablespoons shiro miso
12 ounces firm tofu
2 eggs, beaten
1 garlic clove, minced
⅛ teaspoon cayenne pepper
1 cup panko bread crumbs, for dredging
Vegetable oil, for frying
12 ounces soba noodles
8 scallions, thinly sliced, for garnish
Crumbled, toasted nori, for garnish

Make the broth. Heat the sesame oil in a large saucepot over high heat. When the oil is hot, add the mushrooms, and sauté until they brown, about 4 minutes. Lower the heat to medium-high. Add the vegetable stock, mirin, sugar, 4 tablespoons of the soy sauce, and the ginger, and stir. Bring to a simmer. Combine a ladleful of the hot broth and the miso in a separate bowl, and whisk to dissolve the miso. Add the miso mixture back to the pot of broth. Keep the broth very hot while you prepare the rest of the dish, but do not allow it to boil.

Bring 6 quarts of lightly salted water to a boil.

While the water is coming to a boil, make the tofu. Set the tofu between two paper towels, and press it gently to remove excess moisture. Cut the tofu into bite-size cubes. In a medium bowl, combine the beaten eggs with the garlic, cayenne, and remaining 1 tablespoon soy sauce, and whisk to mix. Place the panko in a wide-bottomed shallow bowl. Dip the tofu cubes in the egg mixture, then dredge them in the panko. Set aside.

Heat about ¼ inch of vegetable oil in a skillet to frying temperature, about 360°F. If you don't have a candy/deep-fry thermometer,

test the oil by dropping a small piece of bread in it. If it doesn't sizzle immediately, the oil isn't yet hot enough. Carefully add the tofu cubes to the oil, taking care not to crowd the pan, and fry until crisp and brown on all sides. (Fry them in batches if they do not all fit comfortably.) Drain on paper towels, and keep warm.

When almost all the tofu cubes are fried, drop the soba into the boiling water. Stir to submerge the noodles. Be gentle. Soba noodles are more delicate than those made from semolina. Reduce the heat to a bare simmer, and cook until *katame ni yuderu* (al dente). Cooking time varies according to the brand of noodle. Taste for doneness after 5 or 6 minutes. Drain the noodles.

Divide the soba noodles among serving bowls. Ladle a portion of the broth on each. Top with the fried tofu, garnish with scallions and crumbled toasted nori, and ring in the New Year with a slurp instead of a bang.

CAULIFLOWER-POTATO CURRY WITH SPAGHETTI SQUASH

AQUARIUS

Carnival, literally "farewell to meat," is a moveable feast that usually falls in mid-February. After Fat Tuesday comes Ash Wednesday, the cold, sober realization of transience and the beginning of the purification process in preparation for the Resurrection. The understanding of mid-winter as a cleansing period dates back to long before the current era. Its symbol is the Aquarian Water-Bearer, Ganymede, beautiful youth, sweet angel who stole Zeus's heart. A modest servant, he kneels and pours forth a free flow of purifying light that cleanses the spirit and enlightens the mind. This dish, satisfying to the appetite, but clean, pure, and unassuming, has the Water-Boy's spirit. Humility is nobility. Simplicity is sophistication.

SERVES 4

2 spaghetti squash (2 to 3 pounds total), cut in half lengthwise
4 tablespoons olive oil, divided
3 tablespoons butter
1 medium yellow onion, chopped (about 1 cup)
2 garlic cloves, minced
1 small head cauliflower, cut into ½-inch florets (core and stalk discarded)
1 pound Yukon gold potatoes, peeled, cut into ½-inch dice
3 tablespoons curry powder
½ teaspoon turmeric
⅛ teaspoon cayenne pepper
1 teaspoon salt
1 cup tomato juice or mixed vegetable juice

Preheat the oven to 375°F.

Rub the cut side of the squash halves with 1 tablespoon of the olive oil, and place cut-side down on a baking sheet. Bake until a paring knife, inserted, meets little resistance, about 30 minutes. Set aside until cool enough to handle.

While the squash bakes, heat the butter and olive oil in a large skillet over medium-high heat. When the butter melts, add the onion and garlic. Sauté until transparent, about 5 minutes.

Add the cauliflower, potatoes, curry powder, turmeric, cayenne, and salt. Sauté 1 minute, coating the vegetables with the spices. Add the tomato juice, stir, and cover. Lower the heat to a simmer, and cook until the cauliflower and potatoes are tender, about 20 minutes.

To serve, spoon half of the curry into four bowls. Using a large spoon, scoop the seeds out of the squash, and discard them. Scoop the pulp out of each half, separating and lightly fluffing the strands with a fork, and place some over the curry. Top with equal portions of the remaining curry, and serve immediately.

EGGPLANT PARMIGIANA
PISCES

As the days lengthen and the reality of imminent spring becomes stronger, all remnants of the past must be washed away. The revolutionary social fantasies and utopian ideals of Aquarius fade and are replaced by a focus on the inner self. In Pisces, a mutable water sign, everything is flowing. Nothing is as it was or will be tomorrow. Are those visions mystic peeks into secret spiritual dimensions, or are they illusions? Until the cycle begins again, there is no telling.

So, go with the flow. Don't make waves. Make eggplant parm instead. The meatiest of vegetarian entrées, this unmistakable classic will keep you from getting too carried away on the seas of uncertainty. An extra deep casserole will prevent overflow in the oven.

You may peel the eggplants entirely or leave the skin on for some visual appeal. If leaving the skin on, more baking time will be required. When in doubt, do the mutable thing: peel off strips of skin, leaving the eggplant "striped."

SERVES 8

2 large eggplants (at least 2½ pounds total), sliced lengthwise into ¼-inch-thick slices
Coarse salt
3 eggs
¼ cup half-and-half
⅛ teaspoon cayenne pepper
1 cup all-purpose flour, for dredging
Light olive oil, for frying
4 cups Summer Tomato Sauce (page 107), or more as needed
3 cups grated Parmesan
2 pounds mozzarella, shredded
1 cup panko bread crumbs
¼ cup dried oregano
¼ cup olive oil

Preheat the oven to 375°F.

Place the eggplant in a colander, and salt it generously. Let it sit for 30 minutes. Rinse the salt from the eggplant slices, squeeze them gently, and pat them dry.

Beat together the eggs, half-and-half, and cayenne in a medium bowl until thoroughly mixed. Place the flour in a separate, flat-bottomed bowl.

Pour about ¼ inch of olive oil in a deep skillet. Heat to frying temperature, about 360°F. If you don't have a cooking thermometer, drop a small cube of bread in the oil. If it sizzles right away, the oil is hot enough.

Dust each slice of eggplant in the flour, dip it into the egg mixture, and carefully add it to the hot oil, taking care not to crowd the pan. Fry until golden brown on both sides. Drain the fried eggplant on a paper towel–lined plate. Continue until all the eggplant is fried.

Cover the bottom of a deep casserole with 1 cup of the tomato sauce. Place half of the eggplant slices over the sauce, overlapping as necessary to cover the bottom of the casserole. Sprinkle with 2 cups of the Parmesan and two-thirds of the mozzarella.

Spread another 1 cup of the tomato sauce over the cheese, then layer the remaining eggplant, the rest of the mozzarella, and 1 more cup of sauce, or enough to cover.

Mix together the remaining 1 cup Parmesan, the panko, oregano, and olive oil in a medium bowl. Spread the Parmesan–bread crumb mixture over the layer of sauce, pressing it down lightly as you go.

Bake until the whole dish is bubbling and the topping is brown and crusty, about 45 minutes. Let it cool completely to room temperature before cutting into it so that it comes out in neat wedges.

STEAMED MUSSELS
CAPRICORN

The holiday feasts are behind you, perhaps in more ways than one. The New Year is here. Capricorn heaviness needs some balance. For a light, quick, easy entrée, try steamed mussels. If you need something more substantial, serve with slices of crusty bread or baguette to mop up the broth.

SERVES 4

2 tablespoons butter
2 tablespoons olive oil
½ teaspoon crushed red pepper flakes
2 garlic cloves, minced
8 shallots, finely chopped
2 cups white wine
1 cup chicken stock
½ cup chopped flat-leaf parsley, divided
20 basil leaves
1 teaspoon dried thyme
1 bay leaf
½ teaspoon freshly ground black pepper
4 pounds mussels

Heat the butter and olive oil in a deep, wide-mouth pot set over medium-high heat. When the butter melts, add the crushed red pepper and garlic. Sauté for 1 minute to infuse the oil. Add the shallots, and sauté until they soften, about 5 minutes.

Add the wine, chicken stock, half the parsley, the basil leaves, thyme, bay leaf, and black pepper. Bring to a slow boil, turn the heat to low, and cover. Let simmer while you prepare the mussels.

Rinse the mussels thoroughly several times by placing them in a large pot of cold water, then draining them in a colander. Pull off the beards. Discard mussels with broken shells and any that are open.

Turn up the heat a bit on the broth, and bring to a vigorous boil. Add the mussels and cover, uncovering at 30-second intervals to stir. Cook until the shells open and the meat is just firm, 3 to 5 minutes. Discard any mussels that don't open.

To serve, divide the mussels among four large bowls, and ladle broth over each bowl. Sprinkle with the remaining parsley, and serve.

OYSTER STEW WITH GRUYÈRE AND POTATOES
AQUARIUS

Chemical analysis shows that oysters' reputation for being an aphrodisiac is more than an old wives' tale. Oysters, typical on Valentine's Day, are high in certain amino acids known to set off frisky hormones in both sexes. The taste of the sea and the slippery, sensual mouthfeel also trigger erotic associations.

Stews are one of the joys of cold weather. Classic oyster stew is usually a simpler preparation. Oysters are added to a base of butter, onion, cream, salt, and pepper. While still rather simple to prepare, this recipe replaces the cream with Gruyère, and the addition of potatoes and mushrooms makes it heartier and more complex. With whole-grain crackers, it makes a warm and welcoming supper for lovers.

SERVES 2

4 tablespoons butter, divided
1 garlic clove, minced
2 leeks, trimmed, well-washed, and thinly sliced
1 pound Yukon gold potatoes, peeled and chopped into ½-inch dice
½ cup white wine
2 cups vegetable or chicken stock
1 teaspoon thyme
1 teaspoon hot sauce
½ teaspoon salt
½ teaspoon freshly ground black pepper
8 ounces button mushrooms, sliced (about 2 cups)
4 ounces Gruyère, grated
16 ounces shucked fresh oysters
Crackers, for the table

Melt 2 tablespoons of the butter in a soup pot over medium-high heat. Add the garlic and leeks. Sauté until the leeks soften, about 5 minutes. Add the potatoes, wine, stock, thyme, hot sauce, salt, and pepper. Bring to a boil, reduce the heat, and simmer until the potatoes are very tender, 10 to 15 minutes. Remove from the heat.

Melt the remaining 2 tablespoons butter in a skillet over medium-high heat. Add the mushrooms and sauté until they wilt, about 5 minutes.

Puree the leeks and potatoes using an immersion blender, or transfer to the bowl of a food processor and puree in batches. Return the pureed potato-leek mixture to the soup, and set over low heat. Add the Gruyère, and stir. Add the mushrooms, and continue simmering over low heat. Add the oysters and their liquid. Simmer until the oysters firm up and their edges begin to curl. Stir to ensure even cooking.

Serve with crackers.

VALENTINE'S DAY

On February 14, the Ides of February, the ancient Romans celebrated a festival known as the Lupercalia. The name derives from *lupus,* the Latin word for wolf, and the festival was in honor of the God Faunus, the horned forest deity who was the Roman counterpart to Pan. Faunus is not only associated with the libido, he was also a god of prophecy, who revealed the future in dreams given to those who bedded down on the fleecy pelts of the lambs sacrificed in his honor.

Appropriating yet another pagan festival and "cleaning it up," the Church instituted the feast of Saint Valentine. Saint Valentine was a Christian martyr from the third century. Not much about the historical person is known. He was decapitated on February 14, 270, for refusing to worship pagan gods. As the legend goes, when he died, the birds began to sing their mating songs. It seems rather ironic that Valentine's Day occurs when the sun is in Aquarius. Aquarius is not known for being romantic or sentimental. The archetypal Aquarian is detached, platonic, and rational; a cool, fixed air personality who values independence and novelty. But a look into the origins of the Lovers' Holiday reveals an Aquarian avoidance of emotional involvement.

During the Middle Ages, when Courtly Love was in flower, Valentine Clubs sprang up. They were Christian in name only. Membership was limited to couples. Every year on February 14, the members of the club would convene and celebrate a parody of the Mass. At the "Communion" the couples would part. The gentlemen would write their names on small pieces of parchment, and these would be placed in a receptacle resembling a large chalice. The ladies would reach in and draw a name. That gentleman would become her Valentine for the following year. They were lovers, not life partners. Marriage of a pair of Valentines was prohibited and punished by expulsion from the club. What could be more Aquarian than a new lover every year?

FLOUNDER ALMONDINE
PISCES

Pisces, a time of preparation for regeneration, of fasting and repentance, of working through the illusions and idealism of Aquarius, of compassion for others, may also be a time of confusion, uncertainty, and struggle, a time of excess and indiscretion, of feeling lost in the vast psychic ocean. Waves of wild energy are followed by periods of floundering. For smoother sailing through the troubled waters, a simplicity of being helps.

Here is a simple recipe that works well with any flat fish fillet, including fresh water trout. Flounder, abundant in the cold waters of March and caught in the wild, is seasonally and symbolically appropriate. A generous pinch of cayenne will keep the delicately flavored, tender, and mild white meat from being boring. At the fish counter, winter flounder is sometimes called lemon sole. Pisces communicates nonverbally. It does not matter what the fish is called, so long as it is fresh!

Tarragon, *Artemisia dracunculus,* is sacred to the goddess Artemis, the Greek Diana. Her epithets are Queen of the Wild and Mistress of Animals. The Virgin Goddess of the Hunt, at home in the wilderness, is the protector of women.

SERVES 4

2 lemons
2 pounds flounder fillets
½ teaspoon salt
½ teaspoon freshly ground black pepper
1 cup all-purpose flour, for dredging
2 tablespoons unsalted butter
2 tablespoons olive oil
½ cup white wine
⅛ teaspoon cayenne pepper, or to taste
½ teaspoon dried tarragon
½ cup slivered, toasted almonds (page 199, Roasting Seeds and Nuts)
2 tablespoons chopped parsley

Squeeze the juice from 1 lemon into a bowl. Cut the other widthwise into thin slices, removing and discarding the ends and the seeds. Put the lemon slices in the bowl with the juice.

Season the fillets with salt and pepper. Then dredge them in flour. Shake off any excess.

Heat the butter and olive oil in a large skillet over medium-high heat. When the butter and oil are very hot, but not smoking, add the fillets. Don't crowd them; panfry in batches if necessary. (If you must batch-fry, use only a portion of the butter and oil at a time.)

Panfry the fish until the undersides turn golden brown, about 3 minutes. Turn and brown the other side similarly. Transfer to a platter, and keep warm.

Pour the wine into the skillet. Simmer briefly to deglaze, scrapping up any bits that may have stuck to the bottom of the pan. Add the lemon juice and lemon slices. Season with the cayenne, tarragon, and an additional dash of salt and pepper, if you like. Add the almonds. Boil until the sauce thickens, about 1 minute. Spoon the sauce over the fillets.

Serve immediately, with a sprinkle of chopped parsley.

ROASTED DUCKLINGS IN ORANGE SAUCE
CAPRICORN

Rich, succulent duck is an appropriate centerpiece for the Yuletide feast, the time of year when the trees come inside to light the darkness, and the table sags under the fat of the land.

Long Island ducklings, descended from Peking forebears, have quite a bit of fat. Boiling them before roasting reduces the roasting time and ensures a crisper, less fatty finished product. Some ducks are fattier than others. The modern trend toward raising ducks more naturally tends to lead to leaner birds. In any case, a good amount of fat will remain to be rendered after boiling. With three months of Big Chill in the forecast, you may want to save it. Rendered duck fat can be a comfort on a lean day in February—it's precious stuff, doing miraculous things for roasted potatoes or roasted chicken.

Roasting the ducks on a bed of vegetables raises them up a bit, out of the fat. Not only does this help the ducks to roast evenly, the vegetables add their flavor to the pan juices. Celery stalks, fennel leaves, and potato slices will work just as well as onions and carrots.

In southern lands, December is the beginning of the orange harvest, the fruit that smacks of the sun's shine.

God bless us one and all!

SERVES 8

FOR THE DUCKS

2 ducklings, about 5 pounds each, giblets saved for the sauce
1 tablespoon coarse salt
1 bunch fresh thyme
1 bunch fresh rosemary
6 garlic cloves, peeled
2 oranges, one quartered and seeded; the other sliced in ¼-inch-thick rounds
2 to 3 onions sliced in ½-inch-thick rounds
1 bunch carrots, peeled and halved lengthwise
¼ cup Cointreau or other orange liqueur
1 teaspoon salt
2 teaspoons freshly ground black pepper

FOR THE SAUCE

16 ounces beef or chicken stock
Giblets and necks from the ducklings
2 to 3 tablespoons rendered duck fat (from the roasting ducklings)
2 tablespoons all-purpose flour
½ cup Cointreau or other orange liqueur
¼ cup red wine vinegar
¼ cup balsamic vinegar
¼ cup fresh orange juice
1 cup orange marmalade
2 tablespoons thinly sliced orange peel

1 orange, sliced into thin rounds, for garnish

Preheat the oven to 425°F. If convection is an option, choose it.

Make the ducks. Cut away the flap of fatty skin from the neck, and scrape any loose fat from inside the cavities. Prick the skin all over gently with a sharp fork, or cross-hatch it with a sharp knife. Be careful not to pierce the meat.

Fill an 18-quart stock pot (or as large as you have) about two-thirds full with water, and add the salt. Place the bunches of thyme and rosemary and the garlic cloves in it. Bring to a rapid boil. (You may need to use two pots if you do not have a single pot large enough to hold both ducklings at once; if so, divide the thyme and rosemary into smaller held-together bunches, and divide the garlic between the pots.) Place the ducks in the pot. If they pop up, keep them submerged using a smaller pot full of water or some other weight. Be aware of overflow. Bring the water back to a slow boil. Simmer the ducks for about 30 minutes. Remove them, and use paper towels to dry them thoroughly.

Stuff each of the ducks' cavities with half of the boiled thyme, rosemary, and garlic and the quartered orange.

Line the bottom of a large shallow roasting pan with the onions, carrots, and the orange rounds. Place the ducks, breast-side down, on top. Massage them with the Cointreau. This will give them a mahogany finish. Let them sit for 10 minutes for the skin to absorb the liqueur. Sprinkle with salt and pepper.

Roast until the bottoms brown, about 20 minutes. Turn them breast-side up, and lower the oven temperature to 350°F. Several times during roasting, spoon off any excess fat as it accumulates, or suck it up using a baster. Use some of the fat to baste the ducks, and set the rest aside, saving some for the sauce.

Depending on how long you boiled the ducks and the size of the ducks, roasting time will be another hour or longer. The ducks are done when a meat thermometer inserted into the thickest part of the thigh registers at least 180°F, or until the juices run clear and the leg bones wiggle easily. You want the meat to slide off the bones. Don't be afraid of overcooking these. Ducks don't dry out easily. The skin should be crisp. If not, no worries. You will pass the pieces under the broiler before serving. (If the ducks are too crisp and the meat is not finished cooking, cover them with foil as you continue roasting.) Once the ducks are ready, remove them from the oven, and cover them with aluminum foil while you finish the sauce.

Meanwhile, make the sauce. Combine the stock, giblets, and necks in a saucepot over

(continued)

ROASTED DUCKLINGS IN ORANGE SAUCE

(continued)

medium-high heat, and bring to a boil. Reduce the heat to medium-low to maintain a gentle boil, until the stock is reduced by half.

Finish the sauce when you have retrieved rendered duck fat from the roasting duck. In a medium saucepan, warm the duck fat over medium heat. Add the flour, whisking with a fork as you do so. Remove the giblets and necks from the stock reduction, and discard. Add the stock to the duck fat–flour mixture, raise the heat to medium-high, and stir continuously to prevent lumps as you bring it to a slow boil. Add the Cointreau, vinegars, orange juice, marmalade, and orange peel to the pan. Bring back to a boil, melting the marmalade, then simmer uncovered on low heat until the sauce thickens and is reduced.

Preheat a broiler with the rack set a notch or two down from the top position.

When the ducks have rested at least 20 minutes, use a sharp knife or poultry scissors to split them and cut the breasts from the legs. Discard the orange quarters, herbs, wings, and any pockets of fat that remain. Slip the breast meat from the bones. Leave the legs intact. Put a little sauce in a broiling pan, and lay the duck pieces on top. Spoon a little sauce on top of each piece. Put them under the broiler for about 1 minute to crisp and glaze. Watch them carefully; the sugar in the sauce caramelizes quickly.

Place the pieces on a platter, and decorate with thin, round slices of orange. Serve with additional sauce on the side.

SATURNALIA

Saturn rules Capricorn. To mark the sun's return, the Romans celebrated the Saturnalia, a weeklong festival observed during the last week of the year, during the time of the Winter Solstice. During the first week of Capricorn, the Goat capered. All hell broke loose. Social norms and conventions were suspended. There were orgiastic celebrations, undisciplined eating and drinking, gambling, gift-giving, and role reversals. Masters served slaves, and slaves ruled their masters until the masters got tired of the game.

CHOUCROUTE GARNI

AQUARIUS

Because of the long, slow cooking, this filling wintertime Alsatian specialty—braised sauerkraut with a selection of meats—fills the kitchen with the hearty aroma of northern lands, juniper berries, and caraway seeds. You may not find it on a spa menu, but the essence of warmth and comfort nourishes the soul.

A little Aquarian inventiveness and autonomy go a long way in this recipe. In Alsatian restaurants, choucroute is on the menu the way pizza or pasta is on trattoria menus. The basic braised sauerkraut base is the same, but there are a variety of toppings to choose from, all sorts of meats and even some versions using seafood.

Let Aquarian creativity, inventiveness, and egalitarian ideals come into play. But here are some suggestions. Tradition calls for you to make your own sauerkraut. Practicality calls for buying a high-quality ready-made version. In this version, ordinary bacon is substituted for the more customary ham hocks or pork knuckles, and butter is called for instead of the usual duck fat. But by all means, if you saved duck fat from the Yule feast, this is the time to use it. The toppings are up to you. Alsatians use Montbeliard and Strasbourg sausages. Since these are not readily available outside Alsace, you may substitute a selection of other sausages: bratwurst, knockwurst, weisswurst, kielbasa, cotechino (for a northern Italian twist), andouille (for a Cajun slant), chorizo (for Spanish style), even chicken or turkey sausage for the red meat–free or franks if you have children at the table. Slices of boneless boiled ham are also an option. Use the apples you prefer. Gala or Delicious adds some sweetness to the sauerkraut. You will need a large Dutch oven or similar casserole.

SERVES 6 TO 8

(*continued*)

CHOUCROUTE GARNI

(*continued*)

½ pound bacon

4 tablespoons butter

2 garlic cloves, minced

2 medium yellow onions, roughly chopped (about 2 cups)

3 medium carrots, peeled and grated (about 1 cup)

3 pounds sauerkraut

1 cup dry, sweet, or semisweet white wine, such as Reisling

1 cup chicken stock

3 apples, unpeeled, cored, and cut into wedges

3 bay leaves

1 tablespoon juniper berries

1 tablespoon black peppercorns

1 teaspoon caraway seeds

1½ teaspoons salt, divided

1 tablespoon prepared mustard, Dijon or whole-grain

3 to 4 pounds mixed sausages

1 to 2 tablespoons olive oil

2 pounds Yukon gold potatoes, peeled and quartered

Assorted mustards, for serving

Horseradish sauce, for serving

Preheat the oven to 275°F.

Fry the bacon in a skillet until lightly crisp. Drain on paper towels.

Melt the butter in the Dutch oven or casserole over medium heat, substituting some for the rendered bacon fat (or duck fat, if you have it), if you wish. Add the garlic, onion, and carrot, and cook, stirring occasionally, until the onion is thoroughly soft, about 10 minutes.

Meanwhile, use your hands to squeeze as much liquid as you can from the sauerkraut. Once the onion has softened, add the sauerkraut to the Dutch oven, and stir. Add the wine and stock, cover, and bring to a slow boil. Once the liquid comes to a boil, crumble the bacon, and add it to the Dutch oven, along with the apple wedges, bay leaves, juniper berries, black peppercorns, caraway seeds, ½ teaspoon of the salt, and mustard, and stir. Cover and place in the oven for 1½ to 2 hours.

While the sauerkraut braises, cook the sausages (in batches if necessary). Cut some of the sausages in half and leave others whole, for variety. In a large skillet, heat

1 tablespoon of olive oil over medium-high heat. When the oil is hot, add the sausages, and sear on all sides. Lower the heat, cover the pan, and cook, turning the sausages occasionally, until they are fully cooked through, 10 to 15 minutes. Repeat with the remaining oil and sausages, if cooking in batches.

Meanwhile, place the potatoes in a large pot, cover them with cold water, add the remaining 1 teaspoon salt, and bring to a boil over high heat. Drain when fully tender.

After the sauerkraut has finished cooking, nestle the sausages and the potatoes on top, and cover again. Return the casserole to the oven, but turn off the heat. Leave the sauerkraut, sausages, and potatoes in the oven for 20 to 30 minutes, allowing the meats to warm up and the flavors to mingle.

Discard the juniper berries, peppercorns, and bay leaves. To serve, mound the hot sauerkraut in the center of a large platter. Arrange the meat and potatoes around the edges, and bring to the table, along with the assorted mustards and horseradish sauce.

 If you put the bay leaves, juniper berries, and peppercorns in a metal tea infuser or tie them up in cheesecloth, they will be easier to remove before serving.

BEEF BOURGUIGNON
PISCES

The final phase of Earth's Zodiacal journey is Pisces. Leading up to the balance of the Vernal Equinox, the crystallizations of winter are beginning to break up, the ice is melting, and the sap is beginning to flow. But while there is hope, there is also uncertainty. In preparation for the new, there must be the disintegration of the old. As there is no left without right, there are no beginnings without ends. As a vital part of the process, the dissolution of structure, the letting-go of the previous cycle, difficult as it might be at times, should be celebrated.

In Pisces we give ourselves up, back to that vast, mutable water-world, the stew of life that lies behind and before our life on land. While you're in the stew, you might as well make it deluxe. But don't be intimidated. The food of the rich originated with the poor. Beef bourguignon, a stew prepared with beef, vegetables, and herbs slowly braised in red wine, started as peasant fare from the Bourgogne region of France. The long simmering was to tenderize tough cuts of meat. Now it has an elevated, refined status, but underneath the haughty reputation, beef bourguignon is at home on a rustic table.

SERVES 6 TO 8

2 tablespoons olive oil

6 ounces chunk bacon, cut into 1-inch cubes

3 pounds stew beef or chuck, cut into 1-inch cubes

½ teaspoon salt, plus extra as needed

1 teaspoon freshly ground black pepper

3 garlic cloves, minced

2 yellow onions, sliced

3 medium carrots, peeled, cut into 1-inch diagonals

½ cup Cognac

1 bottle burgundy or other full-bodied red such as a Côte du Rhone or Pinot Noir

2 to 3 cups beef stock

2 tablespoons tomato paste

Bouquet garni (page 230, Bouquet Garni)

4 tablespoons butter

1 pound pearl onions, peeled (see note on facing page)

1 teaspoon sugar

1 pound button mushrooms, sliced

Preheat the oven to 250°F.

Heat the olive oil over medium-high heat in a large Dutch oven or large casserole. When the oil is hot, add the bacon, and cook until lightly browned, about 10 minutes. Remove with a slotted spoon to a medium bowl, and set aside.

Pat the beef dry, using paper towels. Season the beef with the salt and black pepper. Heat the bacon drippings in the Dutch oven over medium-high heat. Sear the beef in batches, turning until browned on all sides, 3 to 4 minutes total, per batch. Remove the seared beef with a slotted spoon, and transfer to the same bowl as the bacon.

Add the garlic, onions, and carrots to the Dutch oven, and sauté over medium heat until the onion is soft, 7 to 10 minutes. At this point, if there is excess fat in the pot, spoon or pour it off.

Add the Cognac to the Dutch oven, and very carefully ignite it with a long match or fire starter. Let it burn for a few seconds, then add the bacon and beef cubes back to the pot, along with any juices that have accumulated. Add the bottle of wine and enough beef stock to barely cover the meat. Add the tomato paste, and stir. Immerse the bouquet garni in the liquid, and bring to a simmer.

Cover and braise in the oven until the beef is very tender, about 1½ hours. Check occasionally, skimming off fat if it rises.

While the beef is cooking, melt 2 tablespoons of the butter in a large skillet over medium-high heat. Add the pearl onions, and lightly brown them on all sides, about 5 minutes. Lower the heat to medium. Scoop out ¼ cup of the stew from the Dutch oven, and add it to the onions. Add the sugar and a dash of salt, and stir to mix. Bring to a boil,

(continued)

If you use prepeeled frozen or canned pearl onions, you will not have to peel them. But it is better to use fresh. You can peel them by blanching them in boiling water for 1 minute. Run them under cold water, cut off a thin slice from the stem end, and slip off the peel.

BEEF BOURGUIGNON

(*continued*)

then lower the heat to a simmer, and cover. Simmer until the onions are tender, about 20 minutes. Transfer to a bowl.

Melt the remaining 2 tablespoons butter in the same skillet, unwiped, over medium-high heat. Add the mushrooms. Sauté until they start to brown and release some of their juices, about 5 minutes. Add them to the onions, and set aside until the stew is finished.

When the meat is cooked tender, a fork should pierce it without resistance. The sauce should be thick enough to form a light coating on a knife or spoon. Return the stew to the stovetop. If the stew is too thin, bring to a boil over medium-high heat, then lower the heat and simmer for a bit, uncovered, to reduce the stew.

Discard the bouquet garni. Add the onions and mushrooms to the Dutch oven, stir, and simmer for a few more minutes. Taste for seasoning, and adjust as necessary.

Serve with a loaf of rustic country bread and butter on the table.

BOUQUET GARNI

A bouquet garni is a bouquet of herbs. Sprigs of varying herbs such as thyme, rosemary, chervil, savory, basil, and bay leaves are tied together with cooking twine, and steeped in the stew to flavor it. You can probably get the same flavor by packing the herbs in cheesecloth or wrapping them in a coffee filter, but it is not nearly as satisfying. For this dish, make the bouquet garni with 6 thyme sprigs, 4 parsley sprigs, 4 basil sprigs, and 1 rosemary sprig.

CRANBERRY RELISH
CAPRICORN

The cranberry has the chthonic element that relates to Capricorn. Their final harvest occurring around the Winter Solstice, these red berries make an edible decoration at the Yule feast. A sweet and sour cranberry relish mates well with any pork or poultry entrée.

Like many sour foods, cranberries cleanse the palate and stimulate the appetite. Some like them tart, but for most tastes, cranberries need to be sweetened. The amount of sugar recommended (¼ cup) should not make the relish too sweet. If you use unsweetened cherries, you will probably want to add more sugar.

SERVES 8

½ pound fresh or frozen cranberries, plus extra for adjusting taste
4 ounces sweetened dried cherries
¼ cup brown sugar
2 tablespoons balsamic vinegar
1 orange, peeled, sectioned, seeds discarded
¼ cup apple cider
¼ cup apple liqueur
2 tablespoons orange zest, plus extra, julienned, for garnish
2 tablespoons grated fresh ginger
2 cinnamon sticks
1 garlic clove, peeled
⅛ teaspoon cayenne pepper

Combine all ingredients, except for the garnishing zest, in a saucepot, and bring to a gentle boil over medium heat. Turn the heat to low, and simmer until the cranberries and cherries are soft and just starting to lose their shape and the liquid is reduced by half. This can take anywhere from 20 to 35 minutes. After 10 minutes, taste for sweetness/tartness. If too tart, add more sugar. If too sweet, add more cranberries. Discard the cinnamon sticks and garlic clove before serving.

CRANBERRY

The name cranberry came about from a perceived similarity of the plant's blossom to the head of a crane. Hermes, the Greek Mercury, Messenger of the Gods and the Educator of Humanity, is often depicted with a crane by his side. As the legend goes, the Patron of Communication, fascinated by the crane's exotic courtship dance, invented the alphabet, patterning the letters on the birds' suggestive gyrations.

WILD RICE PILAF
AQUARIUS

Wild rice is semi-aquatic. This indigenous American grass grows abundantly in the lakes, rivers, and wetlands of the Great Lakes region. It roots in the mud and develops delicate stems and leaves that float on the water's surface. It is essential that the water remain at a relatively constant depth. With a sudden rise in depth, the plant will be torn out by the root. If the water suddenly becomes too shallow, the stems, unable to bear the weight of the leaves, break. Even in the wild, constancy promotes survival.

A little bit wild and different, young-at-heart Aquarius can go to extremes with impossible dreams. The Water Bearer tends to see things as black and white, not because he is narrow of mind, but because he shuns gray, that symbol of later years when the lively, colorful positive attitudes of youth are replaced by the cares of aging and the disappointment of having seen many of those youthful dreams never materialize.

No pie in the sky, wild rice has a down-to-earth chewy texture and a gutsy flavor. You can eat the shiny black grains "straight up," but many find wild rice's huskiness

unpalatable on its own. It is often mixed with tamer grains and dried mushrooms, another long-shelf-life staple of the winter larder.

A simple, black and white rice pilaf makes a suitable accompaniment to any meat or fish entrée and serves as a reminder to laugh when your dreams fall apart at the seams.

SERVES 6 TO 8

2 cups chicken or vegetable stock
1 ounce dried porcini mushrooms
½ cup wild rice
3 tablespoons butter, divided
½ teaspoon salt, plus extra as needed
1 to 2 medium yellow onions, minced (about 1 cup)
2 medium carrots, peeled and minced (about 1 cup)
3 ounces (about 4 or 5) button mushrooms, sliced (about 1 cup)
½ cup carnaroli rice
1 teaspoon dried thyme

Combine the stock and 1 cup water in a medium saucepan, and bring to a boil over high heat. Add the dried mushrooms, stir, cover, and remove from the heat. Let sit for 30 minutes.

Meanwhile, rinse the wild rice under cold running water. Place it in a pot with 1½ cups of the stock (reserving the porcini). Add 1 tablespoon of the butter and the salt, and bring to a boil over high heat. Reduce the heat to low, and cover. Cook until the grains begin to burst, about 45 minutes. Check several times. Add more stock or water, if necessary.

While the wild rice cooks, melt the remaining 2 tablespoons butter in a separate pot over medium-high heat. Add the onions, carrots, and button mushrooms, and sauté until they begin to sweat, about 5 minutes. Add the carnaroli rice, and sauté until it gives off a nutty aroma, about 2 or 3 minutes. Add

the remaining stock, along with the reserved porcinis. Add the thyme and a few dashes of salt, and stir. Raise the heat to high, and bring to a boil. Cover and reduce the heat to low. Cook for 15 minutes, then remove from the heat, keep covered, and let rest for 5 to 10 minutes. Fluff with a fork.

Add the (cooked) wild rice to the carnaroli rice. Fluff together, and serve.

HAZELNUT SWEET POTATOES
PISCES

Under the seductive power of Neptune, as the Zodiac winds back to Aries, Pisces must accept the final dissolution of the old cycle. The past is washing away in a cleansing Lenten flux. Sentimental thoughts and impressions arise subjectively, of their own accord, rather than through the conscious efforts of the intellect. In the wash, things may be nonspecific, unclear, and impossible to categorize. Where is the stability? Insecurity is built into this phase of the cycle. Nothing lasts forever. Things falling apart is prerequisite to resurrection. Awareness of this creates some necessary objectivity in the chaos. Tossed about in the turbulence, the fluid mind is not attached to distinctions. Root vegetables, earthy ballast, solid and nourishing, also help counteract the excess fluidity of this phase. Sweet potatoes may be served as a side dish for pork or poultry, a la mode as a dessert, or with pancakes at a late winter brunch.

If you wish, use yams instead of sweet potatoes. Both sweet potatoes and yams belong to the same genus and are related to the morning glory. The sweet potato grows on the vine, while the yam is a tuberous root.

SERVES 4 TO 6

2 sweet potatoes, peeled and sliced into
    ½-inch-thick rounds
2 cups chicken stock
2 tablespoons butter
¼ cup maple syrup
¼ cup Frangelico or other hazelnut liqueur
½ cup toasted hazelnuts, coarsely chopped
    (page 199, Roasting Seeds and Nuts)

Combine the sweet potato with the stock in a large saucepan, and bring to a gentle boil over medium-high heat. Boil gently until just tender, about 8 minutes. Strain, reserving the stock.

Rinse and dry the pot. Add the butter, and melt over low heat. Add the sweet potato rounds gently so as not to break them. Turn to distribute the butter. Add the maple syrup and liqueur. If necessary, raise the heat a notch, and simmer slowly until a knife prick pierces them without resistance, about 5 minutes. Add a drizzle or two of the stock if the mixture seems dry.

Transfer the sweet potatoes to a serving dish, top with the chopped hazelnuts, and serve.

CHEESECAKE AND CHERRY SAUCE
CAPRICORN

Creamy and comforting, a cheesecake is a special occasion dessert. Like Capricorn, it is reliable, cool, and in no way thin or shallow. This recipe is made even more distinctive with the addition of a pair of unusual sweeteners—new to us, perhaps, but used for ages in other places, and recently making their re-entry into the mainstream global pantry. Lucuma powder, a sweetener milled from a dried fruit native to Peru, adds notes of maple and melon. As an ingredient in ancient Incan fertility rituals, it has a hint of cosmic vision in its sweetness. Mahleb, the ground seed of the Mahaleb cherry, is an intense spice that has been used in Greek and Middle Eastern bakeries for millennia. It gives the Greek Christmas cake its distinctive bitter almond and sharp wild cherry flavor. A little bit goes a long way.

SERVES 8 TO 10

2 cups graham cracker crumbs
4 tablespoons melted butter
2 8-ounce packages cream cheese, softened
8 ounces of mascarpone
½ cup lucuma powder
½ cup coconut sugar
1 teaspoon vanilla extract
4 eggs, beaten
1 cup dried cherries
1 tablespoon honey
2 tablespoons fruit preserves, such as cherry or apricot
½ teaspoon ground mahleb
Pinch of salt
1 tablespoon brandy

Make the crust. Combine the graham cracker crumbs and the butter in a large bowl, and mix well. Grease the bottom of a 9-inch springform pan, and line it with a circle of parchment paper. Press the crumb mixture onto the bottom of the pan, and spread it upward about 2 inches around the side of the pan. Refrigerate for 1 hour.

Preheat the oven to 350°F.

Make the filling. Combine the cream cheese and mascarpone in a mixing bowl, and beat until smooth with an electric mixer. Add the lucuma, coconut sugar, and vanilla to the bowl, and mix in with a wooden spoon. Add the beaten eggs a little at a time, mixing thoroughly between each addition. Pour the filling into the chilled crust. Place the springform pan on a baking sheet, and bake for 1 hour until set. Cool to room temperature.

Meanwhile, make the cherry sauce. Combine the cherries, ½ cup water, the honey, fruit preserves, mahleb, and salt in a small saucepan over medium heat. Bring to a boil.

Once boiling, turn the heat to low, cover the saucepan, and simmer for 7 minutes, stirring occasionally. Turn off the heat, and stir in the brandy, then cover and let sit for 5 minutes (the cherries will plump a bit more). The sauce can be used warm, cold, or at room temperature.

When the cheesecake is cooled to room temperature, carefully run a knife around the edge of the pan to loosen it before opening the spring. Spoon the cherry sauce over the cheesecake, spreading it out in a smooth layer with the back of the spoon.

CHOCOLATE CHESTNUT MOUSSE
AQUARIUS

Folklore dating back to Mesoamerica tells us chocolate is an aphrodisiac. Chemical analysis does show that the cocoa bean contains small amounts of tryptophan, phenylethylamine, and several other substances that are released in the brain when we experience physical attraction. By clinical standards, however, the amounts of these chemicals in chocolate are rather low. Too low to produce desire? Attraction is a force of Nature. It defies logic and has contradictory qualities that are at odds with the quantitative principles and methods of science.

The mind, with its inherent imagination, is our most erogenous zone. Physical love is often entirely psychological. The right shoes, cologne, hairdo, or tone of voice can trigger deep emotional reactions that cause the mind to see an all-too-human female or male as a Venus or an Adonis. Who can say how much of a chemical is needed to effect this miraculous transformation? Perhaps it only takes the taste, or even the smell, to do the trick. If you think that quantity influences quality, however, use unsweetened chocolate, which is 99 percent cacao, or bittersweet chocolate, which is typically at minimum

70 percent cacao. The amount of sugar recommended below supposes you are using bittersweet.

In the archetype, Aquarius is detached, clearheaded, and not easily beguiled. The Aquarian passion is for independence. But aphrodisiacs can come in all forms: for some idealism, freedom to act on one's own, moderation, and a meeting of the minds are more of a turn-on than unbridled animal passion. This dessert is a little bit different from the average heavy cream mousse, and it is also quick and easy to prepare, leaving more time for an Aquarius to explore the mind-body connections. Happy Valentine's Day!

SERVES 2

½ cup almond milk
½ cup dark chocolate chips
6 ounces firm silken tofu
½ cup roasted, peeled chestnuts
2 teaspoons brandy
8 coarsely chopped chocolate-covered
   espresso beans

Combine the almond milk and chocolate chips in a microwave-safe bowl, and microwave on medium-high about 2 minutes, stirring midway through. Stir again once the chocolate is fully melted and the chocolate and almond milk are fully blended to a rich, milky consistency. Or you can combine the almond milk and chocolate in a small saucepan and melt gently over low heat on your stovetop. Whisk together and let cool.

Combine the chocolate mixture, tofu, chestnuts, and brandy in the bowl of a food processor, and pulse until pureed and very creamy. Pour into 1-cup ramekins or small dishes. Depending on the volume your ramekins hold, the mix will fill 2 or more. (If you have extra, mousse is even yummier the second time around.)

Cover the ramekins with plastic wrap, and refrigerate until thoroughly chilled, at least 2 hours.

When ready to serve, garnish with the chocolate-covered coffee beans.

POACHED PEARS IN MAPLE SYRUP
PISCES

There is a silent, invisible spring that goes on behind the scenes of winter. The vacillating temperatures, deep freezes at night followed by the thawing days as February progresses, cause tree sap to flow. The maple syrup season typically lasts for about a month, roughly coinciding with Pisces. When the nights warm above freezing and spring is imminent, the sap goes to fatten the buds and loses its woody sweetness. The tapping is over.

Pisces is represented by two fish swimming in opposite directions. Vacillation is key to the Piscean time of year. Thoughts and actions may be pulled in opposite directions. Although we may not be aware of our roots in the plant world, like the trees, the late winter variations in temperature cause our psychic sap to start flowing. Tap that for a sweet treat! As it can take more than forty gallons of sap to make one gallon of syrup, you might boil down a cauldron of raw psychic material to produce one sweet hour of rounded awareness, blessed relief in the seasonal fluctuations.

Poached pears are an easy, wholesome winter dessert, or with yogurt, a satisfying way to start the day. Use the pears of your choice. Crisp ones such as Bosc, Concorde, or Seckel will take a little extra time softening than juicier varieties such as Anjou, Bartlett, or Comice.

SERVES 4

3 cups apple juice
½ cup maple syrup
1 cinnamon stick
1 teaspoon whole cloves
2 tablespoons fresh ginger slices
4 pears, peeled, cored, and quartered
½ cup raisins

Combine the apple juice, maple syrup, cinnamon stick, cloves, and ginger slices in a large skillet over medium-low heat. Add the pears, bring to a slow boil, and simmer until the pears are cooked through, 15 to 20 minutes, depending on the type of pear used. Test by poking them carefully with a sharp knife.

Remove the pears with a slotted spoon. Raise the heat to medium-high, and reduce the liquid by half. It should be quite syrupy by this point. Discard the cinnamon stick, the cloves, and the ginger slices. Add the raisins and simmer, covered, for a few minutes longer to plump them.

To serve, place the pears in bowls, and spoon the syrup over the top. Serve warm or at room temperature.

HOLIDAY CELEBRATIONS AND FEASTS

Holiday celebrations come to us from ancient observances of the cycles of the seasons and the movements of heaven and earth. In various social contexts, our holidays and holy days might go by different names, but the inner frames of mind and outer circumstances they commemorate are essentially the same all over the world. They are times to get together with family and dear friends, to share a meal and share the love, to channel peace and happiness. Ideally, there should be something on the table for everyone to feel welcome and well-fed. Feel free to adapt and add or subtract from these suggested menus. The more dishes, the merrier—and the more memorable the feast will be. For special times of the year, no matter the month, let magnanimous Jupiter reign: too much of a good thing is even better.

SPRING RENEWAL CELEBRATION

Blossoming flowers, chirping birds, and warm sunshine all combine to make this a magical time of year. It's a time for new beginnings, so take some time to share a ceremony or two with your friends and family. Acknowledge that you made it through another winter, a symbolic passage through the darkness to the light. Honor old traditions and create new ones with special gatherings, delicious food, rituals, and prayers.

Easter, formerly known as "Eoster," is the name of the Goddess of the Dawn, from which we derive the word *east,* the direction from which the sun rises, a symbol of resurrection if ever there were one. Though some people believe that practicing Christianity means rejecting astrology and "pagan" goddess rites, they have unwittingly honored them since Christianity began, by celebrating many of their main events on days sacred to the Goddess and based on astrological calculations. A primary example is Easter. Easter is celebrated on the Sunday following the full moon that follows or falls on the Spring Equinox.

SPRING RENEWAL FEAST

Deviled Eggs and Diablo Slaw (page 42)

Watercress-Parsley Soup (page 44)

Baby Arugula Pesto and Baby Peas Conchiglie (page 56)

Sriracha Salmon Cakes (page 66)

Classic Passover Brisket (page 74)

Stir-Fried Snap Peas (page 80)

Mashed Baby Limas (page 79)

Carrot Cupcakes (page 81)

SUMMER SOLSTICE CELEBRATION

The enchantments of summer: an abundance of lush growth, dazzling flowers, fruits, and vegetables and the promise of a truly exciting time to celebrate life. The Summer Solstice, also known as Litha, is the first day of summer and the longest day of the year—the sun moves into the sign of Cancer, also known as the Crab. You might feel your more sensitive, nurturing side come to the surface during this period. We recommend that you schedule in more relaxing and pampering time for yourself to make sure you keep yourself feeling refreshed and renewed.

Midsummer is a time for divination and healing rituals. Put beautiful flowers and shells on your altar. Pull out the tarot cards, your pendulum, or your talking board. Get your chakras into balance. Midsummer is a time to celebrate both what we have and what we intend to manifest.

SUMMER SOLSTICE FEAST

Watermelon Gazpacho (page 93)

Haricot Verts and New Potato Salad (page 98)

Lobster and Roasted Corn Orecchiette (page 100)

Zucchini Barzini (page 106)

Golden Turmeric Chicken (page 122)

Polenta Bites with Sage-Hazelnut Pesto (page 126)

Peaches and Boston Lettuce (page 95)

Berry Mascarpone Tart (page 130)

FALL HARVEST CELEBRATION

This time of year is full of colorful leaves, crisp air, bountiful harvest, and internal change. It brings to us a time of personal growth and rebirth. At the beginning of October, the sun is in Libra. Libras like to enjoy their homes by making them comfortable and beautiful. So the Libran energy just might give you that gentle push to surround yourself with some of the beauty that Mother Nature has to offer. By the twenty-third, the sun moves into Scorpio, which is a very magnetic and powerful sign that likes to be in control of its own destiny. We begin then to prepare for the mysteries and mysticism of All Hallows' Eve, now known as Halloween—that time of year when the veils are lifted between the worlds of those on the earth plane and those who are not.

Take time to evaluate the past year and turn inward, gathering what is meaningful and healing. It is a great time of year to identify what is important to keep, and to release the bad habits and emotional baggage that might be holding us back. Pay attention to forgiveness, nonattachment, and letting go. As we step into this coming season, may we listen to the voices of our ancestors and guiding spirits.

Set the dinner table with candles and a fall centerpiece, and put all the food on the table at once. Consider the dinner table a sacred space. Honor your deceased family members with this feast. Gather photographs, heirlooms, and other mementos of loved ones. Arrange them nearby. Say grace: "Tonight we share the bounty of our harvest and thank the earth for all it has given us this season, and we thank our ancestors for life."

Light the candles in their memory, speak their names out loud, and express well wishes and thanks. By honoring and invoking the ancestors through prayer and veneration, we can magically be with them and allow their wisdom to speak powerfully to us. When we communicate openly with these loving energies, we deepen our sense of wholeness, nourish our spirits, and unburden ourselves from the sense of loss and loneliness that results from feeling cut off from them. We can go on and on, back and farther back, and allow the wise and wonderful people of the past to speak their truth to us. May we be inspired to reflect upon and honor what is truly beautiful in our lives.

FALL HARVEST FEAST

Butternut Squash Soup with Roasted Pepitas
(page 138)

Persimmon Pomegranate Salad (page 148)

Linguine with Cauliflower Two Ways
(page 152)

Apple-Stuffed Pork Tenderloin (page 168)

Scallops and Israeli Couscous (page 162)

Roasted Rosemary Potatoes (page 176)

Roasted Brussels Sprouts (page 174)

Plum Upside-Down Cake (page 184)

WINTER SOLSTICE CELEBRATION

Winter Solstice is of course the longest night and shortest day of the year. *Solstice* in Latin actually means "the sun stands still." And so it does—the sun has stopped retreating but hasn't yet begun to come back. Many different cultures around the world honor the sun and its rebirth. In India, Pongal is the Hindu Solstice celebration. The Hopi Native Americans have a ritual where they light fires to energize and entice the safe return of "the Light." In Japan, Winter Solstice is a time when the sun goddess Amaterasu would come out of her cave. Hanukkah actually means "Festival of Lights." And Christians around the world celebrate Christmas, a time when the Christ child brings back light and a renewal of hope to the world.

Today, many people celebrate the holidays of the season—Christmas, Hanukkah, Kwanzaa—without thinking about their Winter Solstice origins. In fact, most of the holiday customs and traditions of December—miraculous events, giving gifts, celebrating with family, decorating with lights, pinecones, Yule logs, even the colors white, red, and green—are actually connected to ancient Winter Solstice celebrations. We like to say a special prayer to "Welcome the Return of Light." It goes like this:

May darkness give way to Light.
We are awake within the Night.
Turn the Wheel to bring the Light.
With the powers of Fire, Air, Water, and Earth,
We welcome the Light.
Strengthen our hope.
Fill us with Peace.

WINTER SOLSTICE FEAST

Sage Pea Soup (page 196)

Angel Hair with Fennel Pesto (page 204)

Flounder Almondine (page 220)

Roasted Ducklings in Orange Sauce
    (page 222)

Wild Rice Pilaf (page 232)

Kale Salad (page 198)

Cranberry Relish (page 231)

Cheesecake and Cherry Sauce (page 236)

NEW YEAR MEDITATION MEAL

There is much to be said for the time of year when the rhythm of life naturally slows down, giving us ample time to take those important steps in putting our plans into place. For us, this is an ideal time to methodically go through papers in our studios and organize and, most important, get rid of what we don't need. It feels good to pare down and begin the New Year on a fresh note.

Orderly and constructive Capricorn at the start of January helps you tap into your self-discipline and assists you in these endeavors. It will also enable you to steadily focus on the things you want to bring about in your life. The open-minded and inventive Aquarian influence, which takes over on January 21, will give you the ability to come up with creative solutions to begin achieving your desires.

The Gregorian calendar, used internationally for civil and business purposes, has the first day of January as New Year's Day. The Chinese ring in the New Year on the new moon following January 21. Rosh Hashanah, the Jewish New Year, also timed by lunar phase, falls between mid-September and mid-October. The Maori see the rising of the Pleiades in late May as the start of the New Year. As individuals we mark the New Year on our birthdays. We always have a reason to celebrate: every night is New Year's Eve; every day is New Year's Day.

We like to say a special New Year's grace: "Bless us on the beginning of this New Year, and bless our beginnings throughout the year."

NEW YEAR MEDITATION MEAL

Baby Spinach and Radicchio Salad (page 96)

Roasted Golden Beets and Walnuts
(page 146)

Toshikoshi Soba (page 210)

Eggplant Parmigiana (page 214)

Lemony Grilled Shrimp with White Beans
(page 116)

Beef Bourguignon (page 228)

Hazelnut Sweet Potatoes (page 234)

Chocolate Chestnut Mousse (page 238)

ACKNOWLEDGMENTS

We especially want to thank Claudia Boutote, publisher, and Libby Edelson, senior editor, at HarperElixir, and Lisa Sharkey, director of creative development at HarperCollins, for supporting our vision and helping to bring this book to life, while encouraging and guiding us to make magic. We would also like to thank the team at HarperElixir, including Anissa Elmerraji, Adrian Morgan, Noël Chrisman, Julia Kent, and Jane Chong. Gratitude to Dan V. Romer for his artful skills and assistance on the twelve food mandalas. And appreciation for our dear friends and family of all signs who make eating, cooking, and entertaining a true pleasure and a blessing.

UNIVERSAL CONVERSION CHART

OVEN TEMPERATURE EQUIVALENTS

250°F = 120°C   400°F = 200°C

275°F = 135°C   425°F = 220°C

300°F = 150°C   450°F = 230°C

325°F = 160°C   475°F = 240°C

350°F = 180°C   500°F = 260°C

375°F = 190°C

MEASUREMENT EQUIVALENTS

Measurements should always be level unless directed otherwise.

⅛ teaspoon = 0.5 mL

¼ teaspoon = 1 mL

½ teaspoon = 2 mL

1 teaspoon = 5 mL

1 tablespoon = 3 teaspoons = ½ fluid ounce = 15 mL

2 tablespoons = ⅛ cup = 1 fluid ounce = 30 mL

4 tablespoons = ¼ cup = 2 fluid ounces = 60 mL

5⅓ tablespoons = ⅓ cup = 3 fluid ounces = 80 mL

8 tablespoons = ½ cup = 4 fluid ounces = 120 mL

10⅔ tablespoons = ⅔ cup = 5 fluid ounces = 160 mL

12 tablespoons = ¾ cup = 6 fluid ounces = 180 mL

16 tablespoons = 1 cup = 8 fluid ounces = 240 mL

INDEX

Acorn Squash with Mushrooms and Hazelnuts,
   140–41
advent, 137
air signs, 9–10
al kimia (black earth), 136
alla Cacciatora, Pappardelle, 206–7
almond flour, 81, 182, 184
almond meal, 84
Anchovies, Linguine Fine with Broccoli and,
   154–55
Angel Hair with Fennel Pesto, 204–5
aphrodisiacs, 218, 238
appetizers
   Cauliflower Sformati, 192–93
   Chorizo-Stuffed Figs, 94
   Endives with Parmesan, Olives, and Walnuts,
      46–47
   Roasted Acorn Squash, 140–41
   Rösti with Smoked Salmon, 142–43
   White Bean–Parsnip Dip, 194–95
   See also salads; soups
apple-celery salad, 144–45
Apple Crumble, 180–81
Apple-Stuffed Pork Tenderloin, 168–69
apricots, 76–77
Aquarius
   classification, 8–10, 32
   food profile, 32–33
   recipes reflecting, 194–95, 200, 206–7,
      212–13, 218, 225–27, 232–33,
      238–39
   seasonal associations, 7, 189–90
Arancini and Ceci Arrabiata, 60–61
Aries
   classification, 7–8, 9, 12
   food profile, 12–13
   recipes reflecting, 42–43, 48–49, 54–55, 60–61,
      66–67, 72–73, 78, 81
   seasonal associations, 3, 38
arugula, 56–57, 62–63, 92, 118–19, 158, 192
Arugula Pesto, Baby, 56–57
asparagus, 54–55, 98–99
Asparagus and Fresh Favas Fettucine, 54–55
astrology. *See* Zodiac
Autumnal Equinox, 91, 246–47
Avocado Dressing, Green Goddess, 50–51
Avocado-Lime Pie, 82–83

Baby Arugula Pesto and Baby Peas Conchiglie,
   56–57
Baby Spinach and Radicchio Salad, 96–97
Beef Bourguignon, 228–30
beef brisket, 74–75
Beef Tenderloin with Scallions and Horseradish,
   120–21
Beets and Walnuts, 146–47
Belgian endive, 46–47, 49, 146–47
Berry Mascarpone Tart, 130
black beans, 160–61
Black Cod and Sesame Spinach, 68–69
blueberry and peach crisp, 128
bouquet garni, 230
Branzino, Grilled, 114–15
Broccoli and Anchovies, Linguine Fine with,
   154–55
Broccoli Rabe, Sausage, and White Beans with
   Penne, 150–51
Brussels Sprouts, Roasted, 174
Brussels Sprouts and Chestnut Slaw, 200–201
Bucatini alla Norma, 104–5
Bucheron cheese, 54

buckwheat noodles, 210–11
Butternut Squash Lasagna, 156–57
Butternut Squash Soup with Roasted Pepitas,
    138–39

cabbage slaw, Savoy, 42–43
Cajun Slaw, 164–65
Cake, Plum Upside-Down, 184–85
Cancer
    classification, 8, 10, 18
    food profile, 18–19
    recipes reflecting, 92, 95, 100–101, 106–7,
        112–13, 118–19, 124, 128
    seasonal associations, 4–5, 88
cannellini beans, 116–17, 150–51
capers, 114
Capricorn
    classification, 8, 10, 30
    food profile, 30–31
    recipes reflecting, 192–93, 198–99, 204–5,
        210–11, 216–17, 222–24, 231, 236–37
    seasonal associations, 6–7, 188–89
cardinal signs, 8
carnaroli rice, 178–79
Carrot Cupcakes, 81
Cauliflower-Potato Curry with Spaghetti Squash,
    212–13
Cauliflower Sformati, 192–93
Cauliflower Two Ways, Linguine with, 152–53
celery-apple salad, 144–45
Cheesecake and Cherry Sauce, 236–37
Chestnut Mousse, Chocolate, 238–39
Chestnut Slaw, Brussels Sprouts and, 200–201
Chicken, Golden Turmeric, 122–23
Chicken, Pomegranate, 170–71

chicken tagine, 76–77
chickpea falafel, 158–59
chickpeas arrabiata sauce, 60–61
Chocolate Chestnut Mousse, 238–39
Chocolate Chip Cookies, 182–83
Chorizo-Stuffed Figs, 94
Choucroute Garni, 225–27
Clams and Cockles Linguine, 102–3
Classic Passover Brisket, 74–75
coconut flour, 81
coconut nectar, 82–83
Coconut-Peach Crisp, 128
Cod and Sesame Spinach, 68–69
Cointreau, 118
Conchiglie, Baby Arugula Pesto and Baby Peas,
    56–57
constellations, 3
Cookies, Chocolate Chip, 182–83
Corn Orecchiette, Lobster and Roasted, 100–101
cornucopia, 175
Couscous, Scallops and Israeli, 162–63
Couscous and Cracked Wheat Tabbouleh, 48–49
Crabs, Fried Soft-Shell, 112–13
cranberries, 180–81, 198–99, 231
Cranberry Relish, 231
crème fraîche, 50, 120, 142–43
croutons, 93, 202–3
Cucumber Pistachio Soup, 92
Cupcakes, Carrot, 81
Curry with Spaghetti Squash, Cauliflower-Potato,
    212–13

desserts
    Apple Crumble, 180–81
    Avocado-Lime Pie, 82–83

desserts (*continued*)
    Berry Mascarpone Tart, 130
    Carrot Cupcakes, 81
    Cheesecake and Cherry Sauce, 236–37
    Chocolate Chestnut Mousse, 238–39
    Chocolate Chip Cookies, 182–83
    Coconut-Peach Crisp, 128
    Kiwi Ricotta Stacks, 129
    Plum Upside-Down Cake, 184–85
    Poached Pears in Maple Syrup, 240–41
    Tahini Lemon Bars, 84–85
Deviled Eggs and Diablo Slaw, 42–43
Dilled Zucchini and Scallions, 124
Dressing, Lemon–Olive Oil, 51
duckling, 118–19, 222–24
Ducklings in Orange Sauce, Roasted, 222–24

earth signs, 10
egg dishes
    Deviled Eggs and Diablo Slaw, 42–43
    Frittata Caprese, 108–9
    Spaghetti alla Carbonara, 208–9
    Spring Vegetable Quiche, 62–63
eggplant dishes, 72–73, 104–5, 110–11, 214–15
Eggplant Parmigiana, 214–15
elements, 9–10
Endives with Parmesan, Olives, and Walnuts,
    46–47
entertaining tips, 11

Falafel with Sesame Sauce, 158–59
fall, 91, 134–37, 246–47
Farro and Fiddleheads, 52–53
fasting, 191
Faunus, 219

Favas Fettucine, Asparagus and Fresh, 54–55
fennel, 46–47, 116, 122–23, 125, 204–5, 207
Fennel Pesto, Angel Hair with, 204–5
fennel seeds, 112, 120, 125, 204
Fettucine, Asparagus and Fresh Favas, 54–55
Fiddleheads, Farro and, 52–53
figs, 82–83, 94
Figs, Chorizo-Stuffed, 94
fire signs, 9
fish grilling tips, 115
fixed signs, 8–9
Flounder Almondine, 220–21
Fried Oyster Po' Boys with Cajun Slaw, 164–65
Fried Soft-Shell Crabs, 112–13
Frisée, Grilled Magret and, 118–19
Frittata Caprese, 108–9

Gazpacho, Watermelon, 93
Gemini
    classification, 8, 9–10, 16
    food profile, 16–17
    recipes reflecting, 46–47, 52–53, 58–59, 64–65,
        70–71, 76–77, 80, 84–85
    seasonal associations, 4, 40–41
    twins myth, 59
goat cheese, 54, 94
Golden Turmeric Chicken, 122–23
green bean and potato salad, 98–99
Green Goddess Avocado Dressing, 50–51
Grilled Branzino, 114–15
Grilled Magret and Frisée, 118–19

Halibut Tacos, 166–67
Haricot Verts and New Potato Salad, 98–99
Hazelnut Pesto, Sage-, 126–27

Hazelnut Sweet Potatoes, 234–35
Hazelnuts, Roasted Acorn Squash with Mushrooms
    and, 140–41
herbes de Provence, 110
hermetic, 80
Horn of Plenty, 175

Iceberg Wedge with Green Goddess Avocado
    Dressing, 50–51

Jupiter rule, 1, 8, 136–37

Kalamata olives, 46, 48, 64–65, 116, 162
Kale Salad, 198–99
kefalotyri cheese, 72
Kiwi Ricotta Stacks, 129

lamb moussaka, 72–73
Lasagna, Butternut Squash, 156–57
leeks, 44–45, 218
Lemon Bars, Tahini, 84–85
Lemon–Olive Oil Dressing, 51
lemon sole, 220–21
Lemony Grilled Shrimp with White Beans, 116–17
Lentil Salad, 202–3
Leo
    classification, 7, 8–9, 20
    food profile, 20–21
    recipes reflecting, 93, 96–97, 102–3, 108–9,
        114–15, 120–21, 125, 129
    seasonal associations, 5, 89–90
Libra
    classification, 8, 9–10, 24

food profile, 24–25
recipes reflecting, 138–39, 144–45, 150–51,
    156–57, 162–63, 168–69, 174, 180–81
seasonal associations, 5, 134–35
Limas, Mashed Baby, 79
Lime Pie, Avocado-, 82–83
Linguine, Clams and Cockles, 102–3
Linguine and Ramps al Olio, 58–59
Linguine Fine with Broccoli and Anchovies,
    154–55
Linguine with Cauliflower Two Ways, 152–53
Lobster and Roasted Corn Orecchiette, 100–101
lucuma powder, 236
Lupercalia festival, 219

maca powder, 84
mâche, 144–45
Magret and Frisée, 118–19
mahleb, 236
Manchego-Stuffed Peppers with Salbitxada, 160–61
Mango-Citrus Relish, 70–71
Maple Syrup, Poached Pears in, 240–41
Mars rule, 1, 7–8, 38, 135
mascarpone, 130, 148–49, 236–37
Mascarpone Tart, Berry, 130
Mashed Baby Limas, 79
mayonnaise, 112–13
meat dishes
    Apple-Stuffed Pork Tenderloin, 168–69
    Beef Bourguignon, 228–30
    Broccoli Rabe, Sausage, and White Beans with
        Penne, 150–51
    Choucroute Garni, 225–27
    Classic Passover Brisket, 74–75
    Merguez Moussaka, 72–73
    Spaghetti alla Carbonara, 208–9

meat dishes (*continued*)
    Spiced Beef Tenderloin, 120–21
    See also poultry recipes
Mercury rule, 1, 8, 40–41, 91
Merguez Moussaka, 72–73
metric conversion chart, 253
mirin, 68–69
moon, 1, 8, 88, 140, 141
Moussaka, Merguez, 72–73
Mousse, Chocolate Chestnut, 238–39
mushroom appetizer, 140–41
Mussels, Steamed, 216–17
mutable signs, 9

nature connection, 2–7
Neptune rule, 2, 8, 191
New Year's celebration, 250–51
nut roasting tips, 199

oat flour, 182
Orange Sauce, Roasted Ducklings in, 222–24
Orecchiette, Lobster and Roasted Corn, 100–101
Oven-Roasted Ratatouille Spiral, 110–11
Oyster Po' Boys with Cajun Slaw, 164–65
Oyster Stew with Gruyère and Potatoes, 218

Pan-Roasted Tomato and Kalamata Spanakopita, 64–65
Pan-Seared Halibut Tacos and Roasted Tomato–Poblano Salsa, 166–67
Pappardelle alla Cacciatora, 206–7
Parsnip Dip, White Bean–, 194–95
pasta
    Angel Hair with Fennel Pesto, 204–5

Asparagus and Fresh Favas Fettucine, 54–55
Baby Arugula Pesto and Baby Peas Conchiglie, 56–57
Broccoli Rabe, Sausage, and White Beans with Penne, 150–51
Bucatini alla Norma, 104–5
Clams and Cockles Linguine, 102–3
cooking tips, 57
Linguine and Ramps al Olio, 58–59
Linguine Fine with Broccoli and Anchovies, 154–55
Linguine with Cauliflower Two Ways, 152–53
Lobster and Roasted Corn Orecchiette, 100–101
Pappardelle alla Cacciatora, 206–7
Spaghetti alla Carbonara, 208–9
See also vegetarian recipes
Peach Crisp, Coconut-, 128
Peaches and Boston Lettuce, 95
Pears in Maple Syrup, Poached, 240–41
Peas Conchiglie, Baby Arugula Pesto and Baby, 56–57
Penne, Broccoli Rabe, Sausage, and White Beans with, 150–51
Pepitas, Roasted, 138–39
pepper roasting tips, 49
Peppers with Salbitxada, Manchego-Stuffed, 160–61
perciatelli, 104–5
Persephone myth, 170
Persimmon Pomegranate Salad, 148–49
Pesto, Angel Hair with Fennel, 204–5
Pesto, Sage-Hazelnut, 126–27
Pesto and Baby Peas Conchiglie, Baby Arugula, 56–57
Pie, Avocado-Lime, 82–83
pine nuts, 80, 101, 125, 159, 198–99

Pisces
  classification, 8, 9, 10, 34
  food profile, 34–35
  recipes reflecting, 196–97, 202–3, 208–9, 214–
    15, 220–21, 228–30, 234–35, 240–41
  seasonal associations, 7, 190–91
Pistachio Soup, Cucumber, 92
pistachios, 52, 56, 92, 129, 170
planets, 1–2, 7–8, 10
Plum Upside-Down Cake, 184–85
Pluto rule, 2, 8, 135, 136
Po' Boys with Cajun Slaw, Fried Oyster,
    164–65
Poached Pears in Maple Syrup, 240–41
Poblano Salsa, Roasted Tomato–, 166–67
Polenta Bites with Sage-Hazelnut Pesto, 126–27
Pomegranate Chicken, 170–71
pomegranate molasses, 148–49, 170–71
Pomegranate Salad, Persimmon, 148–49
porcini mushrooms, 172–73, 232–33
Pork Tenderloin, Apple-Stuffed, 168–69
Potato, Tagine of Chicken with, 76–77
Potato Curry with Spaghetti Squash, Cauliflower-,
    212–13
potato-leek soup, 44–45
potato pancakes, 142–43
Potato Salad, Haricot Verts and New, 98–99
Potatoes, Arugula, and Cheddar, Spring Vegetable
    Quiche with New, 62–63
Potatoes, Oyster Stew with Gruyère and, 218
Potatoes, Roasted Rosemary, 176–77
poultry recipes
  Golden Turmeric Chicken, 122–23
  Grilled Magret and Frisée, 118–19
  Pappardelle alla Cacciatora, 206–7
  Pomegranate Chicken, 170–71
  Roasted Ducklings in Orange Sauce, 222–24

  Tagine of Chicken, 76–77
  Turkey Saltimbocca, 172–73
Pumpkin Risotto, 178–79
pumpkin seed oil, 178
pumpkin seeds, roasted, 138–39

qualities, 8–9, 10
quiche, potato and cheddar, 62–63
quinoa salad, 198–99

radicchio, 46, 95, 96–97, 118
Radicchio Salad, Baby Spinach and, 96–97
Radishes, Roasted, 78
Ramps al Olio, Linguine and, 58–59
rapini, 150–51
raspberries, 95, 130
Ratatouille Spiral, Oven-Roasted, 110–11
Rice, Saffron, 125
rice malt syrup, 84
Rice Pilaf, Wild, 232–33
ricotta salata, 104
Ricotta Stacks, Kiwi, 129
Risotto, Pumpkin, 178–79
Roasted Acorn Squash with Mushrooms and
    Hazelnuts, 140–41
roasted bell peppers, 49
Roasted Black Cod and Sesame Spinach, 68–69
Roasted Brussels Sprouts, 174
Roasted Ducklings in Orange Sauce, 222–24
Roasted Golden Beets and Walnuts, 146–47
Roasted Radishes, 78
Roasted Rosemary Potatoes, 176–77
Roasted Tomato–Poblano Salsa, 166–67
rock shrimp, 92
rosemary, 99

Rösti with Smoked Salmon and Scallion Crème
    Fraîche, 142–43
ruling planet, 1–2, 7–8, 10

saffron, 100, 101, 125
Saffron Rice, 125
Sage-Hazelnut Pesto, Polenta Bites with,
    126–27
sage leaves, 126–27, 140, 172, 196–97
Sage Pea Soup, 196–97
Sagittarius
    classification, 8, 9, 28
    food profile, 28–29
    recipes reflecting, 142–43, 148–49, 154–55,
        160–61, 166–67, 172–73, 178–79, 184–85
    seasonal associations, 6, 136–37
salads
    Baby Spinach and Radicchio, 96–97
    Brussels Sprouts and Chestnut Slaw, 200–201
    Cajun Slaw, 164–65
    Couscous and Cracked Wheat Tabbouleh,
        48–49
    Deviled Eggs and Diablo Slaw, 42–43
    Farro and Fiddleheads, 52–53
    Haricot Verts and New Potato, 98–99
    Iceberg Wedge, 50–51
    Kale, 198–99
    Lentil, 202–3
    Peaches and Boston Lettuce, 95
    Persimmon Pomegranate, 148–49
    Roasted Golden Beets, 146–47
    Waldorf, 144–45
Salbitxada, Manchego-Stuffed Peppers with,
    160–61
Salmon and Scallion Crème Fraîche, Rösti with
    Smoked, 142–43

Salmon Cakes, Sriracha, 66–67
Salsa, Roasted Tomato–Poblano, 166–67
Saltimbocca, Turkey, 172–73
Saturn rule, 1–2, 8, 188, 192
Saturnalia festival, 224
Sausage, and White Beans with Penne, Broccoli
    Rabe, 150–51
sausage and sauerkraut, 225–27
Savoy cabbage slaw, 42–43
Scallops and Israeli Couscous, 162–63
Scorpio
    classification, 8–9, 10, 26
    food profile, 26–27
    recipes reflecting, 140–41, 146–47, 152–53,
        158–59, 164–65, 170–71, 176–77, 182–83
    seasonal associations, 6, 135–36
seabass, grilled, 114–15
seafood recipes
    Clams and Cockles Linguine, 102–3
    Flounder Almondine, 220–21
    Fried Oyster Po' Boys, 164–65
    Fried Soft-Shell Crabs, 112–13
    Grilled Branzino, 114–15
    Lemony Grilled Shrimp, 116–17
    Lobster and Roasted Corn Orecchiette,
        100–101
    Oyster Stew with Gruyère and Potatoes, 218
    Pan-Seared Halibut Tacos, 166–67
    Roasted Black Cod, 68–69
    Scallops and Israeli Couscous, 162–63
    Sriracha Salmon Cakes, 66–67
    Steamed Mussels, 216–17
    Sweet and Sour Snapper, 70–71
seasonal cycle
    astrology connection, 2–7, 10
    fall phases, 134–37
    spring phases, 38–41

summer phases, 88–91
winter phases, 188–91
seed roasting tips, 199
Sesame Sauce, 158–59
Sesame Spinach, 68–69
Sformati, Cauliflower, 192–93
shiitake mushrooms, 210–11
shrimp, 92, 116–17
Shrimp with White Beans, Lemony Grilled, 116–17
side dishes
    Cranberry Relish, 231
    Dilled Zucchini and Scallions, 124
    Hazelnut Sweet Potatoes, 234–35
    Mashed Baby Limas, 79
    Polenta Bites with Sage-Hazelnut Pesto, 126–27
    Pumpkin Risotto, 178–79
    Roasted Brussels Sprouts, 174
    Roasted Radishes, 78
    Roasted Rosemary Potatoes, 176–77
    Saffron Rice, 125
    Stir-Fried Snap Peas, 80
    Wild Rice Pilaf, 232–33
Snap Peas, Stir-Fried, 80
Snapper with Mango-Citrus Relish, Sweet and
    Sour, 70–71
Soba, Toshikoshi, 210–11
Soft-Shell Crabs, Fried, 112–13
soups
    Butternut Squash, 138–39
    Cucumber Pistachio, 92
    Oyster Stew, 218
    Sage Pea, 196–97
    Watercress-Parsley, 44–45
    Watermelon Gazpacho, 93
Spaghetti alla Carbonara, 208–9
Spaghetti Squash, Cauliflower-Potato Curry with,
    212–13

Spanakopita, Pan-Roasted Tomato and Kalamata,
    64–65
Spiced Beef Tenderloin with Scallions and
    Horseradish, 120–21
Spinach, Sesame, 68–69
Spinach and Radicchio Salad, 96–97
spinach spanakopita, 64–65
split pea soup, 196–97
spring, 38–41, 72, 244
Spring Vegetable Quiche with New Potatoes,
    Arugula, and Cheddar, 62–63
sprouts, 146, 201
Sriracha Salmon Cakes, 66–67
starters. See appetizers; soups
Steamed Mussels, 216–17
Stir-Fried Snap Peas, 80
summer phases, 88–91
Summer Solstice, 123, 245
Summer Tomato Sauce, 107
sun rule, 1, 7, 89
Sweet and Sour Snapper with Mango-Citrus Relish,
    70–71
Sweet Potatoes, Hazelnut, 234–35

Tabbouleh, Couscous and Cracked Wheat, 48–49
Tacos, Pan-Seared Halibut, 166–67
Tagine of Chicken with Potato, Preserved Lemon,
    and Apricot, 76–77
Tahini Lemon Bars, 84–85
tahini sauce, 158–59
tapioca flour, 182
tarragon, 220
Tart, Berry Mascarpone, 130
Taurus
    classification, 8–9, 10, 14
    food profile, 14–15

Taurus (*continued*)
   recipes reflecting, 44–45, 50–51, 56–57, 62–63, 68–69, 74–75, 79, 82–83
   seasonal associations, 4, 38–40
tofu dishes, 210–11, 238–39
Tomato and Kalamata Spanakopita, 64–65
Tomato-Poblano Salsa, 166–67
Tomato Sauce, Summer, 107
tomatoes, 60–61, 76–77, 93, 107, 108–11, 116
tomatoes, dried, 98–99
Toshikoshi Soba, 210–11
Turkey Saltimbocca, 172–73
Turmeric Chicken, Golden, 122–23

universal conversion chart, 253
Uranus rule, 2, 8, 189

Valentine's Day, 219
vanilla beans, 130, 131
vegetable dishes. *See* salads; side dishes
vegetarian recipes
   Arancini and Ceci Arrabiata, 60–61
   Butternut Squash Lasagna, 156–57
   Cauliflower-Potato Curry with Spaghetti Squash, 212–13
   Eggplant Parmigiana, 214–15
   Falafel with Sesame Sauce, 158–59
   Frittata Caprese, 108–9
   Manchego-Stuffed Peppers with Salbitxada, 160–61
   Oven-Roasted Ratatouille Spiral, 110–11
   Pan-Roasted Tomato and Kalamata Spanakopita, 64–65
   Spring Vegetable Quiche, 62–63
   Toshikoshi Soba, 210–11
   Zucchini Barzini, 106–7

Venus rule, 1, 8, 39–40, 134–35
Vernal Equinox, 38, 72, 244
Vesta, 123
Virgo
   classification, 8, 9, 10, 22
   food profile, 22–23
   recipes reflecting, 94, 98–99, 104–5, 110–11, 116–17, 122, 126–27, 130–31
   seasonal associations, 5, 90–91

Waldorf Salad, 144–45
water signs, 10
watercress, 44–45, 52–53, 192
Watercress-Parsley Soup, 44–45
Watermelon Gazpacho, 93
White Bean–Parsnip Dip, 194–95
White Beans, Lemony Grilled Shrimp with, 116–17
White Beans with Penne, Broccoli Rabe, and Sausage, 150–51
Wild Rice Pilaf, 232–33
winter phases, 188–91
Winter Solstice, 6, 224, 248–49

Zodiac
   astrology basics, 1–3
   elements, 9–10
   food connection, 2–3, 10–11
   qualities, 8–9
   ruling planets, 7–8
   term definition, 3
   twelve-month seasonal cycle, 2–7, 10
Zucchini and Scallions, Dilled, 124
Zucchini Barzini, 106–7

ABOUT THE AUTHORS

AMY ZERNER AND MONTE FARBER

Internationally known self-help author Monte Farber's inspiring guidance and empathic insights impact everyone he encounters. Amy Zerner's exquisite, one-of-a-kind spiritual couture creations, available exclusively from Bergdorf Goodman and Neiman Marcus, and collaged fabric paintings exude her profound intuition and deep connection with archetypal stories and healing energies.

Amy is an Aries, and Monte is an Aquarius. For more than forty years, they've combined their deep love for each other with the work of inner exploration and self-discovery to build The Enchanted World of Amy Zerner and Monte Farber: astrology books, tarot card decks, and oracles that have helped millions answer questions, be more mindful, find deeper meaning, and follow their own spiritual paths.

Together they've made their love for each other a work of art and their art the work of their lives. Their bestselling titles include *Karma Cards; Sun Sign Secrets; The Soulmate Path; Psychic Circle; Chakra Meditation Kit; Enchanted Tarot; Enchanted Spellboard;*

Little Reminders: The Law of Attraction; Goddess, Guide Me!; Instant Tarot; The Truth Fairy; Tarot Secrets; the *Enchanted Tarot* coloring book; the *Enchanted Worlds* coloring book; and *Quantum Affirmations.*

They have created the entirety of their prodigious output working from home in East Hampton, New York, which Monte affectionately refers to as "a factory with bedrooms and a kitchen." They both enjoy cooking for each other as often as possible. Monte has been eating with awareness of food as medicine since he was sixteen, and was taught by his uncle Morris Harth, former European news editor for Reuters. Amy's mother, Jessie Spicer Zerner, was also an artist and a fantastic cook who passed on her talents to her daughter. They claim to be living proof that adding love, light, and laughter to everything one cooks is essential to creating great meals and a great life.

Their websites are:

www.TheEnchantedWorld.com
www.AmyZerner.com
www.MonteFarber.com

JOHN OKAS

John Okas, an Aries, was born in Brooklyn, New York, in 1949. He unknowingly began his culinary career as a child growing up in an American-Italian household. He showed some talent and was enlisted as kitchen help. Working alongside his Sicilian grandmother, he saw the way things were done in the Old Country.

As a young adult, a struggling writer and musician, he relied on his cooking talents to make ends meet. He worked in such diverse venues as Paradox, a macrobiotic restaurant in Manhattan; Georgette's in Easthampton, which offered a fusion menu; and the Captiva Inn in Florida, where classic French cuisine was served.

In his thirties, he began private chefing both in Eastern Long Island and South Florida. Catering to a variety of specific tastes and needs, he expanded his versatility, skills, and knowledge of ingredients. His first and truest love, however, is Mediterranean food.

Under the name John Penza, he is the author of *Sicilian-American Pasta* and *Sicilian Vegetarian Cooking*. He is also a novelist with four published works. He continues to work as a personal chef; lives in Bridgehampton, New York; and is a consultant at the Highway Restaurant in East Hampton.